Effective Debugging

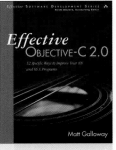

Effective Debugging

66 SPECIFIC WAYS TO DEBUG
SOFTWARE AND SYSTEMS

Diomidis Spinellis

♦♦ Addison-Wesley

Boston • Columbus • Indianapolis • New York • San Francisco • Amsterdam • Cape Town
Dubai • London • Madrid • Milan • Munich • Paris • Montreal • Toronto • Delhi • Mexico City
São Paulo • Sydney • Hong Kong • Seoul • Singapore • Taipei • Tokyo

For information about buying this title in bulk quantities, or for special sales opportunities (which may include electronic versions; custom cover designs; and content particular to your business, training goals, marketing focus, or branding interests), please contact our corporate sales department at corpsales@pearsoned.com or (800) 382-3419.

For government sales inquiries, please contact governmentsales@pearsoned.com.

For questions about sales outside the U.S., please contact intlcs@pearson.com.

Visit us on the Web: informit.com/aw

Library of Congress Control Number: 2016937082

ISBN-13: 978-0-13-439479-4
ISBN-10: 0-13-439479-8

Text printed in the United States at RR Donnelley in Crawfordsville, Indiana.

1   16

To my mentors, past and future

Contents

Figures

Listings

Preface

When you develop software or administer systems that run it, you often face failures. These can range from a compiler error in your code, which you can fix in seconds, to downtime in a large-scale system, which costs your company millions (pick your currency) each hour. In both cases, as an effective professional, you'll need to be able to quickly identify and fix the underlying fault. This is what debugging is all about, and that is this book's topic.

The book is aimed at experienced developers. It is not introductory, in the sense that it expects you to be able to understand small code examples in diverse programming languages and use advanced GUI and command-line-based programming tools. On the other hand, the debugging techniques included in the book are described in detail, for I've seen that even experienced developers who are experts on some methods may well need some hand-holding on others. Furthermore, if you've debugged problems on non-toy software for at least a few months, you'll find it easier to appreciate the context behind some of the book's more advanced items.

What This Book Covers

Debugging, as treated in this book, encompasses strategies, tools, and methods you can use to deal with the whole spectrum of problems that can arise when developing and operating a modern, sophisticated computing system. In the past, debugging mainly referred to detecting and fixing a program's faults; however, nowadays a program rarely works in isolation. Even the smallest program will link (often dynamically) to external libraries. More complex ones can run under an application server, call web services, use relational and NoSQL databases, obtain data from a directory server, run external programs, utilize other middleware, and incorporate numerous third-party packages. The operation of complete systems and services depends on the failure-free functioning of many in-house-developed and third-party components running on hosts that may span the whole planet. DevOps, the software development discipline that addresses this reality, emphasizes the roles of both developers and other IT professionals. This book aims to equip you for a similarly holistic view when facing failures, because in the most challenging problems you'll rarely be able to immediately identify the software component that's the culprit.

The material progresses from general topics to more specific ones. It starts with strategies (Chapter 1), methods (Chapter 2), and tools and techniques (Chapter 3) that can help you debug diverse software and systems failures. It then covers techniques that you apply at specific stages of your debugging work: when you use a debugger (Chapter 4), when you program (Chapter 5), when you compile the software (Chapter 6), and when you run the system (Chapter 7). A separate chapter (Chapter 8) focuses on the specialized tools and techniques you can use to hunt down those pesky bugs that are associated with multi-threaded and concurrent code.

How to Use This Book

Read the left page, read the right page, flip the right page, until you reach the end. Wait! Actually, there's a better way. The advice contained in this book can be divided into three categories.

- **Strategies and methods** you should know and practice when you face a failure. These are described in Chapter 1: "High-Level Strategies" and Chapter 2: "General-Purpose Methods and Practices." In addition, many techniques included in Chapter 5: "Programming Techniques" also fall in this category. Read and understand these items, so that applying them gradually becomes a habit. While debugging, systematically reflect on the method you're using. When you reach a dead end, knowing the avenue you've explored will help you identify other ways to get out of the maze.

- **Skills and tools** you can invest in. These are mainly covered in Chapter 3: "General-Purpose Tools and Techniques" but also include elements that apply to the problems you face on an everyday basis; for example, see Item 36: "Tune Your Debugging Tools." Find time to learn and gradually apply in practice what these items describe. This may mean abandoning the comfort of using tools you're familiar with in order to conquer the steep learning curve of more advanced ones. It may be painful in the beginning, but in the long run this is what will distinguish you as a master of your craft.

- **Ideas for techniques** to apply when things get tough. These are not things you'll be using regularly, but they can save your day (or at least a few hours) when you encounter an unfathomable problem. For instance, if you can't understand why your C and C++ code fail to compile, see Item 50: "Examine Generated Code." Quickly go through these items to be aware of them as options. Study them carefully when the time comes to apply them.

How to Live Your Life

Although all items in this book offer advice for diagnosing failures and debugging existing faults, you can also apply many of them to minimize the number of bugs you encounter and make your life easier when one crops up. Rigorous debugging and software development practices feed on each other in a virtuous circle. This advice covers your (current or future) roles in software construction, software design, and software management.

When **designing** software, do all of the following:

- Use the highest-level mechanisms suitable for its role (Item 47: "Consider Rewriting the Suspect Code in Another Language" and Item 66: "Consider Rewriting the Code Using Higher-Level Abstractions")

- Offer a debugging mode (Item 6: "Use the Software's Debugging Facilities" and Item 40: "Add Debugging Functionality")

- Provide mechanisms to monitor and log the system's operation (Item 27: "Use Monitoring Tools on Systems Composed of Independent Processes," Item 41: "Add Logging Statements," and Item 56: "Examine Application Log Files")

- Include an option to script components with Unix command-line tools (Item 22: "Analyze Debug Data with Unix Command-Line Tools")

- Make internal errors lead to visible failures rather than to instability (Item 55: "Fail Fast")

- Provide a method to obtain postmortem memory dumps (Item 35: "Know How to Work with Core Dumps" and Item 60: "Analyze Deadlocks with Postmortem Debugging")

- Minimize the sources and extent of nondeterminism in the software's execution (Item 63: "Isolate and Remove Nondeterminism")

When **constructing** software, take the following steps:

- Obtain feedback from your colleagues (Item 39: "Go Over Your Code and Reasoning with a Colleague")

- Create a unit test for each routine you write (Item 42: "Use Unit Tests")

- Use assertions to verify your assumptions and the code's correct functioning (Item 43: "Use Assertions")

- Strive to write maintainable code—code that is readable, stable, and easy to analyze and change (Item 46: "Simplify the Suspect Code" and Item 48: "Improve the Suspect Code's Readability and Structure")

- Avoid sources of nondeterminism in your builds (Item 52: "Configure Deterministic Builds and Executions")

Finally, when **managing** software development and operations (either a team or your own process), do the following:

- Have issues recorded and followed through a suitable system (Item 1: "Handle All Problems through an Issue-Tracking System")

- Triage and prioritize the issues you work on (Item 8: "Focus Your Work on the Most Important Problems")

- Have software changes properly recorded in a well-maintained revision management system (Item 26: "Hunt the Causes and History of Bugs with the Revision Control System")

- Deploy software in a gradual fashion, allowing the old version to be compared with the new one (Item 5: "Find the Difference between a Known Good System and a Failing One")

- Strive for diversity in the tools you use and the environments you deploy (Item 7: "Diversify Your Build and Execution Environment")

- Update tools and libraries on a regular basis (Item 14: "Consider Updating Your Software")

- Purchase source code for any third-party libraries you use (Item 15: "Consult Third-Party Source Code for Insights on Its Use") and buy the sophisticated tools needed to pin down elusive faults (Item 51: "Use Static Program Analysis"; Item 59: "Use Dynamic Program Analysis Tools"; Item 62: "Uncover Deadlocks and Race Conditions with Specialized Tools"; Item 64: "Investigate Scalability

Issues by Looking at Contention"; Item 65: "Locate False Sharing by Using Performance Counters")

- Supply any specialized kit required for debugging hardware interfaces and embedded systems (Item 16: "Use Specialized Monitoring and Test Equipment")

- Enable developers to debug software remotely (Item 18: "Enable the Debugging of Unwieldy Systems from Your Desk")

- Provide sufficient CPU and disk resources for demanding troubleshooting tasks (Item 19: "Automate Debugging Tasks")

- Encourage collaboration between developers through practices such as code reviews and mentoring (Item 39: "Go Over Your Code and Reasoning with a Colleague")

- Promote the adoption of test-driven development (Item 42: "Use Unit Tests")

- Include in the software's build performance profiling, static analysis, and dynamic analysis, while maintaining a fast, lean, and mean build and test cycle (Item 57: "Profile the Operation of Systems and Processes"; Item 51: "Use Static Program Analysis"; Item 59: "Use Dynamic Program Analysis Tools" and Item 53: "Configure the Use of Debugging Libraries and Checks"; Item 11: "Minimize the Turnaround Time from Your Changes to Their Result")

A Few Notes on Terminology

In this book, I use the term *fault* according to the following definition, which appears in ISO-24765-2010 (*Systems and software engineering—Vocabulary*): "an incorrect step, process, or data definition in a computer program." This is also often called a *defect*. In everyday language, this is what we call a *bug*. Similarly, I use the term *failure* according to the following definition from the same standard: "an event in which a system or system component does not perform a required function within specified limits." A failure can be a program that crashes, freezes, or gives a wrong result. Thus, a *failure* may be produced when a *fault* is encountered or used. Confusingly, sometimes the terms *fault* and *defect* are also used to refer to failures, something that the ISO standard acknowledges. In this book I maintain the distinction I describe here. However, to avoid having the text read like a legal document when the meaning is clear from the context, I often use the word "problem" to refer to either faults (as in "a problem in your code") or failures (as in "a reproducible problem").

Nowadays the shell, libraries, and tools of the Unix operating system are available on many platforms. I use the term *Unix* to refer to any system following the principles and APIs of Unix, including Apple's *Mac OS X*, the various distributions of *GNU/Linux* (e.g., Arch Linux, CentOS, Debian, Fedora, openSUSE, Red Hat Enterprise Linux, Slackware, and Ubuntu), direct Unix descendants (e.g., *AIX*, *HP-UX*, *Solaris*), the various BSD derivatives (e.g., *FreeBSD*, *OpenBSD*, *NetBSD*), and *Cygwin* running on *Windows*.

Similarly, when I write C++, Java, or Python, I assume a reasonably modern version of the language. I've tried to eschew examples that depend on exotic or cutting-edge features.

In the text I write "your code" and "your software" to refer to the code you're debugging and the software you're working on. This is both shorter and also implies a sense of ownership, which is always important when we develop software.

I use the term *routine* for callable units of code such as member functions, methods, functions, procedures, and subroutines.

I use the terms *Visual Studio* and *Windows* to refer to the corresponding Microsoft products.

I use the terms *revision control system* and *version control system* to refer to tools such as Git that are used for software configuration management.

Typographical and Other Conventions

- Surprise! Code is written in so-called `typewriter font`, key points are set in **bold**, and terms and tool names are set in *italics*.

- Listings of interactive sessions use colors to distinguish the prompt, the user input, and the resultant output.

  ```
  $ echo hello, world
  hello world
  ```

- Unix command-line options appear like `--this` or as their single-letter equivalent (e.g., `-t`). Corresponding Windows tool options appear like `/this`.

- Key presses are set as follows: Shift–F11.

- File paths are set as follows: /etc/motd.

- Links to the web are formatted *like this*. If you're reading this on paper, you can find the URL listed in the "Web Resources" appendix. If you're reading this as an e-book, you know what to do.

- Menu navigation appears as follows: *Debug – New Breakpoint – Break at Function*.

- In the interests of brevity, in C++ code listings I omit the `std::` qualifiers of the `std` namespace.

- When describing GUI tools, I refer to the functionality in the form it's available in the most recent tool at the time of writing. If you're using a different version, look at related menus or windows, or consult the documentation on how to access this functionality. Interestingly, command-line tools retain their interface stable for decades, but GUIs move things around on every new version. The many conclusions that can be reached from this observation are left as an exercise to the reader.

Where to Get the Code and Errata

The code appearing in the book's examples and fixes associated with the text are available through the book's web site at www.spinellis.gr/debugging.

Register your copy of Effective Debugging at informit.com for convenient access to downloads, updates, and corrections as they become available. To start the registration process, go to informit.com/register and log in or create an account. Enter the product ISBN (9780134394794) and click Submit. Once the process is complete, you will find any available bonus content under "Registered Products."

Acknowledgments

First, I want to thank the book's editor at Addison-Wesley, Trina Fletcher MacDonald, and the series' editor, Scott Meyers, for their expert guidance and management of the book's development. I'm also grateful to the book's technical reviewers, Dimitris Andreadis, Kevlin Henney, John Pagonis, and George Thiruvathukal. They provided literally hundreds of top-notch ideas, comments, and suggestions that considerably improved the book. Special thanks to the book's copy editor, Stephanie Geels, for her eagle eyes and featherlight touch. Thanks to the quality of her work, I ended up enjoying a process that I used to dread. My thanks go also to Melissa Panagos for her amazingly effective production management, Julie Nahil who supervised overall production, LaTeX magician Lori Hughes for the book's composition, Sheri Replin for her editing advice, Olivia Basegio for managing the book's technical review board, Chuti Prasertsith for the brilliant book cover, and Stephane Nakib for her guidance on marketing. I'm grateful to Alfredo Benso, Georgios Gousios, and Panagiotis Louridas, who provided early guidance on the book's concept.

Four items are expanded from material I have published in the *IEEE Software* "Tools of the Trade" column.

- Item 5: "Find the Difference between a Known Good System and a Failing One"—"Differential Debugging," vol. 30, no. 5, 2013, pp. 19–21.

- Item 22: "Analyze Debug Data with Unix Command-Line Tools"—"Working with Unix Tools," vol. 22, no. 6, 2005, pp. 9–11.

- Item 58: "Trace the Code's Execution"—"I Spy," vol. 24, no. 2, 2007, pp. 16–17.

- Item 66: "Consider Rewriting the Code Using Higher-Level Abstractions"—"Faking It," vol. 28, no. 5, 2011, pp. 96, 95.

Furthermore,

- Item 63: "Isolate and Remove Nondeterminism" is based on ideas presented by Martin Fowler in his articles "Eradicating Non-Determinism in Tests" (April 14, 2011) and "TestDouble" (January 17, 2006).

- Most of the refactorings suggested in Item 48: "Improve the Suspect Code's Readability and Structure" are derived from Martin Fowler's *Refactoring* book (Addison-Wesley, 1999).

- The article "Real-World Concurrency" (Bryan Cantrill and Jeff Bonwick, *ACM Queue*, October 2008) prompted me to write Item 60: "Analyze Deadlocks with Postmortem Debugging."

- The Java code in Item 66: "Consider Rewriting the Code Using Higher-Level Abstractions" is based on input provided by Tagir Valeev.

A number of colleagues at the Athens University of Economics and Business have (sometimes unknowingly) contributed to the realization of this project through their gracious support in many aspects of my academic life. These include Damianos Chatziantoniou, Georgios Doukidis, Konstantine Gatsios, George Giaglis, Emmanouil Giakoumakis, Dimitris Gritzalis, George Lekakos, Panagiotis Louridas, Katerina Paramatari, Nancy Pouloudi, Angeliki Poulymenakou, Georgios Siomkos, Spyros Spyrou, and Christos Tarantilis.

Debugging is a craft, which you learn by doing. I'd therefore like to thank the coworkers and colleagues who over the past four decades have endured my bugs, have supplied me with helpful issue reports, have reviewed and tested my code, and have taught me how to avoid, track down, and fix problems. In roughly reverse chronological order, in my employment and collaboration history, these are the following:

- In the Ads SRE FE team at Google: Mark Bean, Carl Crous, Alexandru-Nicolae Dimitriu, Fede Heinz, Lex Holt, Thomas Hunger, Thomas Koeppe, Jonathan Lange, David Leadbeater, Anthony Lenton, Sven Marnach, Lino Mastrodomenico, Trevor Mattson-Hamilton, Philip Mulcahy, Wolfram Pfeiffer, Martin Stjernholm, Stuart Taylor, Stephen Thorne, Steven Thurgood, and Nicola Worthington.

- At CQS: Theodoros Evgeniou, Vaggelis Kapartzianis, and Nick Nassuphis.

- In the Department of Management Science and Technology at the Athens University of Economics and Business, current and former research and lab associates: Achilleas Anagnostopoulos, Stefanos Androutsellis-Theotokis, Konstantinos Chorianopoulos, Marios Fragkoulis, Vaggelis Giannikas, Georgios Gousios, Stavros Grigora-kakis, Vassilios Karakoidas, Maria Kechagia, Christos Lazaris, Dimitris Mitropoulos, Christos Oikonomou, Tushar Sharma, Sofo-klis Stouraitis, Konstantinos Stroggylos, Vaso Tangalaki, Stavros Trihias, Vasileios Vlachos, and Giorgos Zouganelis,

- In the General Secretariat for Information Systems at the Greek Ministry of Finance: Costas Balatos, Leonidas Bogiatzis, Paraskevi Chatzimitakou, Christos Coborozos, Yannis Dimas, Dimitris Dimi-triadis, Areti Drakaki, Nikolaos Drosos, Krystallia Drystella, Maria Eleftheriadou, Stamatis Ezovalis, Katerina Frantzeskaki, Voula Hamilou, Anna Hondroudaki, Yannis Ioannidis, Christos K. K. Loverdos, Ifigeneia Kalampokidou, Nikos Kalatzis, Lazaros Kaplan-oglou, Aggelos Karvounis, Sofia Katri, Xristos Kazis, Dionysis Kefal-linos, Isaac Kokkinidis, Georgios Kotsakis, Giorgos Koundourakis, Panagiotis Kranidiotis, Yannis Kyriakopoulos, Odyseas Kyriakop-oylos, Georgios Laskaridis, Panagiotis Lazaridis, Nana Leisou, Ioanna Livadioti, Aggeliki Lykoudi, Asimina Manta, Maria Mara-velaki, Chara Mavridou, Sofia Mavropoulou, Michail Michal-opoulos, Pantelis Nasikas, Thodoros Pagtzis, Angeliki Panayiotaki, Christos Papadoulis, Vasilis Papafotinos, Ioannis Perakis, Kanto Petri, Andreas Pipis, Nicos Psarrakis, Marianthi Psoma, Odyseas Pyrovolakis, Tasos Sagris, Apostolos Schizas, Sophie Sehperides, Marinos Sigalas, George Stamoulis, Antonis Strikis, Andreas Svo-los, Charis Theocharis, Adrianos Trigas, Dimitris Tsakiris, Niki Tsouma, Maria Tzafalia, Vasiliki Tzovla, Dimitris Vafiadis, Achil-leas Vemos, Ioannis Vlachos, Giannis Zervas, and Thanasis Zervopoulos.

- At the FreeBSD project: John Baldwin, Wilko Bulte, Martin Cra-causer, Pawel Jakub Dawidek, Ceri Davies, Brooks Davis, Ruslan Ermilov, Bruce Evans, Brian Fundakowski Feldman, Pedro Gif-funi, John-Mark Gurney, Carl Johan Gustavsson, Konrad Jan-kowski, Poul-Henning Kamp, Kris Kennaway, Giorgos Keramidas, Boris Kovalenko, Max Laier, Nate Lawson, Sam Leffler, Alexander Leidinger, Xin Li, Scott Long, M. Warner Losh, Bruce A. Mah, David Malone, Mark Murray, Simon L. Nielsen, David O'Brien, Johann 'Myrkraverk' Oskarsson, Colin Percival, Alfred Perlstein, Wes Peters, Tom Rhodes, Luigi Rizzo, Larry Rosenman, Jens Schweik-hardt, Ken Smith, Dag-Erling Smørgrav, Murray Stokely, Marius

Strobl, Ivan Voras, Robert Watson, Peter Wemm, and Garrett Wollman.

- At LH Software and SENA: Katerina Aravantinou, Michalis Belivanakis, Polina Biraki, Dimitris Charamidopoulos, Lili Charamidopoulou, Angelos Charitsis, Giorgos Chatzimichalis, Nikos Christopoulos, Christina Dara, Dejan Dimitrijevic, Fania Dorkofyki, Nikos Doukas, Lefteris Georgalas, Sotiris Gerodianos, Vasilis Giannakos, Christos Gkologiannis, Anthi Kalyvioti, Ersi Karanasou, Antonis Konomos, Isidoros Kouvelas, George Kyriazis, Marina Liapati, Spyros Livieratos, Sofia Livieratou, Panagiotis Louridas, Mairi Mandali, Andreas Massouras, Michalis Mastorantonakis, Natalia Miliou, Spyros Molfetas, Katerina Moutogianni, Dimitris Nellas, Giannis Ntontos, Christos Oikonomou, Nikos Panousis, Vasilis Paparizos, Tasos Papas, Alexandros Pappas, Kantia Printezi, Marios Salteris, Argyro Stamati, Takis Theofanopoulos, Dimitris Tolis, Froso Topali, Takis Tragakis, Savvas Triantafyllou, Periklis Tsahageas, Nikos Tsagkaris, Apostolis Tsigkros, Giorgos Tzamalis, and Giannis Vlachogiannis.

- At the European Computer Industry Research Center (ECRC): Mireille Ducassé, Anna-Maria Emde, Alexander Herold, Paul Martin, and Dave Morton.

- At Imperial College London in the Department of Computer Science: Vasilis Capoyleas, Mark Dawson, Sophia Drossopoulou, Kostis Dryllerakis, Dave Edmondson, Susan Eisenbach, Filippos Frangulis Anastasios Hadjicocolis, Paul Kelly, Stephen J. Lacey, Phil Male, Lee M. J. McLoughlin, Stuart McRobert, Mixalis Melachrinidis, Jan-Simon Pendry, Mark Taylor, Periklis Tsahageas, and Duncan White.

- In the Computer Science Research Group (CSRG) at the University of California at Berkeley: Keith Bostic.

- At Pouliadis & Associates: Alexis Anastasiou, Constantine Dokolas, Noel Koutlis, Dimitrios Krassopoulos, George Kyriazis, Giannis Marakis, and Athanasios Pouliadis.

- At diverse meetings and occasions: Yiorgos Adamopoulos, Dimitris Andreadis, Yannis Corovesis, Alexander Couloumbis, John Ioannidis, Dimitrios Kalogeras, Panagiotis Kanavos, Theodoros Karounos, Faidon Liampotis, Elias Papavassilopoulos, Vassilis Prevelakis, Stelios Sartzetakis, Achilles Voliotis, and Alexios Zavras.

Finally, I want to thank my family, which has for years ungrudgingly endured my debugging of systems at home and which has graciously supported my writing, sometimes even over (what should have been) vacations and weekend rest. Special thanks go to Dionysis, who created Figure 5.2, and Eliza and Eleana, who helped select the book's cover.

About the Author

Diomidis Spinellis is a professor in the Department of Management Science and Technology at the Athens University of Economics and Business. His research interests include software engineering, IT security, and cloud systems engineering. He has written two award-winning, widely translated books: *Code Reading* and *Code Quality: The Open Source Perspective*. Dr. Spinellis has also published more than 200 technical papers in journals and refereed conference proceedings, which have received more than 2,500 citations. He served for a decade as a member of the *IEEE Software* editorial board, authoring the regular "Tools of the Trade" column. He has contributed code that ships with OS X and BSD Unix and is the developer of *UMLGraph*, *CScout*, and other open-source software packages, libraries, and tools. He holds an MEng in Software Engineering and a PhD in Computer Science, both from Imperial College London. Dr. Spinellis is a senior member of the ACM and the IEEE. Since January 2015, he has been serving as editor-in-chief for *IEEE Software*.

High-Level Strategies

When you set out to fix a problem, it's important to select the most appropriate strategy. This is the option that will allow you to succeed with the least amount of effort. If your choice doesn't pan out, immediately adopt the next most promising approach.

Item 1: Handle All Problems through an Issue-Tracking System

George calls you on the phone complaining loudly that the application you're developing "isn't working." You scribble that on a sticky note, and add it to the collection of similar notes adorning your monitor. You make a mental note to check whether you sent him the latest library required for the new version of the application. This is *not* how you should be working. Here is what you should be doing instead.

First, ensure you have an **issue-tracking system** in place. Many source code repositories, such as GitHub and *GitLab*, provide a basic version of such a system integrated with the rest of the functionality they provide. A number of organizations use JIRA, a much more sophisticated proprietary system, that can be licensed to run on premise or as a service. Others opt to use an open-source alternative, such as *Bugzilla*, *Launchpad*, *OTRS*, *Redmine*, or *Trac*. The system that is chosen is not as important as using it to file all issues in it.

Refuse to handle any problem that's not recorded in the issue-tracking system. The unswerving use of such a system

- Provides visibility to the debugging effort
- Enables the tracking and planning of releases
- Facilitates the prioritization of work items
- Helps document common issues and solutions

- Ensures that no problems fall through the cracks

- Allows the automatic generation of release notes

- Serves as a repository for measuring defects, reflecting on them, and learning from them

For persons too senior in the organization's hierarchy to be told to file an issue, simply offer to file it for them. The same goes for issues that you discover yourself. Some organizations don't allow any changes to the source code, unless they reference an associated issue.

Also, ensure that each issue contains a precise description on **how to reproduce** it. Your ideal here is a short, self-contained, correct (compilable and runable) example (SSCCE), something that you can readily cut and paste into your application to see the problem (Item 10: "Enable the Efficient Reproduction of the Problem"). To improve your chances of getting well-written bug reports, create instructions of how a good report should look, and brainwash all bug reporters to follow them religiously. (In one organization, I saw these instructions posted on the lavatory doors.)

Other things you should be looking for in a bug report are a **precise title**, the bug's **priority** and **severity**, and the affected **stakeholders**, as well as details about the **environment** where it occurs. Here are the key points concerning these fields.

- A precise short title allows you to identify the bug in a summary report. "Program crashes" is a horrible title; "Crash when clicking on Refresh while saving" is a fine one.

- The severity field helps you prioritize the bugs. Problems where a data loss occurs are obviously critical, but cosmetic issues or those where a documented workaround is possible are less so. A bug's severity allows a team to *triage* a list of issues, deciding which to address now, which to tackle later, and which to ignore.

- The result of triaging and prioritization can be recorded as the issue's *priority*, which provides you the order on which to work (see Item 8: "Focus Your Work on the Most Important Problems"). In many projects, the bug's priority is set by the developer or project lead because end-users tend to set top priority to all the bugs they submit. Setting and recording realistic priorities fends off those managers, customer representatives, developers in other teams, and salespeople who claim that everything (or, at least, their pet issue) is a top priority.

- Identifying an issue's stakeholders helps the team get additional input regarding an issue and the product owner prioritize the issues. Some organizations even tag stakeholders with the yearly revenue they bring in. (For example, "Submitted by Acme, a $250,000 customer.")

- A description of the environment can provide you with a clue on how to reproduce an elusive bug. In the description, avoid the kitchen sink approach in which you demand everything, from the PC's serial number and BIOS date to the version of each library installed on the system. This will overburden your users, and they may just skip those fields. Instead, ask only the most relevant details; for a web-based app, the browser is certainly important. For a mobile app, you probably want the device maker and model. Even better, automate the submission of these details through your software.

When you work with an issue-tracking system, an important good practice is to use it to **document your progress**. Most tracking systems allow you to append to each entry successive free-form comments. Use these to document the steps you take for investigating and fixing the bug, including dead ends. This brings transparency to your organization's workings. Write down the precise command incantations you use to log or trace the program's behavior. These can be invaluable when you want to repeat them next day, or when you (or some colleagues) hunt a similar bug a year later. The notes can also help refresh your memory when, blurry eyed and phased out from a week-long bug-hunting exercise, you try to explain to your team or manager what you've been doing all those days.

Things to Remember

+ Handle all problems through an issue-tracking system.

+ Ensure each issue contains a precise description on how to reproduce the problem with a short, self-contained, correct example.

+ Triage issues and schedule your work based on the priority and severity of each issue.

+ Document your progress through the issue-tracking system.

Item 2: Use Focused Queries to Search the Web for Insights into Your Problem

It's quite rare these days to work in a location lacking Internet access, but when I find myself in one of these my productivity as a developer takes a dive. When your code fails, the Internet can help you find a solution by searching the web and by collaborating with fellow developers.

A remarkably effective search technique involves pasting the error message reported by a failing third-party component into the browser's search box enclosed in double quotes. The quotes instruct the search engine to look for pages containing the exact phrase, and this increases the quality of the results you'll get back. Other useful things to put into the search box include the name of the library or middleware that gives you trouble, the corresponding name of the class or method, and the returned error code. The more obscure the name of the function you look for, the better. For example, searching for `PlgBlt` will give you far better results than searching for `BitBlt`. Also try synonyms, for instance "freezes" in addition to "hangs," or "grayed" in addition to "disabled."

You can often solve tricky problems associated with the invocation of APIs by looking at how other people use them. Look for open-source software that uses a particular function, and examine how the parameters passed to it are initialized and how its return value is interpreted. For this, using specialized code search engine, such as *Black Duck Open Hub Code Search*, can provide you better results than a generic Google search. For example, searching for `mktime` on this search engine, and filtering the results for a specific project to avoid browsing through library declarations and definitions, produces the following code snippet.

```
nowtime = mktime(time->tm_year+1900, time->tm_mon+1,
    time->tm_mday, time->tm_hour, time->tm_min,
    time->tm_sec);
```

This shows that the `mktime` function, in contrast to `localtime`, expects the year to be passed in full, rather than as an offset from 1900, and that the numbering of months starts from 1. These are things you can easily get wrong, especially if you haven't read carefully the function's documentation.

When looking through the search results, pay attention to the site hosting them. Through considerable investment in techniques that motivate participants, sites of the *StackExchange* network, such as *Stack Overflow*, typically host the most pertinent discussions and answers. When looking at an answer on *Stack Overflow*, scan beyond the accepted one, looking for answers with more votes. In addition, read the answer's comments because it is there that people post updates, such as newer techniques to avoid an error.

If your carefully constructed web searches don't come up with any useful results, it may be that you're barking up the wrong tree. For popular libraries and software, it's quite unlikely that you'll be the first to experience a problem. Therefore, if you can't find a description of your problem online, it may be the case that you've misdiagnosed what the problem is. Maybe, for example, the API function that you think is crashing due to a bug in its implementation is simply crashing because there's an error in the data you've supplied to it.

If you can't find the answer online, you can also post on *Stack Overflow* your own question regarding the problem you're facing. This, however, requires considerable investment in creating an SSCCE. This is the golden standard regarding question asking in a forum: a short piece of code other members can copy-paste and compile on its own to witness your problem (see Item 10: "Enable the Efficient Reproduction of the Problem"). For some languages you can even present your example in live form through an online IDE, such as *SourceLair* or *JSFiddle*. You can find more details on how to write good examples for specific languages and technologies at *sscce.org*. Also worth reading is Eric Raymond's guide on this topic titled *How To Ask Questions The Smart Way*.

I've often found that simply the effort of putting together a well-written question and an accompanying example led me to my problem's solution. But even if this doesn't happen, the good example is likely to attract knowledgeable people who will experiment with it and, hopefully, provide you with a solution.

If your problem is partly associated with an open-source library or program, and if you have strong reasons to believe that there's a bug in that code, you can also get in contact with its developers. Opening an issue on the code's bug-tracking system is typically the way to go. Again here, make sure that there isn't a similar bug report already filed, and that you include in your report precise details for reproducing the problem. If the software doesn't have a bug-tracking system, you can even try sending an email to its author. Be even more careful, considerate, and polite here; most open-source software developers aren't paid to support you.

Things to Remember

✦ Perform a web search regarding error messages by enclosing them in double quotes.

✦ Value the answers from StackExchange sites.

✦ If all else fails, post your own question or open an issue.

Item 3: Confirm That Preconditions and Postconditions Are Satisfied

When repairing electronic equipment, the first thing to check is the power supplied to it: what comes out of the power supply module and what is fed into the circuit. In far too many cases, this points to the failure's culprit. Similarly, in computing, you can pinpoint many problems by examining what must hold at the routine's entry point (*preconditions*—program state and inputs) and at its exit (*postconditions*—program state and returned values). If the preconditions are wrong, then the fault lies in the part that set them up; if the postconditions are wrong, then there's a problem with the routine. If both are correct, then you should look somewhere else to locate your bug.

Put a breakpoint (see Item 30: "Use Code and Data Breakpoints") at the beginning of the routine, or the location where it's called, or the point where a crucial algorithm starts executing. To verify that the preconditions have been satisfied, examine carefully the algorithm's arguments, including parameters, the object on which a method is invoked, and the global state used by the suspect code. In particular, pay attention to the following.

- Look for values that are null when they shouldn't be.

- Verify that arithmetic values are within the domain of the called math function; for example, check that the value passed to log is greater than zero.

- Look inside the objects, structures, and arrays passed to the routine to verify that their contents match what is required; this also helps you pinpoint invalid pointers.

- Check that values are within a reasonable range. Often uninitialized variables have a suspect value, such as 6.89851e-308 or 61007410.

- Spot-check the integrity of any data structure passed to the routine; for example, that a map contains the expected keys and values, or that you can correctly traverse a doubly linked list.

Then, put a breakpoint at the end of the routine, or after the location where it's called, or at the point where a crucial algorithm ends its execution. Now examine the effects of the routine's execution.

- Do the computed results look reasonable? Are they within the range of expected results?

- If yes, are the results actually correct? You can verify this by executing the corresponding code by hand (see Item 38: "Review and Manually Execute Suspect Code"), by comparing them with known good values, or by calculating them with another tool or method.

- Are the routine's side effects the expected ones? Has any other data touched by the suspect code been corrupted or set to an incorrect value? This is especially important for algorithms that maintain their own housekeeping information within the data structures they traverse.

- Have the resources obtained by the algorithm, such as file handles or locks, been correctly released?

You can use the same method for higher-level operations and setups. Verify the operation of an SQL statement that constructs a table by looking at the tables and views it scans and the table it builds. Work on a file-based processing task by examining its input and output files. Debug an operation that is built on web services by looking at the input and output of each individual web service. Troubleshoot an entire data center by examining the facilities required and provided by each element: networking, DNS, shared storage, databases, middleware, and so on. In all cases *verify, don't assume.*

Things to Remember

✦ Carefully examine a routine's preconditions and postconditions.

Item 4: Drill Up from the Problem to the Bug or Down from the Program's Start to the Bug

There are generally two ways to locate a source of a problem. You can either start from the problem's manifestation and work up toward its source, or you can start from the top level of your application or system and work down until you find the source of the problem. Depending on the type of the problem, one approach is usually more effective than the other. However, if you reach a dead end going one way, it may be helpful to switch directions.

Starting from the place where the problem occurs is the way to go when there's a clear sign of the problem. Here are three common scenarios.

First, troubleshooting a **program crash** is typically easy if you run your program in a debugger, if you attach a debugger to it when it has crashed, or if you obtain a memory dump (see Item 35: "Know How to Work with Core Dumps"). What you need to do is examine the values of the variables at the point where the crash occurred, looking for null, corrupted, or uninitialized values that could have triggered the crash. On some systems you can easily recognize uninitialized values through their recurring byte values, such as 0xBAADF00D—*bad food.* You can find a complete list of such values in the *Magic Number* Wikipedia article. Having located a variable with an incorrect value, then try to determine the underlying reason either within the routine where the crash occurred or by moving up the stack of routine calls looking for incorrect arguments or other reasons associated with the crash (see Item 3: "Confirm That Preconditions and Postconditions Are Satisfied" and Item 32: "Navigate along the Calls between Routines").

If this search doesn't help you find the problem, begin a series of program runs, again under a debugger. Each time, set a breakpoint near the point where the incorrect value could have been computed. Continue by placing breakpoints earlier and further up the call sequence until you locate the problem.

Second, if your problem is a **program freeze** rather than a crash, then the process of bottom-up troubleshooting starts a bit differently. Run your program within a debugger, or attach one to it, and then break its execution with the corresponding debugger command (see Item 30: "Use Code and Data Breakpoints") or force it to generate a memory dump (see Item 35: "Know How to Work with Core Dumps"). Sometimes you will realize that the executing code is not your own but that of a library routine. No matter where the break occurred, move up the call stack until you locate the loop that caused your program to freeze. Examine the loop's termination condition, and, starting from it, try to understand why it never gets satisfied.

Third, if the problem is manifesting itself through an **error message**, start by locating the message's text within the program's source code. Your friend here is `fgrep -r` (see Item 22: "Analyze Debug Data with Unix Command-Line Tools") because it can quickly locate the wording within arbitrarily deep and complex hierarchies. In modern localized software, this search will often not locate the code associated with the message, but rather the corresponding string resource. For example, assume you live in a Spanish-speaking country and you're debugging a problem that displays the error "Ha ocurrido un error al procesar el archivo XCF" in the *Inkscape* drawing program. Searching for this string in the *Inkscape* source code will drive you to the Spanish localization file es.po.

```
#: ../share/extensions/gimp_xcf.py:43
msgid "An error occurred while processing the XCF file."
msgstr "Ha ocurrido un error al procesar el archivo XCF."
```

From the localization file, you can obtain the location of the code (share/extensions/gimp_xcf.py, line 43) associated with the message. You then set a breakpoint or log statement just before the point where the error message appears in order to examine the problem at the point where it occurs. Again, be prepared to move back a few code statements and up in the call stack to locate the problem's root cause. If you're searching for non-ASCII text, ensure that your command-line locale settings match the text encoding (e.g., UTF-8) of the source code you'll be searching.

Working from the top level of your failing system down toward the location of the fault is the way to go when you can't clearly identify the code associated with the failure. By definition, this is often the case with so-called *emergent properties*: properties (failures) of your system that you can't readily associate with a specific part of it. Examples include performance (your software takes up too much memory or takes too long to respond), security (you find your web application's web page defaced), and reliability (your software fails to provide the web service it was supposed to).

The way to work top down is to decompose the whole picture into parts, examining the likely contribution of each one to the failure you're debugging. With performance problems, the usual approach is *profiling*: tools and libraries that help you find out which routines clog the CPU or devour memory. In the case of a security problem you would examine all the code for typical vulnerabilities, such as those that lead to buffer overflows, code injections, and cross-site scripting attacks. Again, there are tools that can help analyze the code for such problems (see Item 51: "Use Static Program Analysis"). Finally, in the case of the failing web service, you would dig into each of its internal and external dependencies, verifying that these work as they're supposed to.

Things to Remember

+ Work bottom up in the case of failures that have a clearly identifiable cause, such as crashes, freezes, and error messages.

+ Work top down in the case of failures that are difficult to pin down, such as performance, security, and reliability.

Item 5: Find the Difference between a Known Good System and a Failing One

Often, you may have access both to a failing system and similar one that's working fine. This might happen after you implement some new functionality, when you upgrade your tools or infrastructure, or when you deploy your system on a new platform. If you can still access the older working system, you can often pinpoint the problem by looking at differences between the two systems (as you will see here) or by trying to minimize them (see Item 45: "Minimize the Differences between a Working Example and the Failing Code").

This *differential* mode of debugging works because, despite what our everyday experience suggests, deep down computers are designed to work deterministically; the same inputs produce identical results. Probe sufficiently deep within a failing system, and sooner or later you'll discover the bug that causes it to behave differently from the working one.

It's surprising how many times a system's failure reason stares you right in the eye, if only you would take the time to open its **log file** (see Item 56: "Examine Application Log Files"). This could have a line, such as the following, which indicates an error in the clients.conf configuration file.

```
clients.conf: syntax error in line 92
```

In other cases, the reason is hidden deeper, so you must increase the system's log verbosity in order to expose it.

If the system doesn't offer a sufficiently detailed logging mechanism, you have to tease out its runtime behavior with a **tracing tool**. Besides general-purpose tools such as *DTrace* and *SystemTap*, some specialized tools I've found useful are those that trace calls to the operating system (*strace, truss, Procmon*), those that trace calls to the dynamically linked libraries (*ltrace, Procmon*), those that trace network packets (*tcpdump, Wireshark*), and those that allow the tracing of SQL database calls (see Item 58: "Trace the Code's Execution"). Many Unix applications, such as the *R Project*, start their operation through complex shell scripts, which can misbehave in wonderfully obscure ways. You can trace their operation by passing the -x option to the corresponding shell. In most cases, the trace you obtain will be huge. Thankfully, modern systems have both the storage capacity to save the two logs (the one of the correctly functioning run as well as the one of the failing one) and the CPU oomph to process and compare them.

When it comes to the **environments** in which your systems operate, your goal is to make the two environments as similar as possible. This will make your logs and traces easy to compare, or, if you're lucky, it will lead you directly to the cause behind the bug. Start with the obvious things, such as the program's inputs and command-line arguments. Again, *verify, don't assume*. Actually compare the input files of the two systems against each other or, if they're big and far away, compare their MD5 sums.

Then focus on the code. Start by comparing the source code, but be ready to delve deeper, for this is where the bugs often lurk. Examine the dynamic libraries associated with each executable by using a command such as *ldd* (on Unix) or *dumpbin* with the /dependents option (when using *Visual Studio*). See the defined and used symbols using *nm* (on Unix), *dumpbin* with /exports /imports (*Visual Studio*), or *javap* (when developing Java code). If you're sure the problem lies in the code but can't see any difference, be prepared to dig even deeper, comparing the assembly code that the compiler generates (see Item 37: "Know How to View Assembly Code and Raw Memory").

But before you go to such an extreme, consider other elements that influence the setup of a program's execution. An underappreciated factor is **environment variables**, which even an unprivileged user can set in ways that can wreak havoc on a program's execution. Another is the **operating system**. Your application might be failing on an operating system that's a dozen years newer or older than the one on which it's functioning properly. Also consider the compiler, the development framework, third-party linked libraries, the browser (oh, the joy), the application server, the database system, and other middleware. How to locate the culprit in this maze is the topic we'll tackle next.

Given that in most cases you'll be searching for a needle in a haystack, it makes sense to **trim down** the haystack's size. Therefore, invest the time to find the simplest possible test case in which the bug appears (see Item 10: "Enable the Efficient Reproduction of the Problem"). (Making the needle—the buggy output—larger is rarely productive.) A svelte test case will make your job easier through shorter logs, traces, and processing times. Trim down the test case methodically by gradually removing either elements from the case itself or configuration options from the system until you arrive at the leanest possible setting that still exhibits the bug.

If the difference between the working and failing system lies in their source code, a useful method is to conduct a **binary search** through all the changes performed between the two versions so as to pinpoint the culprit. Thus, if the working system is at version 100 and the failing one is at version 132, you'll first test version 116, and then, depending on the outcome, versions 108 or 124, and so on. The ability to perform such searches is one reason why you should always commit each change separately into your version control system. Thankfully, some version control systems offer a command that performs this search automatically; on Git, it's the git bisect command (see Item 26: "Hunt the Causes and History of Bugs with the Revision Control System").

Another highly productive option is to **compare the two log files** (see Item 56: "Examine Application Log Files") with Unix tools to find the difference related to the bug. The workhorse in this scenario is the *diff* command, which will display the differences between the two files.

However, more often than not, the log files differ in nonessential ways, thus hiding the changes that matter. There are many ways to filter these out. If the leading fields of each line contain varying elements, such as timestamps and process IDs, eliminate them with the *cut* or *awk* commands. As an example, the following command will eliminate the timestamp from the Unix `messages` log file by displaying the lines starting from the fourth field.

```
cut -d ' ' -f 4- /var/log/messages
```

Select only the events that interest you—for instance, files that were opened—using a command such as `grep 'open('`. Or eliminate noise lines (such as those thousands of annoying calls to get the system's time in Java programs) with a command such as `grep -v gettimeofday`. You can also eliminate parts of a line that don't interest you by specifying the appropriate regular expression in a *sed* command.

Finally, a more advanced technique that I've found particularly useful if the two files aren't ordered in a way in which *diff* can yield useful results is to extract the fields that interest you, sort them, and then find the elements that aren't common in the two sets with the *comm* tool. Consider the task of finding which files were only opened in only one of two trace files `t1` and `t2`. In the Unix *Bash* shell, the incantation for finding differences in the second field (the filename) among lines containing the string `open(` would be as follows:

```
comm -23 <(awk '/open\(/{print $2}' t1 | sort) \
         <(awk '/open\(/{print $2}' t2 | sort)
```

The two elements in brackets generate an ordered list of filenames that were passed to open. The *comm* (find common elements) command takes the two lists as input and outputs the lines appearing only in the first one.

Things to Remember

+ Compare the behavior of a known good system with that of a failing one to find the failure's cause.

+ Consider all of the elements that can influence a system's behavior: code, input, invocation arguments, environment variables, services, and dynamically linked libraries.

Item 6: Use the Software's Debugging Facilities

Programs are complex beasts, and for this reason they often contain built-in debugging support. (See Item 40: "Add Debugging Functionality" for how to add such features to software you're developing.) This can, among other things, achieve the following:

- Make the program easier to debug by disabling features such as background or multi-threaded execution

- Allow the precise targeting of a failing test case through its selective execution

- Provide reports and other intelligence regarding performance

- Introduce additional logging

Therefore, invest some effort to find what debugging facilities are available in the software you're debugging. Searching the program's documentation and source code for the word *debug* is an excellent starting point. This can point you to command-line options, configuration settings, build options, signals (on Unix systems), registry settings (on Windows), or command-line interface commands that will enable the program's debug mode.

Typically, setting debugging options will make the program's operation more transparent through verbose output and, sometimes, simpler operation. (Unfortunately, these settings can also cause some bugs to disappear.) Use the expanded log output to explore the reasons behind a failure you're witnessing (see Item 56: "Examine Application Log Files"). Here are a few examples.

A simple case of debugging functionality involves having a command detail its actions. For example, the Unix shells offer the -x option to display the commands they execute. This is useful for debugging tricky text substitution problems. The following is an example of shell loop.

```
find-git-repos |
while read repo ; do
  data=$(echo $repo | sed 's/repos/data/')
  # Skip if done
  test -r $data.out && continue
  # Obtain time series
  qtimeseries $(pwd)/$repo >$data.out 2>$data.err
done
```

Invoking the shell on the script containing the loop with command tracing enabled

```
sh -x script.sh
```

will generate output such as the following, which details the command-output and variable substitutions made.

```
+ read repo
+ echo repos/mysql-server
+ sed s/repos/data/
+ data=data/mysql-server
+ test -r data/mysql-server.out
+ continue
```

Often, a number of options can be combined to set up an execution that's suitable for debugging a problem. Consider troubleshooting a failed *ssh* connection. Instead of modifying the global *sshd* configuration file or keys, which risks locking everybody out, you can invoke *sshd* with options that specify a custom configuration file to use (-f) and a port distinct from the default one (-p). (Note that the same port must also be specified by the client.) Adding the -d (debug) will run the process in the foreground, displaying debug messages on the terminal. These are the commands that will be run on the two hosts where the connection problem occurs.

```
# Command run on the server side
sudo /usr/sbin/sshd -f ./sshd_config -d -p 1234
# Command run on the client side
ssh -p 1234 server.example.com
```

Running them will generate debug output such as that appearing in Figure 1.1. The last line shown indicates the reason for the connection failure.

```
debug1: sshd version OpenSSH_6.6.1p1_hpn13v11 FreeBSD-20140420,
OpenSSL 1.0.1p-freebsd 9 Jul 2015
debug1: read PEM private key done: type RSA
[...]
Server listening on :: port 1234.
debug1: Server will not fork when running in debugging mode.
debug1: rexec start in 5 out 5 newsock 5 pipe -1 sock 8
debug1: inetd sockets after dupping: 3, 3
Connection from 10.212.168.34 port 57864
debug1: Client protocol version 2.0; client software version
OpenSSH_6.7p1 Debian-5
[...]
debug1: trying public key file /home/dds/.ssh/authorized_keys
debug1: fd 4 clearing O_NONBLOCK
Authentication refused: bad ownership or modes for directory
/home/dds/.ssh
```

Figure 1.1 Output of the ssh daemon with debugging enabled

Debugging facilities can also help you pinpoint performance problems. Consider the following two SQL queries.

```
select count(*) from commits where au_id = 1;
select count(*) from commits where
  created_at = '2012-08-01 16:25:36';
```

The first executes in less than 10ms; the second one takes more than three minutes. Using the SQL explain statement uncovers the (obvious in this case) reason for the high execution time of the second query.

```
explain select count(*) from commits where au_id = 1;
explain select count(*) from commits where
  created_at = '2012-08-01 16:25:36';
```

The output of the two statements can be seen in Figure 1.2. The first query is using an index, and is thus only scanning the 21 matching

```
+----+-------------+---------+------+---------------+-------+
| id | select_type | table   | type | possible_keys | key   |
+----+-------------+---------+------+---------------+-------+
|  1 | SIMPLE      | commits | ref  | au_id         | au_id |
+----+-------------+---------+------+---------------+-------+

+---------+-------+------+------------------------+
| key_len | ref   | rows | Extra                  |
+---------+-------+------+------------------------+
| 5       | const |   21 | Using where; Using index |
+---------+-------+------+------------------------+

+----+-------------+---------+------+---------------+------+
| id | select_type | table   | type | possible_keys | key  |
+----+-------------+---------+------+---------------+------+
|  1 | SIMPLE      | commits | ALL  | NULL          | NULL |
+----+-------------+---------+------+---------------+------+

+---------+------+-----------+-------------+
| key_len | ref  | rows      | Extra       |
+---------+------+-----------+-------------+
| NULL    | NULL | 222526953 | Using where |
+---------+------+-----------+-------------+
```

Figure 1.2 The output of an SQL explain statement on a query using an index (top) and a query that doesn't use one (bottom)

rows. The second query is not using an index, and is therefore scanning the table's 222 million rows to find the four matching ones.

Another type of debugging functionality allows you to target a precise case. Consider trying to understand why a specific email message out of the thousands being delivered on a busy host faces a delivery problem. This can be examined by invoking the *Postfix sendmail* command with the verbose (-v) and message delivery (-M) options followed by the identifier of the failing message.

sudo sendmail -v -M 1ZkIDm-0006BH-OX

This will generate output such as the following. Again, the last line in the listing identifies the problem.

```
delivering 1ZkIDm-0006BH-OX
LOG: MAIN
  Unfrozen by forced delivery
R: smarthost for root@example.com
T: remote_smtp_smarthost for root@example.com
Connecting to blade-a1-vm-smtp.servers.example.com
[10.251.255.107]:25 ... connected
  SMTP<< 220 blade-a1-vm-smtp.servers.example.com ESMTP
  SMTP>> EHLO parrot.example.com
  SMTP<< 250-blade-a1-vm-smtp.servers.example.com Ok.
        250-AUTH LOGIN
        250-STARTTLS
        250-XEXDATA
        250-XSECURITY=NONE,STARTTLS
        250 DSN
  SMTP>> STARTTLS
  SMTP<< 220 Ok
  SMTP>> EHLO parrot.example.com
  SMTP<< 250-blade-a1-vm-smtp.servers.example.com Ok.
        250-AUTH LOGIN
        250-XEXDATA
        250-XSECURITY=NONE,STARTTLS
        250 DSN
  SMTP>> MAIL FROM:<> SIZE=2568
  SMTP>> RCPT TO:<root@example.com>
  SMTP>> DATA
  SMTP<< 535 Authentication required.
```

Things to Remember

✦ Identify what debugging facilities are available in the software you're troubleshooting, and use them to investigate the problem you're examining.

Item 7: Diversify Your Build and Execution Environment

Sometimes you can pin down subtle, elusive bugs by changing the playing field. You can do this by building the software with another compiler, or by switching the runtime interpreter, virtual machine, middleware, operating system, or CPU architecture. This works because the other environment may perform stricter checks on the inputs you supply to some routines or because its structure amplifies your mistake (see Item 17: "Increase the Prominence of a Failure's Effects"). Therefore, if you experience application instability, crashes that you can't replicate, or portability problems, try testing your software on another setup. Such a change can also allow you to use more advanced debugging tools, such as a nifty graphical debugger or *dtrace* (see Item 58: "Trace the Code's Execution").

Compiling or running your software on another operating system can unearth incorrect assumptions regarding API usage. As an example, some C and C++ header files often declare more entities than are strictly needed, which may lull you into forgetting to include a required header, resulting, again, in portability problems for your customers. Also, some API implementations can vary significantly between operating systems: *Solaris*, *FreeBSD*, and *GNU/Linux* ship with different implementations of the C library, while the Windows API on the desktop and mobile versions is currently relying on a different code base. Note that these differences can also affect interpreted languages that use the underlying C libraries and APIs, such as JavaScript, Lua, Perl, Python, or Ruby.

On languages that run close to the hardware, such as C and C++, the underlying processor architecture can influence a program's behavior. Over the past decades, the dominance of Intel's x86 processor architecture on the desktop and the ARM architecture on mobile devices has reduced the popularity of architectures with significant differences in byte ordering (*SPARC*, *PowerPC*) or even the handling of null pointer indirection (VAX). Nevertheless, differences in the handling of misaligned memory accesses and memory layout still exist between x86 architecture and ARM. For example, accessing a two-byte value on an odd memory address can generate a fault on some ARM CPUs and may result in non-atomic behavior. On other architectures, misaligned memory accesses may severely affect an application's performance. Furthermore, the size of structures and offsets of their members can differ among the two architectures, especially when using earlier compiler versions. More importantly, the sizes of primitive elements, such as `long` and pointer values, change as you move code from 32-bit to 64-bit architectures or from one operating system to another. Consider the following program, which displays the sizes of five primitive elements.

```
#include <stdio.h>

int
main()
{
    printf("S=%zu I=%zu L=%zu LL=%zu P=%zu\n", sizeof(short),
        sizeof(int), sizeof(long),
        sizeof(long long), sizeof(char *));
}
```

Here is its output in some representative cases.

Windows, Microsoft C/C++ 80x86	S=2 I=4 L=4 LL=8 P=4
Windows, Microsoft C/C++ x64	S=2 I=4 L=4 LL=8 P=8
GNU/Linux, GCC, x86_64	S=2 I=4 L=8 LL=8 P=8
GNU/Linux, GCC, armv6l	S=2 I=4 L=4 LL=8 P=4
OS X, LLVM, x86_64	S=2 I=4 L=8 LL=8 P=8

Therefore, running your software on another architecture or operating system can help you debug and detect portability problems.

On mobile platforms, there's a huge variation not only on the version of the operating system they run (most phone and tablet manufacturers ship their own modified version of the Android operating system), but also significant hardware differences: screen resolution, interfaces, memory, and processor. This makes it even more important to be able to debug your software on a variety of such platforms. To address this problem, mobile app development groups often maintain a stock of many different devices.

There are three main ways to debug your code in another execution environment.

1. You can use **virtual machine software** on your workstation to install and run diverse operating systems. This approach has the

added advantage of providing you with an easy way to maintain a pristine image of the execution environment: just copy the configured virtual machine image to the "master" file, which you can restore when needed.

2. You can use **small inexpensive computers**. If the architecture you're mainly targeting is x86, an easy way to get your hands on an ARM CPU is to keep at hand a *Raspberry Pi*. This miniature ARM-based device runs many popular operating systems. It's easy to plug into an Ethernet switch or connect it via Wi-Fi so that you can access it over the network. This will also allow you to cut your teeth into the GNU/Linux development environment, which can be beneficial if you're mainly debugging your code on Windows or OS X. Also, if Windows is your regular cup of tea, a Mac mini tucked under your desk can offer you easy access to an OS X development environment.

3. You can rent **cloud-based hosts** running the operating systems you want to use.

It's not always necessary to use another operating system or device to debug your software on diverse compiler and runtime environments. You can easily introduce ecosystem variety on your own development workstation. By doing so, you can regularly benefit from the additional errors and warnings and stricter conformance in some areas that another environment can offer you. As is the case with static analysis tools (see Item 51: "Use Static Program Analysis"), different compilers can typically detect more problems than a single one can. This includes both portability problems, which may inadvertently creep in due to lax checking by a particular compiler, and logical flaws that one compiler may not warn about. Compilers are very good at compiling any legal code into a matching executable but are sometimes not as good at flagging misuse of the language, for example, identifying code that works only if a particular included header file also declares some undocumented elements. A second pair of compiler eyes can help you in this regard. All you need to do is to install—and use as part of your debugging lifecycle—an alternative to your mainstream environment. Here are some suggestions.

- For .NET Framework development, use *Mono* in parallel with Microsoft's tools and environment.

- For the development of Ada, C, C++, Objective C, and other supported languages, use both *LLVM* and *GCC*.

- For Java development, use both the *OpenJDK* (or Oracle's offering from the same code base) and *GNU Classpath*. Also try using more than one Java runtime.

- For Ruby programs, apart from the reference *CRuby* implementation, try other VMs: *JRuby*, *Rubinius*, and *mruby*.

A more radical alternative involves reimplementing part of your code in another language. This can be helpful when you're debugging a tricky algorithm. The typical case involves an initial (failing) implementation written in a relatively low-level language, such as C. Consider implementing an alternative in a more high-level language: Python, R, Ruby, Haskell, or the Unix shell. The alternative implementation achieved by using the language's high-level features, such as operations on sets, pipes and filters, and higher-order functions, may help you arrive at a correctly functioning algorithm. Through this method, you can quickly identify problems in the algorithm's design and also fix implementation faults. Then, if performance is really critical, you can implement the algorithm in the original language or a language that's closer to the CPU and use differential debugging techniques (see Item 5: "Find the Difference between a Known Good System and a Failing One") to make it work.

Things to Remember

+ Diverse compilation and execution platforms can offer you valuable debugging insights.

+ Fix a tricky algorithm by implementing it in a higher-level language.

Item 8: Focus Your Work on the Most Important Problems

Most big software systems ship and operate with countless (known and unknown) bugs. Deciding in an intelligent manner on which bugs to concentrate and which bugs to ignore will increase your debugging effectiveness. Hopefully, you're not being paid to minimize the number of open issues, but to help deliver reliable, usable, maintainable, and efficient software. Therefore, set priorities through an issue-tracking system (see Item 1: "Handle All Problems through an Issue-Tracking System"), and use them to concentrate your work on top-priority issues and to ignore low-priority ones. Here are a few points to help your prioritization.

Give a high priority to the following types of problems.

- **Data loss**: This can occur as a result of either data corruption or usability issues. Users entrust their data to your software. If you lose their data you violate that trust, and trust that is lost is difficult to regain.

- **Security**: This may affect the confidentiality or integrity of the software's data, the integrity of the system where your software is running, or the availability of the service your software is providing. Such problems are often exploited by malicious individuals and can therefore result in large monetary and reputational damage. Security problems can also garner unwelcomed attention from regulatory authorities or extortionists. Consequently, sweeping security issues under the carpet is not an option.

- **Reduced service availability**: If your software is providing a service, the cost of downtime may be measured in dollars (sometimes millions of them). Lost goodwill, late-night phone calls from irate managers, and clogged support desks are additional consequences you want to avoid.

- **Safety**: These are issues that may result in death or serious injury to people, loss or severe damage to property, or environmental harm. All consequences of the preceding problems apply here. If your software can fail in such a way, you should have more rigorous processes than this list to guide your actions.

- **Crash or freeze**: This may result in data loss or downtime, and it may also signify an underlying security problem. Thankfully, you can often easily debug a crashed or non-responding application through postmortem debugging (see Item 35: "Know How to Work with Core Dumps"). Consequently, it makes little sense to give such issues a low priority.

- **Code hygiene**: Compiler warnings, failed assertions, unhandled exceptions, memory leaks, and, in general, inferior code quality provide a fertile ground for serious bugs to develop and hide. Therefore, don't let such issues persist and accumulate (see Item 20: "Houseclean Before and After Debugging").

The following are types of problems you may decide to relegate to a lower priority. These issues are not by themselves unworthy of your attention. However, they are issues you may be able to set aside in order to deal with more urgent ones.

- **Legacy support**: Support for outdated hardware, API, and file formats is commendable, but, from a business perspective, it won't get you very far because, by definition, you're serving a shrinking market.

- **Backward compatibility**: Here the case is less clear-cut because if your software evolves in a way that leaves behind past users, you're losing customer goodwill. Some companies, such as Nikon, have established a stellar reputation by maintaining backward compatibility through many generations of their product: you can still use a 1970s Nikkor lens on high-end modern Nikon cameras. On the other hand, some successful software firms are known for their "take no prisoners" approach, where they ditch support for older software and services without any qualm. Sometimes it may be worth eliminating support for an old feature in order to focus on the future.

- **Cosmetic issues**: These may be devilishly hard to get right and easy to ignore. You are unlikely to lose business over a truncated bubble-help item, but dynamically adjusting the size of the item's panel based on the screen's dpi setting can be a nightmare.

- **Documented workarounds**: You may be able to avoid debugging some tricky issues by documenting a workaround. After switching on my TV, the first time I try to use the TV's remote to operate the media player I get a "Please try again" prompt. I suspect that properly fixing this minor problem may be a major project.

- **Rarely used features**: For problems associated with an exotic, rarely used feature of your software, it may be more productive to yank the corresponding feature (and deal with the small, if any, fallout), than to actually solve the problem. Collecting usage data regarding your software can make it easier for you to reach such decisions.

Note that you should be explicit when you decide to ignore a low-priority issue. File it in the issue-tracking system, and then close it with an action such as "*won't solve.*" This documents the decision you've made and helps avoid the management overhead of future duplicate issues.

Things to Remember

+ Not all problems are worth solving.

+ Fixing a low-priority issue may deprive you of the time required to address a high-priority one.

General-Purpose Methods and Practices

The way you debug a failure often depends on the underlying technology and development platform. Yet, there are methods that you can use on a wide variety of cases.

Item 9: Set Yourself Up for Debugging Success

Software is often extremely complex. The movement of a mechanical watch comprises just over a hundred parts; the wiring of your entire home can have a few times as many simple components. Compare that with typical software systems, which easily consist of tens of thousands of complex statements. At the high end, consider the 9 million lines of code in the Linux kernel against the 4 million physical components in an A380 airliner. Your mind needs all the help it can get to conquer this complexity.

First you need to **believe that the problem can be found and fixed**. Your state of mind affects your debugging performance; this is what the experts call *a match between perceived challenges and skills*. If you don't believe you can conquer the problem, your mind will wander around or give up. In such a case, you may also end up harming the code by patching the symptom, instead of the problem. Here is what you should keep in mind.

If a problem is reproducible, then make no mistake, you can fix it! (Often by following the advice in this book.) If it's not reproducible, there are ways to make it so. In debugging you typically have two important allies: access to all the data you may require and powerful computers to process it. You can examine the problem manifestation, logs, source code, even machine instructions. You can also add detailed log statements (or at least monitoring probes) in any place of the software stack you want, and then use tools or short scripts to sift through volumes of data to locate the culprit. It is this combined ability to cast a wide net and dive arbitrarily deep when needed that makes debugging possible and, also, a uniquely satisfying experience.

To be effective in debugging you also need to **set aside ample time.** Debugging is a very demanding activity, more complex than programming, because it requires you to maintain in your brain both the program's logic and its underlying effects—often at a low level. It also requires you to set up your environment, breakpoints, logging, windows, and test cases exactly right if the problem is to be reproduced in a productive fashion. Don't squander all your invested time by stopping before you've squashed the bug, or at least until you've understood precisely what you need to do.

The complexity of debugging also requires you to **work without distractions.** Your brain needs time to enter a state called *flow* in which you become fully immersed and involved in an activity. According to Mihály Csíkszentmihályi, who termed it, in the state of flow you align your emotions with the task you perform. Flow can boost your persistence and performance through a sense of accomplishment. These are critical success factors for dealing with the immense difficulty of debugging complex systems. Distractions, such as a popup message, a phone call, a running chat, rolling social network updates, or a colleague asking for help will drag you out of the flow state, depriving you of its benefits. Avoid them! Quit unneeded applications, enable your phone's silent mode, and hang a *do not disturb sign* on your monitor (or your office door, should you be so lucky as to have one).

Another helpful strategy is to **sleep on a difficult problem.** Researchers have found that during sleep our neurons make connections that generalize across seemingly unrelated paths. This can be a great help during debugging. You can often escape from what appears to be a dead end by trying an outside-the-box debugging strategy. Sleep is exactly the process needed to make this new connection. However, for this to work, you need to do it properly. Work hard on the problem before going to sleep to give your mind all the necessary data needed in order to find a novel solution to the problem. Giving up and going for a beer and then to bed at the first difficulty won't help you a lot. Also, get plenty of sleep so that on the next day the conscious part of your brain can work effectively with the recommendations of its subconscious sibling.

Nobody said that debugging is easy, so to be effective in it you must **persist.** At the lowest level computers are deterministic, so they allow you to dig down until you isolate the error. At higher levels, nondeterminism (apparent randomness) is introduced to increase expressiveness and efficiency (think of threads). For nondeterministic errors, you can use the fact that computers are fast and programmable to run zillions of cases until you isolate the error. Therefore, debugging dead ends are mostly due to a lack of persistence: a missing test case, an ignored log file, or an unexplored angle of attack.

Finally, as an effective debug engineer, you must continuously **invest in your environment, tools, and knowledge.** Only in this way will you be able to keep your edge over the ever-increasing complexity of the technology stack you're working on. In retrospect, my most common debugging mistake is insufficient investment in setting up my debugging infrastructure. This may involve failing to do any of the following:

- Prepare a robust minimal test case (see Item 10: "Enable the Efficient Reproduction of the Problem")

- Automate the bug's reproduction

- Script a log file's analysis

- Learn how an API or language feature really works

Once I summon the energy to invest in what's needed, my debugging productivity receives a large boost. From that point onward, I can often pinpoint the bug in minutes.

Things to Remember

✦ Believe that the problem can be traced and fixed.

✦ Set aside sufficient time for your debugging task.

✦ Arrange to work without distractions.

✦ Sleep on a difficult problem.

✦ Don't give up.

✦ Invest in your environment, tools, and knowledge.

Item 10: Enable the Efficient Reproduction of the Problem

A key to effective debugging is a problem that you can reliably and easily reproduce. You need this for a number of reasons. First, if you can always reproduce the issue with a single hit of a button, you can focus on tracking down the cause rather than wasting time randomly fumbling to make the problem appear. In addition, if you can provide an easy way to reproduce the problem, you can easily take the description and ask for outside help (see Item 2: "Use Focused Queries to Search the Web for Insights into Your Problem"). Finally, once you fix the fault, you can easily demonstrate that your fix works by running the sequence that demonstrated the problem again and witnessing that the failure no longer occurs.

Creating a short example or a *test case* that reproduces the problem can go a long way in increasing your efficiency. The golden standard is a *minimal* example: the shortest possible that reproduces the problem. The platinum standard, which goes under the name SSCCE (see Item 1: "Handle All Problems through an Issue-Tracking System"), has the example be not only short, but also self-contained and correct (compilable and runable). With a minimal example at hand, you won't waste time exploring code paths that could have been eliminated. Also, any logs and traces you create and must examine won't be longer than what's actually needed. And, a short example will also execute more quickly than a longer one, especially when executed in a debugging mode that imposes a significant performance overhead.

To shorten your example, you can proceed top-down or bottom-up (see Item 4: "Drill Up from the Problem to the Bug or Down from the Program's Start to the Bug"). Select the most expedient method. If the code has many dependencies, starting bottom-up from a clean slate may be preferable. If you don't really understand the problem's likely cause, creating a test case in a top-down fashion may help you narrow down the possibilities.

In the bottom-up fashion, you theorize the cause of the problem, for example, a call to a specific API, and you build up a test case that demonstrates the problem. In one case, I was trying to find out why a 27,000-line program was extremely slow in the complex code it used for processing its input files. By looking at the program's invoked system calls, I hypothesized that the problem had something to do with calling `tellg`—a function returning the file stream's offset—while reading the file. Indeed, running the following short snippet confirmed my suspicion (see Item 58: "Trace the Code's Execution") and was also useful to test the workaround (a wrapper class).

```
ifstream in(fname.c_str(), ios::binary);
do {
  (void)in.tellg();
} while ((val = in.get()) != EOF);
```

In the top-down fashion, you remove elements from the scenario that demonstrates the problem, until there's nothing left to remove. A binary search technique is often quite useful. Say you have an HTML file that makes the browser behave in an erratic way. First eliminate the file's head elements. If the problem persists, eliminate the body elements. If that cures the problem, restore the body elements, and then remove half of them. Repeat the process until you've nailed down the elements that cause the problem. Keeping your editor open and using its undo function to backtrack when you follow a wrong path will mightily increase your efficiency.

With a short example at hand, it's also easy to make it **self-contained.** This means that you can take the example and replicate the problem somewhere else without external dependencies, such as libraries, headers, CSS files, and web services. If your test case requires some external elements, you can bundle them with it. Use a portable notation for referring to them, avoiding things such as absolute file paths and hard-coded IP addresses. For instance use ../resources/file.css rather than /home/susan/resources/file.css, and http://localhost:8081/myService rather than http://193.92.66.100:8081/myService. A self-contained example will make it easier for you to try it on the customer's premises, examine it on another platform (say, on Windows instead of Linux), publish it on a Q&A forum (see Item 2: "Use Focused Queries to Search the Web for Insights into Your Problem"), and ship it to a vendor for further help.

In addition, you want to work on a **replicable execution environment.** If you don't nail down the code you're working on and the system it executes in, then you might end up searching for a bug that simply isn't there. Consider the case of debugging a software installer. Every time you install it, it messes up your operating system configuration, which is exactly what you want to avoid when you're trying to debug it. In this case, a useful technique is to create a virtual machine image with a pristine system in a state ready for the software installation. After every failed installation, you can simply start afresh with that image. You can also often achieve a similar result using operating-system-level virtualization or containment with a tool such as *Docker*. Even better, consider adopting a system configuration management tool, such as *Ansible*, *CFEngine*, *Chef*, *Puppet*, or *Salt*. These tools allow you to reliably create a specified system configuration from your high-level instructions. This makes it easy to maintain compatible production, testing, and development environments, and to control their evolution in the same way as you control your software.

You also want to be able to **reliably replicate the failing version** of your software. To do this, first put your software under configuration management with a tool, such as *Git*. Then, make your build process embed into the software an identifier of the source code version used for the build. The following shell command will print a variable initialization with the abbreviated Git hash of the last commit, which you can embed into your source code.

```
git log -n 1 --format='const string version = "%h";'
```

Here is an example of its output.

```
const string version = "035cd45";
```

Add to your software a way to display this version string; a command-line option or a line in the *About* dialog are all that's needed. With this version identifier at hand you can then obtain a copy of the failing source code with a command such as the following:

```
git checkout 035cd45
```

If you want to increase the fidelity of builds you run on old code, don't forget to put under version control all elements that affect what ends up in your distribution, such as the compiler, system and third-party libraries and header files, as well as the build specification (the *Makefile*s or IDE project configuration). As a final step, you may need to remove the variability introduced by your tools and your runtime environment (see Item 52: "Configure Deterministic Builds and Executions").

Things to Remember

+ Reproducible runs simplify your debugging process.

+ Create a short self-contained example that reproduces the problem.

+ Have mechanisms to create a replicable execution environment.

+ Use a revision control system to label and retrieve your software's versions.

Item 11: Minimize the Turnaround Time from Your Changes to Their Result

Debugging is often a process of successive approximation. The time you wait (again and again) for the software to build, run, and fail, and the time you spend (again and again) to cajole it to go through these steps is time you don't devote in solving your problem. Therefore, early on, invest in minimizing the time it takes to go through a debug cycle.

Start with the software build. You should be able to **quickly build** the failing software with a single command or keystroke, such as make, mvn compile, or F5. The build process should track dependencies between files ensuring that only a few files get compiled after you change something. Tools that can help you here include *make*, *Ant*, and *Maven*.

The **efficient deploying and running** of the software is equally important. The steps here vary a lot between projects. You may need to deploy files on a remote host, restart an application server, clear caches, or reinitialize a database. Use the project's build system or write some scripts to automate this process (see Item 12: "Automate Complex Testing Scenarios"). If a typical installation of your software involves a protracted construction of a distribution file and its subsequent slow installation, setup a shortcut where you only copy the modified files to their final location.

Finally, ensure that the software will **quickly fail** (see Item 55: "Fail Fast"). If the failing code comes with unit tests or a regression-testing framework, build a test case that demonstrates the specific failure (see Item 10: "Enable the Efficient Reproduction of the Problem"). Then use features of your IDE or testing environment to run the specific test case. For instance, under *Maven* you can run the `TestFetch` case with the following command.

```
mvn -Dtest=TestFetch test
```

If the program you're debugging can be made to fail by processing a specific file, then construct a minimal file that can trigger this failure. To replicate problems in GUI applications, you can use software automation applications, such as *Selenium* for web browsers, *AutoHotkey* for Windows, *Automator* for OS X, and *AutoKey* for Linux.

Things to Remember

+ A fast turnaround time increases your effectiveness.

+ Set up a fast automated build and deployment process.

+ Minimize the time it takes for your tests to fail.

Item 12: Automate Complex Testing Scenarios

Automate complex scripting scenarios through the use of scripting. There are multiple options for this. For orchestrating processes and files, the Unix shell offers many useful facilities (see Item 22: "Analyze Debug Data with Unix Command-Line Tools"). In addition, with commands such as *cURL* to fetch URLs and *jq* to parse JSON data, you can also use the shell to test web services. In complex cases involving API access and state maintenance, you will benefit from a more sophisticated scripting language, such as Python, Ruby, or Perl. Also, numerous systems come with their own built-in scripting language; for example, the *Apache HTTP Server*, the *Wireshark* network packet analyzer, and the *VLC* media player all support the *Lua* programming language.

If your software does not support a scripting language and you have the ability to modify it, consider bolting a scripting language onto it, and add API bindings that expose the scripting language to your program's functions. As a (simple but contrived) example, say you want to construct a test case associated with a math library you've implemented. The C program in Listing 2.1 will load and run the Lua program debug.lua, exposing to it the functions sin, cos, and tan.

Listing 2.1 Exporting C functions for testing through Lua

```c
#include <math.h>
#include "lua5.2/lua.h"
#include "lua5.2/lauxlib.h"

// Functions exposed to Lua
static int l_sin(lua_State *L) {
    double value_as_number = luaL_checknumber(L, 1);
    // Call the function, and return the result
    lua_pushnumber(L, sin(value_as_number));
    return 1; // Single result
}

static int l_cos(lua_State *L) {
    double value_as_number = luaL_checknumber(L, 1);
    lua_pushnumber(L, cos(value_as_number));
    return 1;
}

static int l_tan(lua_State *L) {
    double value_as_number = luaL_checknumber(L, 1);
    lua_pushnumber(L, tan(value_as_number));
    return 1;
}

int main() {
    // Setup Lua
    lua_State *L = luaL_newstate();
    luaL_openlibs(L);

    // Expose the functions to Lua
    lua_pushcfunction(L, l_sin);
    lua_setglobal(L, "lsin");
    lua_pushcfunction(L, l_cos);
    lua_setglobal(L, "lcos");
    lua_pushcfunction(L, l_tan);
    lua_setglobal(L, "ltan");
```

```
// Load and run the debug file
luaL_dofile(L, "debug.lua");
puts("Done");
return 0;
}
```

On a Debian Linux distribution, I installed Lua by running sudo apt-get install lua5.2-dev and compiled the program with cc myprog.c -llua5.2 -lm. (You can find advice on how to install Lua on other systems in Lua's documentation.) I then wrote the following small Lua program to verify the accuracy of the functions with respect to the definition of the tangent function.

$$\tan \vartheta = \frac{\sin \vartheta}{\cos \vartheta}$$

```
epsilon = 1
errors = 0
while epsilon > 0 and errors < 2 do
    for theta = 0, 2 * math.pi, 0.1 do
        diff = lsin(theta) / lcos(theta) - ltan(theta)
        if (math.abs(diff) > epsilon) then
            print(epsilon, theta, diff)
            errors = errors + 1
        end
    end
    epsilon = epsilon / 10
end
```

Running the C program will load the Lua code and produce output such as the following:

```
1e-14 4.7    1.4210854715202e-14
1e-15 1.5    1.7763568394003e-15
1e-15 4.7    1.4210854715202e-14
```

In a more realistic scenario, the C program would be your large application, the trigonometric functions would be the functions of the application you wanted to check, and the Lua program would make it easy for you to tinker with test cases for these functions.

Things to Remember

✦ Automate the execution of complex test cases through the use of a scripting language.

Item 13: Enable a Comprehensive Overview of Your Debugging Data

Effective debugging entails processing and correlating loads of diverse data: source code, log entries, the values of variables, stack contents, program I/O, and test results, all of these often from multiple processes and computing hosts. Having all those data properly laid out in front of you offers you many benefits. First, it allows you to detect correlations, such as a log entry appearing when a test fails. Then, it minimizes your context switching overhead and the disruptions this brings. Having to enter a command or juggle windows to see the values of some variables when you single-step through code can break the all-important mental flow (see Item 9: "Set Yourself Up for Debugging Success") that might be required to spot a crucial connection. Also, sufficient space to lay out long lines can help you establish patterns that you would otherwise miss. You may have configured your editor windows to match the 70–80 columns prescribed by many code style guides. However, when long lines of log files and stack traces are folded multiple times to fit into such an 80-column line, they become difficult to read and analyze. Lay those lines out on your monitor's glorious full width, and patterns will stand out; see Figure 2.1 for an example. Here are some ways to increase the amount of data you can examine when you debug.

First, **maximize your display area.** Many developers also use two (or more) high-resolution monitors. (Using large cheap TV screens won't cut it, for they will just give you blurry characters.) For this to work, you'll need a correspondingly powerful graphics interface. If you're working on a laptop, you can connect an external monitor, *extend* (rather than *clone*) your display into it, and benefit from the increased screen real estate. In all these cases, don't shy away from switching your editor or terminal window to full-screen mode. It may look silly on a modern full HD monitor, but for some tasks, being able to see the data along and across is an indispensable affordance. If the data still can't fit, decrease the font size (and get a pair of glasses) or use a video projector.

Printing stuff can also be remarkably effective. At just 600-DPI resolution, a laser printer can display 6600 × 5100 pixels on a letter-size paper—many more than your monitor, which you can use to display more and crisper data. You can use printed sheets for items that don't change a lot, such as data structure definitions and listings, and free up your screen to display the more dynamic parts of your debugging session. Finally, the best medium for program listings is surely the 15-inch green bar fanfold paper. There you can print 132-column-wide text of unlimited length. If you've still got access to a printer that can handle this, use it. And guard its existence.

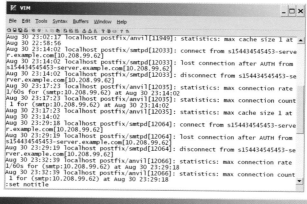

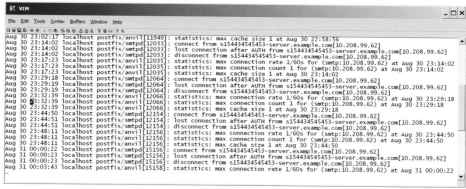

Figure 2.1 A representation of how a log file will look: in the default editor setup (top) and with a wide view (bottom)

Things to Remember

✦ With a lot of data in view, you can concentrate better and spot patterns and correlations.

✦ Use the largest display area you can obtain.

✦ Display relatively static data on printed sheets.

Item 14: Consider Updating Your Software

Guess what? Your code is not the only one that has errors in it. The compiler or interpreter that's processing your code, the libraries you use, the database and application servers you depend on, and the operating systems that are hosting everything all have their own fair share of bugs. For example, at the time of this writing, the Linux source code contained more than 2,700 comments marked with XXX, which typically denotes a questionable construct; some of these are surely bugs.

Consequently, some bugs can be addressed by **updating** your software. Using a newer compiler or library may help you correct an obscure bug in the packaged software you're shipping. If you're delivering a software-based service, then updating middleware, databases, and the operating system can also help. At the very least try building, linking, or running your code with the newest versions to eliminate the possibility that you're witnessing a third-party bug. However, keep in mind that there's a lot to be said for a conservative upgrade policy—working with the devil you know. A lot of middleware suffers from faulty or limited backward compatibility, so experienced users are usually very careful when doing updates, opting for the next earliest bug-fixing release (e.g., 6.4.3) that would solve their problem. Also, new software can introduce new bugs and incompatibilities, so at the very least don't burn your bridges rushing into it: have a sensible back-off plan if the upgrade doesn't work, or if it doesn't address the bug you're witnessing. Updating the third-party code in a sandbox, such as a throw-away cloned virtual machine image, is a reliable and easy way to achieve this. Whatever happens, don't expect too much from software upgrades.

It's best to assume that outside code is innocent until proven guilty. Most of the time, bugs you blame on third-party code are actually problems in your own. Over the course of thirty years, I've fixed thousands of bugs in my own code. Over the same period, I've encountered a single case where a widely used commercial compiler generated incorrect code, a few instances of bugs in libraries, one case of unreliable operating system functionality, a handful of errors in system call documentation, and just tens of errors in tools and other system software. Therefore, the biggest benefit you'll get from using updated software is a new resolve to get your own house in order.

Things to Remember

✦ Try your failing system on an updated environment.

✦ Don't expect too much from this exercise.

✦ Consider the possibility of third-party bugs.

Item 15: Consult Third-Party Source Code for Insights on Its Use

Often problems occur due to the way the code you're debugging uses a third-party library or application (rather than actual bugs in that software—see Item 14: "Consider Updating Your Software").

This is no surprise, because such software gets integrated with your code as a black box, and therefore you have fewer opportunities to coordinate. A powerful way to debug these problems is to consult the source code of third-party libraries, middleware, and even lower-level software.

First, if you need to know why a particular API behaves in an unexpected way or what triggers a cryptic error message, you can find the answer by **browsing the third-party source code** around the area that interests you. To debug functionality related to a library, locate the function or method definition and follow the code from there. You're probably not looking for a bug in the library's code, but rather for a better understanding of how the library works and ties in with your code. To understand an error message, search through all the code for the wording of the error message, and examine the code leading to it (see Item 23: "Utilize Command-Line Tool Options and Idioms" and Item 4: "Drill Up from the Problem to the Bug or Down from the Program's Start to the Bug"). You can quickly locate the function or method you're looking for by indexing the code with the *ctags* or *etags* program (most editors support its output), or with your integrated development environment (IDE). Your IDE is likely to handle sophisticated language features such as overloading, overriding, and templates better than *ctags*. On the other hand, *etags* handles many more languages: 41 in version 5.8. The following command, when run on a source code directory, will create an index for all files lying under it.

```
ctags -R .
```

If the third-party code you're using is open source, you can also search through it through a hosted service, such as the *Black Duck Open Hub Code Search*.

A more powerful technique involves **building the third-party with debugging information** (see Item 28: "Use Code Compiled for Symbolic Debugging"). Then link your code with the debug version of the library you built. Having done that, you can easily step through the third-party code and examine variables with the symbolic debugger (see Chapter 4), just as you can do with your own code. Note that some vendors, such as Microsoft, ship with their code debug builds or symbols. This saves you the effort of debug-building their code on your own.

If you happen to find that a fault lies in the third-party code rather than yours, with access to the source code you can actually **correct** it there. Use this option only in extreme circumstances: if there is no reasonable workaround, and you can't get the vendor to fix it for you. Once you modify third-party code, you'll be responsible for maintaining the change across its new versions for the lifetime of your application.

Also ensure you're legally allowed to modify the code. Some vendors ship their code with a "look, don't touch" license. For open-source software, a reasonable option is to submit your changes to the project responsible for the code. This is also the right thing to do. If the project is hosted on *GitHub*, you can easily do that with a *pull request*.

For all these wonderful things to work, **you need to have the third-party source code at hand**. This is trivial if the library or application you're using is open source. Then, you can download the source code with a click of a button. Open-source operating system distributions also offer you the ability to download the source code as a package; this is the command you would use under Debian Linux to install the C library source code.

```
sudo apt-get install glibc-source
```

In addition, many software development platforms will install important parts of their source code on your system. For instance, you can find the source code for the C runtime library of Microsoft's *Visual Studio* at a location VC\crt\src and for the Java Development Kit in an archive named src.zip. In other cases, you may have to pay extra to obtain the source code when you order the third-party software. Insist on this option if the price is not exorbitant. Getting the source code later when you need it might require a lot of time to budget, place the order, and execute any required agreement. Also, the vendor might have stopped supporting the version you use or might even have gone out of business. Getting the source code for proprietary software beforehand is a reasonable insurance policy against these problems.

Things to Remember

✦ Get the source code for third-party code you depend on.

✦ Explore problems with third-party APIs and cryptic error messages by looking at the source code.

✦ Link with the library's debug build.

✦ Correct third-party code only when there's no other reasonable alternative.

Item 16: Use Specialized Monitoring and Test Equipment

Debugging embedded systems and systems software sometimes requires you to be able to inspect and analyze the whole computing stack, from the hardware to the application. Deep down at the hardware level, debugging involves detecting minute changes in electron flows and the alignment of magnetic moments. In most cases, you can use powerful IDEs as well as tracing and logging software to see what's going on. Yet there are situations where these tools leave you none the wiser. This often happens when software touches hardware: you think your software behaves as it should, but the hardware seems to have its own ideas. For example, you can see that you write the correct data to disk, but the data appears corrupt when you read it. When you debug problems close to the hardware level, some fancy equipment may offer you significant help.

A general-purpose tool that you may find useful is a *logic analyzer*. This captures, stores, and analyzes digital signals coming in at speeds of millions of samples per second. Such devices used to cost more than a new car, but now you can buy a cheap USB-based one for about $100. With such a device you can monitor arbitrary digital signals on a hardware board but also higher communication protocols that components use to talk to each other. The alphabet soup and number of supported protocols is bewildering; quoting from one manufacturer (*saleae*): "SPI, I2C, serial, 1-Wire, CAN, UNI/O, I2S/PCM, MP Mode, Manchester, Modbus, DMX-512, Parallel, JTAG, LIN, Atmel SWI, MDIO, SWD, LCD HD44780, BiSS C, HDLC, HDMI CEC, PS/2, USB 1.1, Midi."

If you specialize in a particular technology, you may want to invest in dedicated equipment, such as a *protocol analyzer* or *bus analyzer*. As an example, vehicle and other microcontrollers often communicate over the so-called CAN (controller area network) bus. A number of companies offer stand-alone self-contained modules that can plug into the bus and filter, display, and log the exchanged traffic. Similar products exist for other widely used or specialized physical interconnections and protocols, such as Ethernet, USB, Fibre Channel, SAS, SATA, RapidIO, iSCSI, sFPDP, and OBSAI. In contrast to software-based solutions, these devices are guaranteed to work at the true line rate, they offer support for monitoring multiple traffic lanes, and they allow you to define triggers and filters based on bit patterns observed deep inside the data packet frame.

If you lack dedicated debugging hardware, don't shy away from **improvising** something to suit your needs. This can help you investigate problems that are difficult to replicate. A few years ago we faced a problem with missing data from a web form drop box. The trouble was that the occurrence of the problem was rare and impossible to reproduce, though it affected many quite vocal users for days. (The application was used by hundreds of thousands.) By looking at the distribution of the affected users, we found that these were often based in remote areas. Hypothesizing that the problem had to do with the quality of their Internet connection, I took a USB wireless modem, wrapped it in tinfoil to simulate a marginal connection, and used that to connect to the application's web interface. I could immediately see the exact problem, and, armed with an easy way to replicate (see Item 10: "Enable the Efficient Reproduction of the Problem") it, we were able to solve it in just a few hours.

If the code you're trying to debug runs as **embedded software** on a device that lacks decent I/O, there are several tricks you can play to communicate with the software you're debugging.

- If the device has a status light or if it can beep, use coded flashes or beeps to indicate what the software is doing. For example, one short beep could signify that the software has entered a particular routine and two that it has exited. You can send more sophisticated messages with *Morse Code*.

- Store log output in non-volatile storage (even on an external USB thumb drive), and then retrieve the data on your own workstation in order to analyze it.

- Implement a simple serial data encoder, and use that to write the data on an unused I/O pin. Then, you can level-convert the signal to *RS-232* levels and use a serial-to-USB adapter and a terminal application to read the data on a modern computer.

- If the device has a network connection, you can obviously communicate through it. If it lacks the software for network logging (see Item 41: "Add Logging Statements") or remote shell access, you can communicate with the outside world through HTTP or even DNS requests.

When you're monitoring **network packets,** you can set up your network's hardware in a way that allows you to use a *software packet analyzer*, such as the open-source *Wireshark* package. The Wireshark version running on my laptop claims to support 1,514 (network and USB) protocols and packet types. If you can run the application you want to debug on the same host as the one you'll use Wireshark, then network packet monitoring can be child's play. Fire up Wireshark, specify the packets you want to capture, and then look at them in detail.

Monitoring traffic between other hosts, such as that between an application server and a database server or a load balancer, can be more tricky. The problem is that *switches*, the devices that connect together

Ethernet cabling, isolate the traffic flowing between two ports from the others. You have numerous options to overcome this difficulty.

If your organization is using a *managed* (read "expensive") switch, then you can set up one port to mirror the traffic on another port. Mirroring the traffic of the server you want to monitor on the port where your computer running Wireshark is connected allows you to capture and analyze the server's traffic.

If you don't have access to a managed switch, try to get hold of an Ethernet *hub*. These are much simpler devices that broadcast the Ethernet traffic they receive on all ports. Hubs are no longer made, and this is why they're often more expensive than cheap switches. Connect the computer you want to monitor and the one running Wireshark to the hub, and you're ready to go.

Yet another way to monitor remote hosts involves using a command-line tool such as *tcpdump*. Remotely log in into the host you want to monitor, and run *tcpdump* to see the network packets that interest you. (You will need administrator privileges to do that.) If you want to perform further analysis with Wireshark's GUI, you can write the raw packets into a file with *tcpdump*'s –w option, which you can then analyze in detail with Wireshark. This mode of working is particularly useful with cloud-based hosts, where you can't easily tinker with the networking configuration.

One last possibility involves setting up a computer to *bridge* network packets between the computer you want to monitor and the rest of the network. You configure that computer with two network interfaces (e.g., its native port and a USB-based one), and bridge the two ports together. On Linux use the *brctl* command; on FreeBSD configure the *if_bridge* driver.

You can also use a similarly configured device to simulate various networking scenarios such as packets coming from hosts around the world, traffic shaping, bandwidth limitations, and firewall configurations. Here the software you'll want to use is *iptables*, which runs under Linux.

Things to Remember

+ A logic, bus, or protocol analyzer can help you pinpoint problems that occur near the hardware level.

+ A home-brew contraption may help you investigate problems related to hardware.

+ Monitor network packets with *Wireshark* and an Ethernet hub, a managed switch, or command-line capture.

Item 17: Increase the Prominence of a Failure's Effects

Making problems stand out can increase the effectiveness of your debugging. You can achieve this by manipulating your software, its input, or its environment. In all cases, ensure you perform the changes under revision control in a separate branch, so that you can easily revert them and they won't end up by mistake in production code.

There are cases where your software simply refuses to behave in the way you expect it to. For example, although certain complex conditions are apparently satisfied, the record that's supposed to appear in the database doesn't show up. A good approach in such cases is to lobotomize the software through **drastic surgery** and see if it falls in line. If not, you're probably barking up the wrong tree.

As a concrete case, consider the following (abridged) code from the Apache HTTP server, which deals with signed certificate timestamps (SCTs). You might be observing that the server fails to react to SCTs with a timestamp lying in the future.

```
for (i = 0; i < arr->nelts; i++) {
    cur_sct_file = elts[i];
    rv = ctutil_read_file(p, s, cur_sct_file, MAX_SCTS_SIZE,
            &scts, &scts_size_wide);
    rv = sct_parse(cur_sct_file,
            s, (const unsigned char *)scts, scts_size, NULL,
            &fields);
    if (fields.time > apr_time_now()) {
        sct_release(&fields);
        continue;
    }
    sct_release(&fields);
    rv = ctutil_file_write_uint16(s, tmpfile,
            (apr_uint16_t)scts_size);
    if (rv != APR_SUCCESS)
        break;
    scts_written++;
}
```

A way to debug this is to temporarily change the conditional so that it always evaluates to *true*.

```
    if (fields.time > apr_time_now() || 1) {
```

This change will allow you to determine whether the problem lies in the Boolean condition you short circuited, in your test data, or in the rest of the future SCT handling logic.

Other tricks in this category are to add a `return true` or `return false` at the beginning of a method, or to disable the execution of some code by putting it in an `if (0)` block (see Item 46: "Simplify the Suspect Code").

In other cases, you may be trying to debug a barely observable effect. Here the solution is to temporarily modify the code to **make the effect stand out.** If, in a game, a character gets a minute increase in power after some event, and that doesn't seem to happen, make the power increase dramatically more so that you can readily observe it. Or, when investigating the calculation of an earthquake's effects on a building in a CAD program, magnify the displayed structure displacement by 1,000 so that you can easily see the magnitude and direction of the structure's movement.

In cases where your software's failure depends on external factors, you can increase your effectiveness by **modifying the environment** where your software executes in order to make it fail more quickly or more frequently (see Item 55: "Fail Fast"). If your software processes web requests, you can apply a *load test* or *stress test* tool, such as *Apache JMeter*, in order to force your application into the zone where you think it starts misbehaving. If your software uses threads to achieve concurrency, you can increase their number far beyond what's reasonable for the number of cores in the computer you're using. This may help you replicate deadlocks and race conditions. You can also force your software to compete for scarce resources by concurrently running other processes that consume memory, CPU, network, or disk resources. A particularly effective way to investigate how your software behaves when the disk fills up is to make it store its data in a puny USB flash drive.

Finally, a testing approach that can also help you investigate rare data validation or corruption problems is *fuzzing.* Under this approach you either supply to your program randomly generated input, or you randomly perturb its input, and see what happens. Your objective is to increase the likelihood of chancing on the data pattern that produces the failure in a systematic way. Having done that, you can use the problematic data to debug the application. This technique may, for example, help you find out why your application crashes when running on your customer's production data but not when it's running on your own test data. You can perform fuzzing operations using a tool such as *zzuf*.

Things to Remember

✦ Force the execution of suspect paths.

✦ Increase the magnitude of some effects to make them stand out for study.

✦ Apply stress to your software to force it out of its comfort zone.

✦ Perform all your changes under a temporary revision control branch.

Item 18: Enable the Debugging of Unwieldy Systems from Your Desk

Jenny and Mike are comparing notes regarding their debugging experiences. "I hate it when I work on a customer's PC," says Jenny. "My tools are missing, I don't have my browser's bookmarks, it's noisy, I can't access my files, their key bindings and shortcuts are all wrong." Mike looks at her with disbelief: "Key bindings? You're lucky, you have a keyboard!"

Indeed, having to work away from your workstation can be a major drain on your productivity. Apart from Jenny's complaints, other nuisances can be constrained Internet or intranet access, an awkward setup (from the screen to the chair, via the mouse and keyboard), a need to travel to a humid, hot (or cold) location in the middle of nowhere, and undersized computing power. These problems are quite common and will become even more widespread as our industry embraces mobile devices and the Internet of Things. Cases where you may need to debug software away from your cozy desk and powerful workstation include cellphone apps, devices with embedded software, problems that occur only on a customer's computer, and crises that occur in the data center. There are workarounds so that you can continue working with your favorite keyboard, but you must plan ahead.

For cellphone apps and some embedded devices, there are *device emulators*, which you can use on your PC to troubleshoot the failing application. However, these typically don't offer much help in the way of debugging, other than some enhanced logging facilities. True, you don't need to fumble with a touchscreen's keyboard any more, but you also can't run your symbolic debugger inside the emulator. Still, you have convenient access to the source code and your editor from the same screen, and you can quickly experiment with code changes and see the results without having to deploy the software on an actual device.

A more powerful approach is to create a software *shim* that will allow you to run the key parts of the application you're debugging on your workstation. Unit tests and mock objects are techniques often used for this (see Item 42: "Use Unit Tests"). The setup typically excludes the user interface, but can easily include tricky algorithmic parts where a lot of debugging may be required. Thus, you hook up the application's algorithms with some simple (e.g., file-based) input/output, so that you can compile and run the code natively on your PC, and then use your powerful debugger to step through and examine the operation of the tricky parts.

As an example, consider a cellphone app that imports into your contacts the pictures of your social network friends. A difficult part of this app is the interaction with the social networks and the contact matching. Therefore, your shim could be a command-line tool that takes as an argument a contact's name, and uses the Facebook/LinkedIn/Twitter API to retrieve and locate matching friends. Once you debug this part, you can integrate it into the cellphone app as a class. Keep the ability to compile and run it again as a stand-alone command (perhaps via a `main` method) in case a problem occurs in the future.

For troubleshooting problems on customers' PCs, arrange for **remote access.** Do that before a crisis strikes because this typically requires administrator privileges and some technical expertise. Many operating systems offer a way to access the desktop remotely, though support people often prefer the use of a dedicated application, such as *TeamViewer*. Also, consider deploying at the customers' PCs other data and tools that may simplify your debugging. This could be a viewer for your application's binary files or an execution tracer. If I'd have to choose one debugging tool to have on a third-party computer, I'd select the Unix *strace* or *truss* command. Incidentally, remote access can also simplify the troubleshooting that all of us who work in IT are routinely asked to do for friends and family.

A lot of back-end computing is nowadays done through commercial cloud offerings, which offer nifty web interfaces for debugging and console access. If the server you may end up debugging isn't hosted on a shiny cloud but in a cold, noisy, inaccessible data center, you need to plan ahead again. If a problem occurs before the server establishes network connectivity, you normally need to access it through its physical screen and keyboard. A solution to this problem is a *KVM over IP* device. This offers remote access to a computer's keyboard, video, and mouse (KVM) over an IP network. By installing, configuring, and testing such a device, you can conveniently debug problems in a remote server's boot process from the luxury of your desk.

Things to Remember

✦ Set up a device emulator so you can troubleshoot using your workstation's screen and keyboard.

✦ Use a shim to debug embedded code with your workstation's native tools.

✦ Arrange for remote access to customers' PCs.

✦ Set up KVM over IP devices to debug remote servers.

Item 19: Automate Debugging Tasks

You may find yourself with many possible discrete causes for a failure and no easy way to deduce which of them is the culprit. To identify it, you can write a small routine or a script that will perform an exhaustive search through all cases that might cause the problem. This works well when the number of cases would make it difficult to test them by hand, but possible to go through them in a loop. Iterating through 500 characters is a case that can be automated; doing an exhaustive search of all strings of user input is not.

Here is an example. After an upgrade, a computer began to delay the execution of the *which* command. Changing the long command search path (the Windows and Unix PATH environment variable) to /usr/bin removed the delay but left the question: Which of the path's 26 elements was causing it? The following Unix shell script (run on the Windows machine through *Cygwin*) displayed the elapsed time for each path's component.

```
# Obtain path
echo $PATH |
# Split the :-separated path into separate lines
sed 's/:/\n/g' |
# For each line (path element)
while read path ; do
  # Display elapsed time for searching through it
  PATH=$path:/usr/bin time -f "%e $path" which ls >/dev/null
done
```

Here is (part of) the script's output:

```
0.01 /usr/local/bin
0.01 /cygdrive/c/ProgramData/Oracle/Java/javapath
0.01 /cygdrive/c/Python33
4.55 /
0.02 /cygdrive/c/usr/local/bin
0.01 /usr/bin
0.01 /cygdrive/c/usr/bin
0.01 /cygdrive/c/Windows/system32
0.01 /cygdrive/c/Windows
0.01 .
```

As you can clearly see, the problem is caused by an element consisting of a single slash, which had inadvertently crept into the path. Tracing the execution of the *which* command (see Item 58: "Trace the Code's Execution"), revealed the problem's root cause: The *which* command appended a slash to each path element, and on Windows a path starting with a double slash triggered a discovery process for network drives.

If it's difficult to perform the exhaustive search by scripting the software you're investigating, you can embed in the program a small routine for the same purpose. The routine can generate all the cases algorithmically (e.g., by iterating through some values). Alternately, it can read them from an external file, where you can generate them via a more sophisticated script or by scrapping data from existing execution logs.

Finally, there are also tools that can instrument your code to detect API violations, memory buffer overflows, and race conditions (see Item 59: "Use Dynamic Program Analysis Tools" and Item 62: "Uncover Deadlocks and Race Conditions with Specialized Tools"). For some of these tools, the analysis of a test run that used to take a few seconds can take tens of minutes. Nevertheless, the debugging time they can save you is well worth the wait.

Things to Remember

✦ Automate the exhaustive searching for failures; computer time is cheap, yours is expensive.

Item 20: Houseclean Before and After Debugging

Ten possible faults in the software you're debugging can manifest themselves in a thousand (2^{10}) possible combinations. Twenty in a million (2^{20}) combinations. Therefore, when you're debugging, consider picking first the low-hanging fruit around the area you're working on. These include the following:

- Issues that tools can find for you (see Item 51: "Use Static Program Analysis")

- Warnings, such as recoverable assertion failures, that the program produces at runtime

- Unreadable code associated with your issue (see Item 48: "Improve the Suspect Code's Readability and Structure")

- Questionable code identified by comments marked with XXX, FIXME, TODO, or containing cop-out words, such as *should*, *think*, *must*

- Other known minor bugs that lie neglected

Debugging a tricky problem without a relatively fault-free environment can mean death from a thousand cuts.

There are counter-arguments to this approach. First, there's the saying "If it ain't broke, don't fix it." Then comes the question of stylistic inconsistencies that will crop up when you upgrade only part of a system's code to use more modern facilities. You have to use your judgment here. If you can see that cleaning the code will definitely help you debug an elusive bug, then you may decide to take the risk. If, on the other hand, you're dealing with fragile code and a bug that you can pinpoint by examining, say, log files, then a code cleanup exercise is probably an unnecessary risk.

After you have located and fixed a fault, you're not done. Two tasks remain. First, search through the code for other similar errors and fix them (see Item 21: "Fix All Instances of a Problem Class"). Second, deal with code changes you made to pinpoint the problem (see Item 40: "Add Debugging Functionality"). Undo any temporary modifications you added to make the fault stand out. This should be easy if you were working on a separate local revision control branch (see Item 26: "Hunt the Causes and History of Bugs with the Revision Control System"). Also clean up and permanently commit other changes that might be useful in the future, such as assertions, logging statements, and new debug commands.

Things to Remember

✦ Ensure a baseline level of code hygiene before embarking on a major debugging task.

✦ When you finish, clean up temporary code changes and commit useful ones.

Item 21: Fix All Instances of a Problem Class

An error in one place is likely to also occur in others, either because a developer behaved in the same way, because a particular API can be easily misused, or because the faulty code was cloned into other places. The debugging process in many mature development cultures and in safety-critical work doesn't stop when a defect is fixed. The aim is to fix the whole class of defects and ensure that similar defects won't occur in the future.

For example, if you have addressed a division by zero problem in the following statement

```
double a = getWeight(subNode) / totalWeight;
```

search through all the code for other divisions by `totalWeight`. You can easily do this with your IDE, or with the Unix *grep* command (see Item 22: "Analyze Debug Data with Unix Command-Line Tools"):

```
# Find divisions by totalWeight, ignoring spaces after
# the / operator
grep -r '/ *totalWeight' .
```

Having done that, consider whether there are other divisions in the code that might fail in a similar way. Find them and fix those that might fail. A simple Unix pipeline can again help your search. I used the following to quickly go over suspect instances of division in a body of four million lines of C code.

```
# Find divisions, assuming spaces around the / operator
grep -r ' / ' . |
# Eliminate those involving sizeof
grep -v '/ sizeof' |
# Color divisors for easy inspection and
# eliminate divisions involving numerical or symbolic constants
grep --color=always ' / [^0-9A-Z][^,;)]*' |
# Remove duplicates
sort -u
```

Amazingly, the filters successively reduced the suspect lines from 5,731 down to 5,045, then 2,032, and finally to 1,923; an amount of data I could go over within a reasonable time. Although the filters are not bulletproof (sizeof can return zero and a symbolic constant can also evaluate to zero), examining the filtered instances is much better than avoiding the task by claiming that looking at all divisions in the code is too much work.

Finally, consider what steps you can take to avoid introducing a similar fault in the future. These may involve changes in the code or in your software development process. Here are some examples. If the fault was the misuse of an API function, consider hiding the original one and providing a safer alternative. For instance, you can add the following to your project's global include file.

```
#define gets(x) USE_FGETS_RATHER_THAN_GETS(x)
```

Under this definition, programs that use gets (which is famously vulnerable to buffer overflows) will fail to compile or link. If the fault occurred through the processing of an incorrectly typed value, introduce stricter type checking. You can also locate many faults by adding static analysis to your build or by tightening its configuration (see Item 51: "Use Static Program Analysis").

Things to Remember

✦ After fixing one fault, find and fix similar ones and take steps to ensure they will not occur in the future.

General-Purpose Tools and Techniques

Although specialized debugging tools can be friendly and efficient, general-purpose ones often have an edge because you can use them to quickly solve a wide variety of development and operations problems in diverse languages and platforms. The tools described in this chapter trace their origin to Unix, but are nowadays available on most systems including GNU/Linux, Windows, and OS X. The flexibility, efficiency, and wide applicability they offer you justifies investing time and effort to master them. A succinct guide you can use for this purpose is Joshua Levy's collaboratively edited text, "*The Art of Command Line*." Assuming you know the basics of Unix command-line use and regular expressions, this chapter focuses on the specific tools and methods you'll use when debugging.

Item 22: Analyze Debug Data with Unix Command-Line Tools

When you're debugging you'll encounter problems no one has ever seen before. Consequently, the shiny IDE that you're using for writing software may lack the tools to let you explore the problem in detail with sufficient power. This is where the Unix command tools come in. Being general-purpose tools, which can be combined into sophisticated pipelines, they allow you the effortless analysis of text data.

Line-oriented textual data streams are the lowest useful common denominator for a lot of data that passes through your hands. Such streams can be used to represent many types of data you encounter when you're debugging, such as program source code, program logs, version control history, file lists, symbol tables, archive contents, error messages, test results, and profiling figures. For many routine, every-day tasks, you might be tempted to process the data using a powerful Swiss Army knife scripting language, such as *Perl*, *Python*, *Ruby*, or the

Windows *PowerShell*. This is an appropriate method if the scripting language offers a practical interface to obtain the debug data you want to process and if you're comfortable to develop the scripting command in an interactive fashion. Otherwise, you may need to write a small, self-contained program and save it into a file. By that point you may find the task too tedious, and end up doing the work manually, if at all. This may deprive you of important debugging insights.

Often, a more effective approach is to combine programs of the Unix tool chest into a short and sweet pipeline that you can run from your shell's command prompt. With the modern shell command-line editing facilities, you can build your command bit by bit, until it molds into exactly the form that suits you.

In this item, you'll find an overview of how to process debug data using Unix commands. If you're unfamiliar with the command-line basics and regular expressions, consult an online tutorial. Also, you can find the specifics on each command's invocation options by giving its name as an argument to the *man* command.

Depending on the operating system you're using, getting to the Unix command line is trivial or easy. On Unix systems and OS X, you simply open a terminal window. On Windows, the best course of action is to install *Cygwin*: a large collection of Unix tools and a powerful package manager ported to run seamlessly under Windows. Under OS X, the *Homebrew* package manager can simplify the installation of a few tools described here that are not available by default.

Many debugging one-liners that you'll build around the Unix tools follow a pattern that goes roughly like this: fetching, selecting, processing, and summarizing. You'll also need to apply some plumbing to join these parts into a whole. The most useful plumbing operator is the pipeline (|), which sends the output of one processing step as input to the next one.

Most of the time your data will be text that you can directly feed to the standard input of a tool. If this is not the case, you need to adapt your data. If you are dealing with object files, you'll have to use a command such as *nm* (Unix), *dumpbin* (Windows), or *javap* (Java) to dig into them. For example, if your C or C++ program exits unexpectedly, you can run *nm* on its object files to see which ones call (import) the `exit` function.

```
# List symbols in all object files prefixed by file name
nm -A *.o |
# List lines ending in U exit
grep 'U exit$'
```

The output, such as the example below, is likely to be more accurate than searching through the source code.

```
cscout.o:          U exit
error.o:          U exit
idquery.o:           U exit
md5.o:         U exit
pdtoken.o:           U exit
```

If you're working with files grouped into an archive, then a command such as *tar*, *jar*, or *ar* will list you the archive's contents. If your data comes from a (potentially large) collection of files, the *find* command can locate those that interest you. On the other hand, to get your data over the web, use *curl* or *wget*. You can also use *dd* (and the special file /dev/zero), *yes* or *jot* to generate artificial data, perhaps for running a quick benchmark. Finally, if you want to process a compiler's list of error messages, you'll want to redirect its standard error to its standard output or to a file; the incantations 2>&1 and 2>*filename* will do this trick. As an example, consider the case in which you've changed a function's interface and want to edit all the files that are affected by the change. One way to obtain a list of those files is the following pipeline.

```
# Attempt to build all affected files redirecting standard error
# to standard output
make -k 2>&1 |
# Print name of file where the error occurred
awk -F: '/no matching function for call to Myclass::myFunc/
  { print $1}' |
# List each file only once
sort -u
```

Given the generality of log files and other debugging data sources, in most cases you'll have on your hands more data than what you require. You might want to process only some parts of each row, or only a subset of the rows. To select a specific column from a line consisting of fixed-width fields or elements separated by space or another field delimiter, use the *cut* command. If your lines are not neatly separated into fields, you can often write a regular expression for a *sed* substitute command to isolate the element you want.

The workhorse for obtaining a subset of the rows is *grep*. Specify a regular expression to get only the rows that match it, and add the -v flag to filter out rows you don't want to process. You saw this in Item 21: "Fix

All Instances of a Problem Class," where the sequence was used to find all divisions apart from those where the divisor was `sizeof`.

```
grep -r ' / ' . |
grep -v '/ sizeof'
```

Use *fgrep* (*grep* for fixed strings) with the `-f` flag if the elements you're looking for are plain character sequences rather than regular expressions and if they are stored into a file (perhaps generated in a previous processing step). If your selection criteria are more complex, you can often express them in an *awk* pattern expression. Many times you'll find yourself combining a number of these approaches to obtain the result that you want. For example, you might use *grep* to get the lines that interest you, `grep -v` to filter out some noise from your sample, and finally *awk* to select a specific field from each line. For example, the following sequence processes system trace output lines to display the names of all successfully opened files.

```
# Output lines that call open
grep '^open(' trace.out |
# Remove failed open calls (those that return -1)
grep -v '= -1' |
# Print the second field separated by quotes
awk -F\" '{print $2}'
```

(The sequence could have been written as a single *awk* command, but it was easier to develop it step-by-step in the form you see.)

You'll find that data processing frequently involves sorting your lines on a specific field. The *sort* command supports tens of options for specifying the sort keys, their type, and the output order. Once your results are sorted, you then efficiently count how many instances of each element you have. The *uniq* command with the `-c` option will do the job here; often you'll postprocess the result with another sort, this time with the `-n` flag specifying a numerical order, to find out which elements appear most frequently. In other cases you might want to compare results between different runs. You can use *diff* if the two runs generate results that should be the same (perhaps the output of a regression test) or *comm* if you want to compare two sorted lists. You'll handle more complex tasks, again, using *awk*. As an example, consider the task of investigating a resource leak. A first step might be to find all files that directly call obtainResource but do not include any direct calls to `releaseResource`. You can find this through the following sequence.

```
# List records occurring only in the first set
comm -23 <(
```

```
# List names of files containing obtainResource
grep -rl obtainResource . | sort) <(
# List names of files containing releaseResource
grep -rl releaseResource . | sort)
```

(The $(...) sequence is an extension of the *bash* shell that provides a file-like argument supplying, as input, the output of the process within the brackets.)

In many cases, the processed data is too voluminous to be of use. For example, you might not care which log lines indicate a failure, but you might want to know how many there are. Surprisingly, many problems involve simply counting the output of the processing step using the humble *wc* (word count) command and its -l flag. If you want to know the top or bottom 10 elements of your result list, then you can pass your list through *head* or *tail*. Thus, to find the people most familiar with a specific file (perhaps in your search for a reviewer), you can run the following sequence.

```
# List each line's last modification
git blame --line-porcelain Foo.java |
# Obtain the author
grep '^author ' |
# Sort to bring the same names together
sort |
# Count by number of each name's occurrences
uniq -c |
# Sort by number of occurrences
sort -rn |
# List the top ones
head
```

The *tail* command is particularly useful for examining log files (see Item 23: "Utilize Command-Line Tool Options and Idioms" and Item 56: "Examine Application Log Files"). Also, to examine your voluminous results in detail, you can pipe them through *more* or *less*; both commands allow you to scroll up and down and search for particular strings. As usual, use *awk* when these approaches don't suit you; a typical task involves summing up a specific field with a command such as sum += $3. For example, the following sequence will process a web server log and display the number of requests and average number of bytes transferred in each request.

```
awk '
# When the HTTP result code is success (200)
# sum field 10 (number of bytes transferred)
```

```
$9 == 200 {sum += $10; count++}
# When input finishes, print count and average
END {print count, sum / count}' /var/log/access.log
```

All the wonderful building blocks of Unix are useless without some way to glue them together. For this you'll use the Bourne shell's facilities. In some cases you might want to execute the same command with many different arguments. For this you'll pass the arguments as input to *xargs*. A typical pattern involves obtaining a list of files using *find* and processing them using *xargs*. So common is this pattern, that in order to handle files with embedded spaces in them (such as the Windows "Program Files" folder), both commands support an argument (-print0 and -0) to have their data terminated with a null character, instead of a space. As an example, consider the task of finding the log file created after you modified foo.cpp that contains the largest number of occurrences of the string "*access failure*." This is the pipeline you would write.

```
# Find all files in the /var/log/acme folder
# that were modified after changing foo.cpp
find /var/log/acme -type f -cnewer ~/src/acme/foo.cpp -print0 |
# Apply fgrep to count number of 'access failure' occurrences
xargs -0 fgrep -c 'access failure' |
# Sort the :-separated results in reverse numerical order
# according to the value of the second field
sort -t: -rn -k2 |
# Print the top result
head -1
```

If your processing is more complex, you can always pipe the arguments into a while read loop (amazingly, the Bourne shell allows you to pipe data into and from all its control structures). For instance, if you suspect that a problem is related to an update of a system's dynamically linked library (DLL), through the following sequence you can obtain a listing with the version of all DLL files in the windows/system32 directory.

```
# Find all DLL files
find /cygdrive/c/Windows/system32 -type f -name \*.dll |
# For each file
while read f ; do
  # Obtain its Windows path with escaped \
  wname=$(cygpath -w $f | sed 's/\\/\\\\/g')
  # Run WMIC query to get its name and version
  wmic datafile where "Name=\"$wname\"" get name, version
done |
# Remove headers and blank lines
grep windows
```

When everything else fails, don't shy away from using a couple of inter-mediate files to juggle your data.

Things to Remember

✦ Analyze debug data through Unix commands that can obtain, select, process, and summarize textual records.

✦ By combining Unix commands with a pipeline, you can quickly ac-complish sophisticated analysis tasks.

Item 23: Utilize Command-Line Tool Options and Idioms

The program you're debugging produces a cryptic "`Missing foo`" error message. Where is the culprit code? Running

```
fgrep -lr 'Missing foo' .
```

in the application's source code directory will recursively (-r) search through all the files and list (-l) those containing the error message. The beauty of performing a textual search with *grep* is that this will work ir-respective of the programming language of the code that produces the error message. This is particularly useful in applications written in mul-tiple languages, or when you lack the time to set up a project within an IDE. Note that the (-r) *fgrep* option is a GNU extension, which purists find distasteful. If you're working on a system lacking this facility, the following pipeline will perform exactly the same task.

```
find . -type f |
xargs fgrep -l 'Missing foo'
```

Often the data you're examining contain a lot of noise: items you don't want to see. Although you could tailor a *grep* regular expression to select the records you want, in many cases it's easier to simply discard the records that bother you using the -v argument of the *grep* command. Particularly powerful is the combination of multiple such commands. For example, to obtain all the log records that include the string "`Missing foo`" but do not contain "`connection failure`" or "`test`," you can use a pipeline such as the following:

```
fgrep 'Missing foo' *.log |
fgrep -v 'connection failure' |
fgrep -v test
```

The output of the *grep* command are lines that match the specified reg-ular expression. However, if those lines are long, it may be difficult to easily see the part of the line where the culprit occurs. For example, you might believe that a display problem associated with a (badly format-ted) HTML file has to do with a `table` tag. How can you quickly inspect all such tags? Passing the `--color` option to *grep*, as in `grep --color table file.html`, will show all the `table` tags in red, simplifying their inspection.

By convention, programs that run on the command line do not send er-rors to their standard output. Doing that might confuse other programs that process their output and also hide the error message from the pro-gram's human operator if the output is redirected into a file. Instead, error messages are sent to a different channel, called the standard error. This will typically appear on the terminal through which the command was invoked; even its output was redirected. However, when you're de-bugging a program you might want to process that output, rather than see it fly away on the screen. Two redirection operators can help you here. First, you can send the standard error (by convention, file descrip-tor 2) into a file for later processing by specifying `2>filename` when run-ning the program. You can also redirect the standard error to the same file descriptor as the standard output (file descriptor 1), so that you can process both with the same pipeline. For example, the following com-mand passes both outputs through *more*, allowing you to scroll through the output at your own pace.

```
program 2>&1 | more
```

When debugging non-interactive programs, such a web servers, all the interesting action is typically recorded into a log file (see Item 56: "Examine Application Log Files"). Rather than repeatedly viewing the file for changes, the best thing to do is to use the *tail* command with the `-f` option to examine the file as it grows. The *tail* command will keep the log file open and register an event handler to get notifications when the file grows. This allows it to display the log file's changes in an efficient manner. If the process writing the file is likely at some point to delete or rename the log file and create a new one with the same name (e.g., to rotate its output), then passing the `--follow=name` to *tail* will instruct *tail* to follow the file with that name rather than the file descriptor as-sociated with the original file. Once you have *tail* running on a log file, it pays to keep that on a separate (perhaps small) window that you can easily monitor as you interact with the application you're debugging. If the log file contains many irrelevant lines, you can pipe the *tail* output into *grep* to isolate the messages that interest you.

```
sudo tail /var/log/maillog | fgrep 'max connection rate'
```

If the failures you're looking for are rare, you should set up a mon-itoring infrastructure to notify you when something goes wrong (see

Item 27: "Use Monitoring Tools on Systems Composed of Independent Processes"). For one-off cases, you can arrange to run a program in the background even after you log off by suffixing its invocation with an ampersand and running it with the *nohup* utility. You will then find the program's output and errors in a file named nohup.out. Or you can pipe a program's output to the *mail* command, so that you will get it when it finishes. For runs that will terminate within your workday, you can set a sound alert after the command.

```
long-running-regression-test ; printf '\a'
```

You can even combine the two techniques to get an audible alert or a mail message when a particular log line appears.

```
sudo tail -f /var/log/secure |
fgrep -q 'Invalid user' ; printf '\a'

sudo tail -f /var/log/secure |
fgrep -m 1 'Invalid user' |
mail -s Intrusion jdh@example.com
```

Modifying the preceding commands with the addition of a while read loop can make the alert process run forever. However, such a scheme enters into the realm of an infrastructure monitoring system for which there are specialized tools (see Item 27: "Use Monitoring Tools on Systems Composed of Independent Processes").

Things to Remember

✦ Diverse *grep* options can help you narrow down your search.

✦ Redirect a program's standard error in order to analyze it.

✦ Use tail -f to monitor log files as they grow.

Item 24: Explore Debug Data with Your Editor

Debuggers may get all the credit, but your code editor (or IDE) can often be an equally nifty tool for locating the source of a bug. Use a real editor, such as *Emacs* or *vim*, or a powerful IDE. Whatever you do, trade up from your system's basic built-in editor, such as *Notepad* (Windows), *TextEdit* (OS X), or *Nano* and *Pico* (various Unix distributions). These editors offer only rudimentary facilities.

Your editor's search command can help you navigate to the code that may be associated with the problem you're facing. In contrast to your IDE's function to find all uses of a given identifier, your editor's search function casts a wider net because it can be more flexible, and also because it includes in the search space text appearing in comments. One way to make your search more flexible is to search with the *stem* of the word. Say you're looking for code associated with an ordering problem. Don't search for "ordering." Rather, search for "order," which will get you all occurrences of order, orders, and ordering. You can also specify a *regular expression* to encompass all possible strings that interest you. If there's a problem involving a coordinate field specified as x1, x2, y1, or y2, then you can locate references to any one of these fields by searching for [xy][12].

In other cases, your editor can help you pinpoint code that fails to behave in the expected way. Consider the following JavaScript code, which will not display the failure message it should.

```
var failureMessage = "Failure!", failureOccurrances = 5;
// More code here
if (failureOccurrences > 0)
    alert(failureMessage);
```

After a long, stressful day, you may fail to spot the small but obvious error. However, searching for "failureOccurrences" in the code will locate only one of the two variables (the other is spelled "failureOccurrances"). Searching for an identifier is particularly effective for locating typos when the name of the identifier you're looking for comes from another source: copy-and-pasted from its definitive definition or a displayed error message or carefully typed in. A neat trick is to use the editor's command to search for occurrences of the same word. With the *vim* editor, you can search forward for identifiers that are the same as the one under the cursor by pressing * (or # for searching backward). In the *Emacs* editor, the corresponding incantation is Ctrl-s, Ctrl-w.

Your editor is useful when you perform differential debugging (see Item 5: "Find the Difference between a Known Good System and a Failing One"). If you have two (in theory) identical complex statements that behave differently, you can quickly spot any differences by copy-and-pasting the one below the other. You can then compare them letter by letter, rather than having your eyes and mind wander from one part of the screen to another. For larger blocks you may want to compare, consider splitting your editor window into two vertical halves and putting one block beside the other: this makes it easy to spot any important differences. Ideally, you'd want a tool such as *diff* to identify differences, but this can be tricky if two files you want to compare differ in nonessential elements, such as IP addresses, timestamps, or arguments passed to routines. Again, your editor can help you here by allowing you to replace the differing nonessential text with identical placeholders. As an example, the following *vim* regular expression substitution command will replace all instances of a Chrome version identifier (e.g., Chrome/45.0.2454.101) appearing in a log file with a string identifying only the major version (e.g., Chrome/45).

```
:%s/\(Chrome\/[^.]*\)[^ ]*/\1
```

Finally, the editor can be of great help when you're trying to pinpoint an error using a long log file chock-full of data. First, your editor makes the removal of nonessential lines child's play. For example, if you want to delete all lines containing the string poll from a log file, in *vi* you'd enter :g/poll/d, whereas in *Emacs* you'd invoke (M-x) delete-matching-lines. You can issue such commands multiple times (issuing undo when you overdo it), until the only things left in your log file are the records that really interest you. If the log file's contents are still too complex to keep in your head, consider commenting the file in the places you understand. For example, you might add "start of transaction," "transaction failed," "retry." If you're examining a large file with a logical block structure you can also use your editor's outlining facilities to quickly fold and unfold diverse parts and navigate between them. At this point, you can also split your editor's window into multiple parts so that you can concurrently view related parts.

Things to Remember

✦ Locate misspelled identifiers using your editor's search commands.

✦ Edit text files to make differences stand out.

✦ Edit log files to increase their readability.

Item 25: Optimize Your Work Environment

Debugging is a demanding activity. If your development environment is not well tuned to your needs, you can easily die the death of a thousand cuts. Many parts of this book present techniques for the effective use of tools: the debugger (see Chapter 4), the editor (see Item 24: "Explore Debug Data with Your Editor"), and command-line tools (see Item 22: "Analyze Debug Data with Unix Command-Line Tools"). Here you'll find additional things you should consider in order to keep your productivity high.

First comes the hardware and software at your disposal. Ensure that you have adequate CPU power, main memory, and secondary storage space at your disposal (locally or on a cloud infrastructure). Some static analysis tools require a powerful CPU and a lot of memory; for other tasks, you may need to store on disk multiple copies of the project or gigabytes of logs or telemetry data. In other cases, you may benefit from being able to easily launch additional host instances on the cloud. You shouldn't have to fight for these resources: your time is (or should be) a lot more valuable than their cost. The same goes for software. Here the restrictions can be associated both with false economies and with excessive restrictions regarding what software you're allowed to download, install, and use. Again, if some software will help you debug a problem, it's inexcusable to have this withheld from you. Debugging is hard enough as it is without additional restrictions on facilities and tools.

Having assembled the resources, spend some effort to make the best out of them. A good personal setup that includes key bindings, aliases, helper scripts, shortcuts, and tool configurations can significantly enhance your debugging productivity. Here are some things you can set up and examples of corresponding *Bash* commands.

- Ensure that your PATH environment variable is composed of all directories that contain the programs you run. When debugging, you may often use system administration commands, so include those in your path.

```
export PATH="/sbin:/usr/sbin:$PATH"
```

- Configure your shell and editor to automatically complete elements they can deduce. The following example for Git can save you many keystrokes as you juggle between various branches.

```
# Obtain a copy of the Git completion script
if ! [ -f ~/.bash_completion.d/git-completion.bash] ; then
  mkdir -p ~/.bash_completion.d
  curl https://raw.githubusercontent.com/git/git/master/\
contrib/completion/git-completion.bash \
    >~/.bash_completion.d/git-completion.bash
fi
# Enable completion of Git commands
source ~/.bash_completion.d/git-completion.bash
```

- Set your shell prompt and terminal bar to show your identity, the current directory, and host. When debugging, you often use diverse hosts and identities, so a clear identification of your status can help you keep your sanity.

```
# Primary prompt
PS1="[\u@\h \W]\\$ "
# Terminal bar
PROMPT_COMMAND='printf "\033]0;%s@%s:%s\007" "${USER}"\
"${HOSTNAME%%.*}" "${PWD/#$HOME/~}"'
```

- Configure command-line editing key bindings to match those of your favorite editor. This will boost your productivity when building data analysis pipelines in an incremental fashion (see Item 22: "Analyze Debug Data with Unix Command-Line Tools").

```
set -o emacs
# Or
set -o vi
```

- Create aliases or shortcuts for frequently used commands and common typos.

```
alias h='history 15'
alias j=jobs
alias mroe=more
```

- Set environment variables so that various utilities, such as the version control system, will use the paging program and editor of your choice.

```
export PAGER=less
export VISUAL=vim
export EDITOR=ex
```

- Log all your commands into a history file so that you can search for valuable debugging incantations months later. Note that you can avoid logging a command invocation (e.g., one that contains a password) by prefixing it with a space.

```
# Increase history file size
export HISTFILESIZE=1000000000
export HISTSIZE=1000000
export HISTTIMEFORMAT="%F %T "
# Ignore duplicate lines and lines that start with space
export HISTCONTROL=ignoreboth
# Save multi line commands as single line with semicolons
shopt -s cmdhist
# Append to the history file
shopt -s histappend
```

- Allow the shell's path name expansion (globbing—e.g., *) to include files located in subdirectories.

```
shopt -s globstar
```

This simplifies applying commands on deep directory hierarchies through the use of the ** wildcard, which expands to all specified files in a directory tree. For example, the following command will

count the number of files whose author is James Gosling, by looking at the JavaDoc tag of Java source code files.

```
$ grep '@author.*James Gosling' **/*.java | wc -l
33
```

Then comes the configuration of individual programs. Invest time to
learn and configure the debugger, the editor, the IDE, the version control
system, and the humble pager you're using to match your preferences
and working style. IDEs and sophisticated editors support many helpful plugins. Select the ones you find useful, and set up a simple way to
install them on each host on which you set up shop. You will recoup the
investment in configuring your tools multiple times over the years.

When debugging, your work will often straddle multiple hosts. There
are three important time savers in this context. First, ensure that you
can log in to each remote host you use (or execute a command there)
without entering your password. On Unix systems you can easily do this
by setting up a public-private key pair (you typically run ssh-keygen for
this) and storing the public key on the remote host in the file named
.ssh/authorized_hosts. Second, set up host aliases so that you can access
a host by using a short descriptive name, rather than its full name,
possibly prefixed by a different user name. You store these aliases in
a file named .ssh/config. Here is an example that shortens the *ssh* host
login specification from testuser@garfield.dev.asia.example.com into
garfield.

```
Host garfield
HostName garfield.dev.asia.example.com
User testuser
```

Third, find out how you can invoke a GUI application on a remote host
and have it display on your desktop. Although this operation can be
tricky to set up, it is nowadays possible with most operating systems.
Being able to run a GUI debugger or an IDE on a remote host can give
you a big productivity boost.

Debugging tasks often span the command line and the GUI world. Therefore, knowing how to connect the two in your environment can be an
important time saver. One common thing you'll find useful is the ability to launch a GUI program from the command line (e.g., the debugged
application with a test file you've developed). The command to use is
start under Windows, open under OS X, gnome-open under Gnome, and
kde-open under KDE. You will also benefit from being able to copy text
(e.g., a long path of a memory dump file) between the command line and
the GUI clipboard. Under Windows you can use the winclip command

of the *Outwit* suite, or, if you have *Cygwin* installed, you can read from or write to the /dev/clipboard file. Under Gnome and KDE you can use the *xsel* command. If you work on multiple GUI environments, you may want to create a command alias that works in the same way across all environments. Here is an example for a command named "s" that will launch a GUI file or application.

```
case $(uname) in
FreeBSD) # KDE
  alias s=kde-open
  ;;
Linux) # Gnome
  alias s=gnome-open
  ;;
Darwin)
  alias s=open
  ;;
CYGWIN*)
  alias s=cygstart
  ;;
esac
```

Also, configure your GUI so that you can launch your favorite editor through a file's context menu and open a shell window with a given current directory through a directory's context menu. And, if you don't know that you can drag and drop file names from the GUI's file browser into a shell window, try it out; it works beautifully.

Having made the investment to create all your nifty configuration files, spend some time to ensure they're consistently available on all hosts where you're debugging software. A nice way to do this is to put the files under version control. This allows you to push improvements or compatibility fixes from any host into a central repository and later pull them back to other hosts. Setting up shop on a new host simply involves checking out the repository's files in your new home directory. If you're using Git to manage your configuration files, specify the files from your home directory that you want to manage in a .gitignore file, such as the following.

```
# Ignore everything
*
# But not these files...
!.bashrc
!.editrc
!.gdbinit
```

```
!.gitconfig
!.gitignore
!.inputrc
```

Note that the advice in this item is mostly based on things I've found useful over the years. Your needs and development environment may vary considerably from mine. Regularly monitor your development environment to pinpoint and alleviate sources of friction. If you find yourself repeatedly typing a long sequence of commands or performing many mouse clicks for an operation that could be automated, invest the time to package what you're doing into a script. If you find tools getting in your way rather than helping you, determine how to configure them to match your requirements, or look for better tools. Finally, look around and ask for other people's tricks and tools. Someone else may have already found an elegant solution to a problem that is frustrating you.

Things to Remember

✦ Boost your productivity through the appropriate configuration of the tools you're using.

✦ Share your environment's configuration among hosts with a version control system.

Item 26: Hunt the Causes and History of Bugs with the Revision Control System

Many bugs you'll encounter are associated with software changes. New features and fixes, inevitably, introduce new bugs. A revision control system, such as Git, Mercurial, Subversion, or CVS, allows you to dig into the history in order to retrieve valuable intelligence regarding the problem you're facing. To benefit from this you must be diligently managing your software's revisions with a version control system (see Item 10: "Enable the Efficient Reproduction of the Problem"). By "diligently" I mean that you should be recording each change in a separate self-contained commit, documented with a meaningful commit message, and (where applicable) linked to the corresponding issue (see Item 1: "Handle All Problems through an Issue-Tracking System").

Here are the most useful ways in which a version control system can help your debugging work. The examples use Git's command-line operations because these work in all environments. If you prefer to use a GUI tool to perform these tasks, by all means do so. If you're using another revision control system, consult its documentation on how you can perform these operations, or consider switching to Git to benefit from all its power. Note that not all version control systems are created equal. In particular, many have painful and inefficient support for local branching and merging—features that are essential when you debug by experimenting with alternative implementations.

When a new bug appears in your software, begin by reviewing what changes were made to it.

```
git log
```

If you know that the problem is associated with a specific file, specify it so that you will only see changes associated with that file.

```
git log path/to/myfile.js
```

If you suspect that the problem is associated with particular code lines, you can obtain a listing of the code with each line annotated with details regarding its last change.

```
git blame path/to/myfile.js
```

(Specify the -C and -M options to track lines moved within a file and between files.)

If the code associated with the problem is no longer there, you can search for it in the past by looking for a deleted string.

```
git rev-list --all | xargs git grep extinctMethodName
```

If you know that the problem appeared after a specific version (say V1.2.3), you can review the changes that occurred after that version.

```
git log V1.2.3..
```

If you don't know the version number but you know the date on which the problem appeared, you can obtain the SHA hash of the last commit before that date.

```
git rev-list -n 1 --before=2015-08-01 master
```

You can then use the SHA hash in place of the version string.

If you know that the problem appeared when a specific issue (say, issue 1234) was fixed, you can search for commits associated with that issue.

```
git log --all --grep='Issue #1234'
```

(This assumes that a commit addressing issue 1234 will include the string "Issue #1234" in its message.)

In all the preceding cases, once you have the SHA hash of the commit you want to review (say, 1cb6e3f6), you can inspect the changes associated with it.

```
git show 1cb6e3f6
```

You may also want see the code changes between two releases.

`git diff V1.2.3..V1.3.2`

Often, a simple review of the changes can lead you to the problem's cause. Alternately, having obtained from the commit descriptions the names of the developers associated with a suspect change, you can have a talk with them to see what they were thinking when they wrote that code.

You can also use the version control system as a time-travel machine. For example, you may want to check out an old correct version (say V1.1.0) to run that code under the debugger and compare it with the current one (see Item 5: "Find the Difference between a Known Good System and a Failing One").

`git checkout V1.1.0`

Even more impressive, if you know that a bug was introduced between, say, V1.1.0 and V1.2.3 and you have a script, say, `test.sh` that will exit with a non-zero code if a test fails, you can ask Git to perform a binary search among all changes until it locates the one that introduced the bug.

```
git bisect start V1.1.0 V1.2.3
git bisect run test.sh
git reset
```

Git also allows you to experiment with fixes by creating a local branch that you can then integrate or remove.

```
git checkout -b issue-work-1234

# If the experiment was successful integrate the branch
git checkout master
git merge issue-work-1234

# If the experiment failed delete the branch
git checkout master
git checkout -D issue-work-1234
```

Finally, given that you may be asked to urgently debug an issue while you're working on something else, you may want to temporarily hide your changes while you work on the customer's version.

```
git stash save interrupted-to-work-on-V1234
# Work on the debugging issue
git stash pop
```

Things to Remember

✦ Examining a file's history with a version control system can show you when and how bugs were introduced.

✦ Use a version control system to look at the differences between correct and failing software versions.

Item 27: Use Monitoring Tools on Systems Composed of Independent Processes

Modern software-based systems rarely consist of a single stand-alone program, which you need to debug when it fails. Instead, they comprise diverse services, components, and libraries. The quick and efficient identification of the failed element should be your first win when debugging such a system. You can easily accomplish this on the server side by using or by setting up and running an infrastructure monitoring system.

In the following paragraphs, I'll use as an example the popular *Nagios* tool. This is available both as free software and through supported products and services. If your organization already uses another system, work on that one; the principles are the same. Whatever you do, avoid the temptation to concoct a system on your own. Over a quick home-brewed solution or a passive recording system such as *collectd* or *RRD-tool*, *Nagios* offers many advantages: tested passive and active service checks and notifiers, a dashboard, a round-robin event database, unobtrusive monitoring schedules, scalability, and a large user community that contributes plugins.

If your setup is running on the cloud or if it is based on a commonly used application stack, you may also be able to use a cloud-based monitoring system offered as a service. For example, Amazon Web Services (AWS) offers monitoring for the services it provides.

To be able to zero in efficiently on problems, you must monitor the whole stack of your application. Start from the lowest-level resources by monitoring the health of individual hosts: CPU load, memory use, network reachability, number of executing processes and logged-in users, available software updates, free disk space, open file descriptors, consumed network and disk bandwidth, system logs, security, and remote access. Moving up one level, verify the correct and reliable functioning of the services your software requires to run: databases, email servers, application servers, caches, network connections, backups, queues, messaging, software licenses, web servers, and directories. Finally, monitor in detail the health of your application. The details here will vary. It's best to monitor

- The end-to-end availability of your application (e.g., if completing a web form will end with a fulfilled transaction)

- Individual parts of the application, such as web services, database tables, static web pages, interactive web forms, and reporting

- Key metrics, such as response latency, queued and fulfilled orders, number of active users, failed transactions, raised errors, reported crashes, and so on

When something fails, *Nagios* will update the corresponding service status on its web interface. Figure 3.1 shows the status of services running on a variety of hosts; a few are in a warning (yellow) state and one is on error (red) state. In addition, you want to be notified of the failure immediately, for example, with an SMS or an email. For services that fail sporadically, the immediate notification may allow you to debug the service while it is in a failed state, making it easier to pinpoint the cause. You can also arrange for *Nagios* to open a ticket so that the issue can be assigned, followed, and documented (see Item 1: "Handle All Problems through an Issue-Tracking System"). *Nagios* also allows you to see a histogram for the events associated with a service over time. Poring over the time where the failures occur can help you identify other factors that lead to the failure, such as excessive CPU load or memory pressure. If you monitor a service's complete stack, some low-level failures will cause a cascade of other problems. In such cases you typically want to start your investigation at the lowest-level failed element (see Item 4: "Drill Up from the Problem to the Bug or Down from the Program's Start to the Bug").

If the available notification options do not suit your needs, you can easily write a custom notification handler. The shell script in Listing 3.1 will open an issue on GitHub when a service fails using the *ghi* tool by Stephen Celis.

Listing 3.1 Example of a *Nagios* plugin

```sh
#!/bin/sh
TITLE="$1"
BODY="$2"

# Unescape newlines
NLBODY="$(printf '%b' \"$BODY\")"
```

```
ghi open -m "$TITLE
$NLBODY
" >/dev/null
```

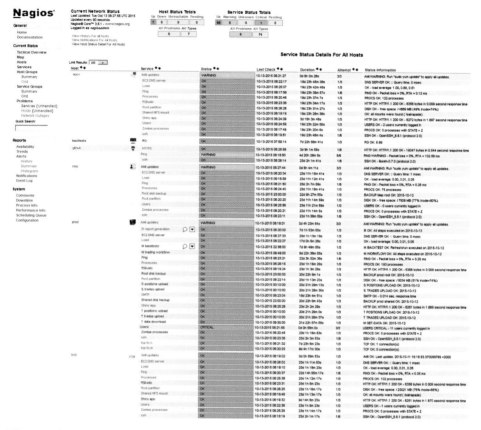

Figure 3.1 *Nagios* monitoring service status details

Setting up *Nagios* is easy. The software is available as a package for most popular operating systems and includes built-in support for monitoring key host resources and popular network services. In addition, more than a thousand plugins allow the monitoring of all possible services, from cloud, clustering, and CMS to security and web forms. Again, if no plugin matches your requirements, you can easily script your own checker. Simply have the script print the service's status and exit with 0 if the service you're checking is OK and with 2 if there's a critical error. As an example, the following shell script verifies that a given storage volume has been backed up as a timestamped AWS snapshot.

```
#!/bin/sh

HOST="$1"
NAME="$2"
TODAY=$(date -I)

LAST_BACKUP=$(ec2-describe-snapshots --filter \
    tag:Name="backup-$HOST-$NAME" \
    --filter tag-key=date |
  awk '
    $1 == "SNAPSHOT" {status = $4}
    $1 == "TAG" && $4 == "date" {
      if (status == "completed" && $5 > latest) latest = $5
    }
    END {print latest}')

if [ "$LAST_BACKUP" = "$TODAY" ]
then
  echo "BACKUP $HOST $NAME OK: $TODAY"
  exit 0
else
  echo "BACKUP $HOST $NAME CRITICAL: last $LAST_BACKUP"
  exit 2
fi
```

Things to Remember

✦ Set up a monitoring infrastructure to check all parts composing the service you're offering.

✦ Quick notification of failures may allow you to debug your system in its failed state.

✦ Use the failure history to identify patterns that may help you pinpoint a problem's cause.

Debugger Techniques

A *debugger*, the specialized tool that allows you to examine in detail the runtime behavior of your software, is probably the most pampered application in existence. No other software can claim specialized support just for its own use both by the CPU and by the operating system. This demonstrates the value that professionals place on it. If you don't learn to use a debugger effectively, you're missing the benefits of the investments made on its behalf. Depending on the language and environment you work in, these may be old news to you. If so, skim through the chapter for techniques you're not using; otherwise, go through it carefully.

Although there are many stand-alone debuggers and integrated development environments (IDEs) with debugger functionality, the methods and techniques for using these to debug your software are roughly the same. The examples of debugging compiled code in this chapter are illustrated with three popular setups: the *Eclipse* IDE for debugging Java and Scala code, the *Visual Studio* IDE for debugging the languages it supports (C, C++, Visual C#, and Visual Basic), and *gdb* for debugging under Unix any of its supported languages (C, C++, D, Go, Objective-C, Fortran, Java, OpenCL C, Pascal, assembly, Modula-2, and Ada). If you're using another tool, for example Google Chrome to debug JavaScript code, look up how you can perform the tasks described here. If your tool doesn't support the functionality you want, consider switching to one that does.

Item 28: Use Code Compiled for Symbolic Debugging

Although a debugger can be used to debug any compiled program, it works best when the program contains debugging information. This information maps the machine instructions to the corresponding source code and memory addresses to variables. For languages compiled into hardware machine instructions, such as C, C++, and Go, the minimum information an application supplies is that which is required to link it at runtime with so-called shared (Unix) or dynamically linked (Windows) libraries. This means that the debugger can identify only a few of the routines used in a program. Here is an example of the call stack (see Item 32: "Navigate along the Calls between Routines") of a C++ program waiting from some input.

```
#0  0xb77c0424 in __kernel_vsyscall ()
#1  0xb75e7663 in read () from /lib/i386-linux-gnu/i686/cmov/
    libc.so.6
#2  0xb758bb3b in _IO_file_underflow ()
    from /lib/i386-linux-gnu/i686/cmov/libc.so.6
#3  0xb758d3db in _IO_default_uflow ()
    from /lib/i386-linux-gnu/i686/cmov/libc.so.6
#4  0xb758e808 in __uflow () from /lib/i386-linux-gnu/i686/
    cmov/libc.so.6
#5  0xb75840ec in getc () from /lib/i386-linux-gnu/i686/cmov/
    libc.so.6
#6  0xb7750345 in __gnu_cxx::stdio_sync_filebuf<char, std::
    char_traits<char> >::uflow() () from /usr/lib/i386-linux
    -gnu/libstdc++.so.6
#7  0xb7737365 in ?? () from /usr/lib/i386-linux-gnu/
    libstdc++.so.6
#8  0xb77386a4 in std::istream::get(char&) ()
    from /usr/lib/i386-linux-gnu/libstdc++.so.6
#9  0x0805083d in ?? ()
#10 0x0804f730 in ?? ()
#11 0x0804b792 in ?? ()
#12 0x08049b13 in ?? ()
#13 0x08049caf in ?? ()
#14 0xb7535e46 in __libc_start_main ()
    from /lib/i386-linux-gnu/i686/cmov/libc.so.6
#15 0x08049a01 in ?? ()
```

The routines displayed with their name are those required for the code to link with the shared library, such as get and read. (Names preceded by an underscore are internally used routines that also require dynamic linking.) The question marks (??) are placeholders for the names of routines that the debugger can't match with their source code.

On Unix systems, by default, the compilation process also includes in the compiled code the names of variables and routines that are resolved during linking (non-*static* symbols). This information is often removed with a command called *strip* in order to save space or hide proprietary information. You can get more informative data by working with non-stripped code. Here is part of the preceding call stack from a non-stripped version of the same program.

```
#8 0xb769e6a4 in std::istream::get(char&) ()
   from /usr/lib/i386-linux-gnu/libstdc++.so.6
#9 0x0805083d in CMetricsCalculator::calculate_metrics_
   switch() ()
#10 0x0804f730 in CMetricsCalculator::calculate_metrics_
    loop() ()
#11 0x0804b792 in CMetricsCalculator::calculate_metrics() ()
#12 0x08049b13 in process_metrics(char const*) ()
#13 0x08049caf in main ()
```

Notice how the question marks have been replaced by function names. You can easily identify whether a Unix program has been stripped or not by applying the *file* command on it. Here is the command's output for a stripped and a non-stripped program.

```
/bin/bash: ELF 64-bit LSB executable, x86-64, version 1 (SYSV),
dynamically linked, interpreter /lib64/ld-linux-x86-64.so.2,
for GNU/Linux 2.6.35, stripped


nethogs: ELF 64-bit LSB executable, x86-64, version 1 (SYSV),
dynamically linked, interpreter /lib64/ld-linux-x86-64.so.2,
for GNU/Linux 2.6.18, not stripped
```

On all systems, you can set compiler and linker options to embed into the code further debugging information: the instruction memory address associated with each file and line number and the location where variables of all kinds are stored. Here are again parts of the preceding call stack listing when the program is compiled with debugging information enabled.

```
#9 0x0804f054 in CharSource::get (this=0xbfa0876c,
   c=@0xbfa08637: 8 '\b') at CharSource.h:32
#10 0x0804fa4d in CMetricsCalculator::calculate_metrics_switch
    (this=0xbfa0876c) at CMetricsCalculator.cpp:160
#11 0x0804eea5 in CMetricsCalculator::calculate_metrics_loop
    (this=0xbfa0876c) at CMetricsCalculator.cpp:868
#12 0x0804b4b2 in CMetricsCalculator::calculate_metrics
    (this=0xbfa0876c) at CMetricsCalculator.h:74
#13 0x08049833 in process_metrics (filename=0x8054dd8 "-")
    at qmcalc.cpp:39
#14 0x080499cf in main (argc=1, argv=0xbfa08b94)
    at qmcalc.cpp:72
```

Notice how you can now see the file and line associated with each method call, as well as the names of the arguments and their values. This is the type of data you want to have when you're debugging. Keep in mind that you may not want to include such data in code that you ship to customers in order to avoid exposing proprietary information.

The way to embed debugging information depends on the tools you're using. Here are some common cases.

- For Java under *Eclipse*, debug symbol generation is enabled by default. You can control it by navigating to *Project – Properties – Java Compiler – Classfile Generation.*

- The Oracle JDK compiler provides the -g option to embed all debugging information (and several arguments to control it).

- Most Unix compilers use the -g option to embed debugging information.

- Microsoft's compilers use the /Zi for the same task.

- In Microsoft's *Visual Studio*, you control whether you want a debug or a release (non-debug) build, by navigating to *Build – Configuration manager – Active solution configuration.* (There's also a corresponding option on the toolbar.)

Another consideration when you're building code for debugging is the level of optimization you enable. Modern compilers perform extensive **optimizations that can alter the generated code** so much that you won't be able to understand how it corresponds to the source code you actually wrote. If you're single-stepping through the source code (see Item 29: "Step through the Code"), the debugger will appear to perform erratically, skipping over statements, or executing them in a different order than what you would expect. To appreciate this, consider the following C program.

```c
#include <stdio.h>
int main()
{
    int a, b, c, d, i;

    a = 12;
    b = 3;
    c = a / b;
    d = 0;

    for (i = 0; i < 10; i++)
        d += c;
    printf("result=%d\n", d);
}
```

Here is the corresponding code that the Microsoft C compiler generates with the maximum level of optimization.

```
$SG2799 DB    'result=%d', 0aH, 00H
_main PROC
      push  40
      push  OFFSET $SG2799
      call  _printf
      add   esp, 8
      xor   eax, eax
      ret   0
_main ENDP
```

What the generated code does is simply to push the final value of d (40) into the stack and call printf to display the result. That's right—no assignments, no calculations, no loop, nothing. The compiler performed all the calculations at compile time so that the generated code just displays the precalculated value. Disappearing code is not something you want to happen when you're debugging a complex algorithm.

Therefore, ensure that your debug build configures the compiler to disable code optimizations. IDEs control this correctly when you select a debug or release configuration. Also, Oracle's Java compiler doesn't perform any optimizations, leaving the job to the just-in-time JVM-to-machine-code compiler, which executes at runtime. Otherwise, to disable optimization on compilers you invoke from the command line, use –O0 under Unix and /0d for Microsoft's tools. Note that even with optimizations disabled, the compiler may still modify your program, for example, by removing dead code and by evaluating constant expressions. Disabled optimization is mostly suitable for debug builds; it is typically avoided in production builds because it can severely slow down the generated code. Still, some organizations ship production code compiled with disabled optimization in order to simplify debugging and to avoid the risk of an immature compiler's incorrect optimizations. Some, also in the name of simplified debugging, even ship their code with debug symbols, accepting the risk of assisting the reverse engineering of their product.

There are two cases in which you might not want to disable optimizations in a debug build. First, you may want to allow the compiler to optimize parts of the program that are critical for its performance but not part of the code you want to debug. Feel free to tweak accordingly your build configuration; thankfully, the common optimization settings allow optimized code to coexist with unoptimized one. Also, you may encounter bugs that only manifest themselves in a production (rather than a debug) build. In this case, you want to tailor a build setup that includes debug information but also optimizes the code in the same way as the production build.

Things to Remember

✦ Configure your build settings to get the required level of debugging information.

✦ Disable compiler code optimizations so that the generated code matches the code you're debugging.

Item 29: Step through the Code

Following a program's detailed execution in real time is impossible because computers process billions of instructions each second. Using a debugger to single-step through the code allows you to execute the code a single program statement (or machine instruction) at a time. With single-stepping, you can pinpoint errors in the sequence of instructions your program executes. You can thus see conditional statements that branch the wrong way, or loops that execute too few or too many times. As you can see in other items in this chapter, through single-stepping you can also examine the detailed state of your program before and after each statement.

The way you start single-stepping through your program depends on the tools you use. Under *Eclipse*, you open the *debug perspective* (*Window – Open Perspective – Debug*), you start running your program (*Run – Debug* or F6), and then you step through each statement by pressing F5. With *Visual Studio* you select *Debug – Step Into* or simply press F11. On the Unix command line, you invoke *gdb* with the program's executable file as an argument (gdb path/to/myprog), you set a breakpoint on the program's entry point—for example, break main; (see Item 30: "Use Code and Data Breakpoints")—and then you execute the step command (or just press Enter to repeat it). Note that many object-oriented languages execute some of your code before the program's "*main*" entry point by running the constructors of static objects.

Often, stepping into the code gives you more than you bargained for. In most of the cases, you don't want to see the detailed execution of every routine inside a loop. Thankfully, debuggers offer the *step over* command (*Eclipse*: F6, *Visual Studio*: F10, *gdb*: next) exactly for this purpose. The way you usually examine an algorithm's steps is that you *step over* unimportant routines, and *step into* the ones you want to troubleshoot. If you realize that you've entered into a routine by mistake, you can also ask the debugger to run all its code until its return point (*Eclipse*: F7, *Visual Studio*: Shift–F11, *gdb*: finish).

Sometimes you find that you wanted in fact to step into a routine only after you've stepped over it. Deal with this situation by adding a breakpoint at the statement calling the routine and rerunning the problematic execution from the program's user interface or restarting the whole program. The program's execution will stop at the point where the routine is about to be called, giving you the opportunity to step into it. This process allows you to narrow down on a problem: you step over large parts of the execution until you find a problematic one. You then add a breakpoint and rerun the execution, repeating the process for the code within that part. Alternately, consider using your debugger's reverse debugging features (see Item 31: "Familiarize Yourself with Reverse Debugging").

Things to Remember

✦ Examine the execution's sequence and the state of the program by stepping through the code.

✦ Speed up your examination by stepping over irrelevant parts.

✦ Narrow down on problems you stepped over by setting a breakpoint, running the code again, and stepping into the key routine.

Item 30: Use Code and Data Breakpoints

Code breakpoints allow you to fine-tune which code you examine. You set a breakpoint by specifying the source code location where you want execution to stop and control to be handed to the debugger (*Eclipse: Run – Toggle Breakpoint* or Ctrl-Shift-B, *Visual Studio: Debug – Toggle Breakpoint* or Shift–F11, *gdb:* break *file-name*:*line-number*). Instead of a source code location, you can also specify the name of a routine (*Eclipse: Run – Toggle Method Breakpoint, Visual Studio: Debug – New Breakpoint – Break at Function, gdb:* break *routine-name*). You then either *run* your program from its beginning (*Eclipse: Run – Run* or Ctrl-F11, *Visual Studio: Debug – Start Debugging* or F5, *gdb:* run) or you *continue* the already running execution (*Eclipse: Run – Resume* or F8, *Visual Studio: Debug – Continue* or F5, *gdb:* continue).

Code breakpoints allow you to quickly focus on the code that concerns you. You set a breakpoint there and run the program until it reaches that point. They also help you avoid wasting time stepping through uninteresting code sequences. You set a breakpoint at their end and continue the execution; the program will stop in the debugger once control reaches that point.

By creatively combining breakpoints, you can also examine cases where a failure occurs only through a specific code path. Consider the case where a problem in a commonly called routine c makes it fail only when it's called as part of test case t. Adding a breakpoint in c would be a waste of time, forcing you to repeatedly continue the program's execution until you reached the point where it is called when t is executing. Instead, what you do is to add (or enable) c's breakpoint during the program's execution: you first set a breakpoint in t, and when that is reached, you add a breakpoint for c.

Code breakpoints are also useful when you want to examine the state of the code just before your program trips over. Modern debuggers will, in general, break the execution and give you control within the debugger when something bad occurs. For example, *Visual Studio* opens a dialog box offering you the possibility to break when an unhandled exception occurs, whereas *gdb* will break the execution when a program aborts (through an exception, a signal, or by calling abort()). In *Eclipse* you have to be explicit: the dialog that opens through *Run – Add Java Exception Breakpoint* allows you to search for any exception and to specify whether you want your program to suspend its operation when such an exception occurs.

Yet, debuggers aren't psychic: if your program has its own code to terminate on some abnormal condition, you end with a stopped program and no easy way to determine its state when that condition occurs. You can handle such a situation by adding a breakpoint in the program's code that handles such events. If you can't find that code, then set up a breakpoint in the routine that's typically used to terminate a program's operation (exit, or _exit, or abort).

If you haven't added a suitable breakpoint and your program hangs (stops responding), then you can use the debugger to force its execution to stop (*Eclipse*: *Run – Suspend*, *Visual Studio*: *Debug – Break All* or Ctrl-Alt-Break, *gdb*: Ctrl-C). Once the program stops, you can find the statements that were executing at that time by examining the program's stack (see Item 32: "Navigate along the Calls between Routines"). Often this will provide you with enough context to understand why the program hung. Alternately, you can then single-step from that point onward (see Item 29: "Step through the Code") to better understand the code's behavior.

Sometimes you're not interested when some code executes, but when some data changes. This is when you use a *data breakpoint* or *watchpoint*. Finding the instruction that modifies the value of a variable in code that executes at a rate of billions of instructions per second is a tall order, especially when (stray) pointers can modify arbitrary memory locations. Thankfully, modern CPUs include clever circuitry in which a debugger can set a data breakpoint by specifying the memory location and the size corresponding to a variable. At every memory write, the CPU checks whether the memory address being written to falls within the range of the specified data breakpoints and, if so, breaks the program's execution, thereby handing control to the debugger. Because these checks happen through the CPU's circuitry concurrently with normal memory writes, the program's execution doesn't normally slow down.

Owing to their closeness with the underlying hardware, data breakpoints are a bit fickle. In *Visual Studio*, in order to set one (*Debug – New Breakpoint – New Data Breakpoint*), your program must already have started its execution, so that the addresses of the global variables are nailed down. Then you don't specify the name of the variable that interests you, but its memory location (&`variable`) and size (e.g., typically 4 for integers and 8 for double precision floating point numbers). In *gdb* you specify just the variable's name as an argument to the `watch` command. (If *gdb* doesn't respond with a line saying `Hardware watchpoint`, it means that your setup or specification doesn't allow a hardware-supported watchpoint. In this case, *gdb* will emulate the functionality in software, slowing down your program by many orders of magnitude.) In both cases, if you want to set a data breakpoint on a dynamically allocated variable (one that is allocated on the heap via *malloc* or *new* or a routine's local variable), you must wait until that variable comes into existence (by setting a suitable code breakpoint) so that when you specify it its address is known. When debugging Java under *Eclipse*, setting a watchpoint is simpler: open the field's context menu and select *Toggle Breakpoint*.

Debuggers allow the qualification of breakpoints with conditions (break only if a specified condition is true), hit counts (break only after the specified number of occurrences), and filters (e.g., set the breakpoint only in the specified thread). Although these goodies are sometimes very useful, stressing them can be a sign that you need more powerful debugging aids, such as a precisely targeted test case (see Item 54: "Find the Fault by Constructing a Test Case") or powerful logging (see Item 40: "Add Debugging Functionality").

Things to Remember

✦ Narrow down on the code that interests you with a code breakpoint.

✦ Skip executions that don't concern you by adding a breakpoint when another is hit.

✦ Debug abnormal terminations by breaking on exceptions or in exit routines.

✦ Troubleshoot a hung program by stopping its execution within the debugger.

✦ Pinpoint mysteriously changing variables with data breakpoints.

Item 31: Familiarize Yourself with Reverse Debugging

The abundant RAM space and fast CPUs that grace modern computers often allow you to execute your program in reverse. This typically works by having each instruction record the changes it makes, and undoing these changes when executing the program backward. Reverse debugging is especially useful when you reach a point in the program's execution where you realize that the failure you're trying to isolate has already occurred. Normally you would execute the program from its beginning, placing a breakpoint earlier in the hope that this time you will catch the failure by single-stepping toward it. The reexecution might even require you to go again through a time-consuming process required to make the program fail. Then, one impatient command to step over a function is all that's needed to miss the failure one more time. With *reverse debugging* all you need to do when you've missed a failure is to execute the program backward (and then maybe again forward) until you pinpoint the failure.

A number of stand-alone debuggers and IDEs support reverse debugging, in one form or another, under diverse names. Examples include *Visual Studio IntelliTrace*, Rogue Wave Software's *TotalView ReplayEngine*, Undo Software's *UndoDB*, and *gdb*—either stand-alone or hidden under *Eclipse CDT*. As reverse debugging is not yet universally available, your mileage (and its cost) will vary.

As seeing is believing, here is a simple walk-through of reverse debugging actions using *gdb*. Consider as an example the following simple program. (To keep the text succinct, the program has no bugs; it serves to demonstrate how you can step back in time when debugging an actual bug.)

```
1   #include <stdio.h>
2   int
3   main()
4   {
5         int i, sum = 0;
6
7         for (i = 0; i < 10; i++)
8               sum += i;
9         printf("%d\n", sum);
10  }
```

Let's first debug the program, breaking at the entry point of main.

```
(gdb) break main
Breakpoint 1 at 0x40050e: file loop.c, line 5.
(gdb) run
Starting program: /home/dds/a.out

Breakpoint 1, main () at loop.c:5
5               int i, sum = 0;
```

At that point you can set *gdb* to display the values of i and sum, and break at the routine's last line. Crucially, you also ask *gdb* to record the program's execution, so that you can later execute it in reverse.

```
(gdb) display i
(gdb) display sum
(gdb) break 10
Breakpoint 2 at 0x400542: file loop.c, line 10.
(gdb) record
```

When the program breaks, the variables i and sum have the expected values.

```
(gdb) cont
Continuing.
45
Breakpoint 2, main () at loop.c:10
10    }
2: sum = 45
1: i = 10
```

At that point you can use the *gdb* reverse-next command to execute the program backward.

```
(gdb) reverse-next
9               printf("%d\n", sum);
2: sum = 45
1: i = 10
(gdb) reverse-next
7               for (i = 0; i < 10; i++)
2: sum = 45
1: i = 9
(gdb) reverse-next
8                   sum += i;
2: sum = 36
1: i = 9
```

The command `reverse-step` works in the same way, but (in common with the `step` command) goes into the execution of routines rather than stepping over them. The command `reverse-continue` allows you to execute the program in reverse until the execution encounters the first preceding breakpoint. In this case, the breakpoint is at the entry point of the `main` function, and you can see that the two variables again have their initial values.

```
(gdb) reverse-continue
Continuing.

No more reverse-execution history.
main () at loop.c:5
5               int i, sum = 0;
2: sum = 0
1: i = 0
```

Note that reverse debugging has a number of limitations. Many stem from the large amount of work the debugger has to do behind the scenes to allow you to time travel. Owing to this, the performance of the program you're debugging is likely to drop substantially, the debugger will require a lot of memory, and the distance you may be allowed to travel back in time may be limited (*gdb*'s default is 200,000 instructions). Also, interaction with other systems and the outside world will typically not be "undone": characters that have appeared on a terminal will stay there, rows that have been removed from a remote database will not reappear. Incoming asynchronous events, such as signals and network packets, are also difficult to replicate when you step forward again. Nevertheless, this is a feature that can occasionally save you hours of dull, painful work.

Things to Remember

✦ Familiarize yourself with reverse debugging.

Item 32: Navigate along the Calls between Routines

While your program is executing, a data structure named *call stack* or simply *stack* is used so that routines can call each other in an orderly manner. When one routine calls another, the following data can be *pushed* or allocated onto the stack. (Sometimes CPU registers are used to optimize performance.)

- The arguments passed to the called routine, (typically in right-to-left order, which easily accommodates routines with a variable number of arguments)

- If the routine is a method, a pointer to the corresponding object

- The address to which the called routine will return when its execution finishes

- The local variables of the called routine

All of these elements are addressed relative to the current stack position, allowing an arbitrary number of calls (even recursive ones) to be made. The stack is the second most important piece of information associated with an executing program. (The most important is the currently executing program location.)

Note that on many CPU architectures, such as x86, x86-64, and 68k, a *calling convention* dictates that the stack is indeed used in exactly the way described. On other CPU architectures, such as ARM, *PowerPC*, and *SPARC*, a routine's arguments and (on some CPUs) the return address are stored in CPU registers. The stack is then only used in cases where there are not enough registers to handle the data.

All debuggers provide a way to view the stack (*Eclipse*: *Window – Show View – Debug*, *Visual Studio*: *Debug – Windows – Call Stack* or Alt-7, *gdb*: where). What you see is one line for each routine invocation. Each line contains the file or class associated with the routine, the routine's name, its arguments, and the line that was last executed. This gives you a snapshot of your program's status. The currently executing routine appears at the topmost line, while near the bottom you should be able to see your program's entry point (often a routine called main) and sometimes the runtime library or even kernel routines that led to it (e.g., wmainCRT-Startup() on Windows programs). On multi-threaded programs, each thread is associated with its own stack.

Some particular stack traces have a story to tell.

- If the top of the stack trace contains unrecognizable routines, then you have interrupted the program while it was executing some third-party code. This often occurs in GUI programs where the low levels of the interaction (e.g., wait for the user to click a button) happen through the framework's libraries. It can also happen when your program calls a third-party library, such as an embedded SQL database, to perform some heavy processing. If the routines appear without arguments and listed through their memory address rather than their name, then that code was not compiled with debugging information (see Item 28: "Use Code Compiled for Symbolic Debugging"). You can scan the stack trace downward to find the point where your program called the third-party code.

- If the stack trace contains only third-party routines, your program is probably executing through a framework that interacts with it via callback routines, retaining the control of the program flow. You probably don't want to debug the framework's code, so you need to add some breakpoints to get a chance to debug your own code.

- If the stack trace is unexpectedly shallow and contains no recognizable routines, then your code has probably corrupted the stack via a stray pointer. You need to carefully step through the code from an earlier point in order to find the place where the stack gets corrupted.

- If the stack trace contains the same routine(s) many times over, then you may have a bug in recursive code.

With the stack on display, you can easily move between its routines. On a graphical debugger, you simply click on the corresponding stack line and the debugger will switch its context to the routine associated with the corresponding *stack frame*. There, you can see the line that was last executed and examine the routine's local variables and arguments. In *gdb*, you can set your context to the *n*th frame with the command frame *n*. You can also move between stack frames with the up and down commands.

Things to Remember

✦ Look at the program's stack to understand its state.

✦ A messed up stack can be the result of a problem in your code.

Item 33: Look for Errors by Examining the Values of Variables and Expressions

A quick and easy way to examine a routine's key variables is to display the values of its local variables: *Window – Show View – Variables* or Alt–Shift–Q V under *Eclipse*, *Debug – Windows – Locals* or Alt-4 under *Visual Studio*, and info locals or info args under *gdb*. In well-written code, these will be few and will provide all the information needed to follow the code's execution. If some expressions are too complex to understand through the values of the local variables, consider simplifying them by introducing appropriately named temporary variables. Don't worry about the performance cost of this change: it will be negligible if any, because the compiler can optimize away your change.

As demonstrated by Gary Bernhardt's CodeMash 2012 hilarious *Wat* (What?) talk, the value of an expression is sometimes different from what you might expect. Therefore, when you're trying to understand why some code behaves in an unfathomable way, look at the value of its expressions. If the expression is part of the code (rather than part of a C/C++ macro), to see its value select it with the mouse, and in *Eclipse* click on *Inspect* from the context menu or simply hover the mouse over the selection in *Visual Studio*. You can also display the value of arbitrary expressions. In *Eclipse* go to the *Window – Show View – Display* window, enter the expression, select it, and click on *Inspect* from the context menu; in *Visual Studio*, open *Debug – QuickWatch* (or press Shift-F9) and enter the expression. Under *gdb*, use the print *expression* command. Keep in mind that the debugger can evaluate the expression only if its variables are defined in the current stack frame.

Often it's useful to observe how an expression's value changes while the code executes. You can do this by entering it in the *Eclipse Window – Show View – Expression* window, or the *Visual Studio Debug – Windows – Watch* window, or execution display *expression* under *gdb*. Under *Visual Studio* the expression will helpfully be colored red every time its value changes, making it even easier to follow an algorithm's execution.

Diverse debugger extensions, libraries, and tools can help you view and comprehend complex data types and structures, such as arbitrary precision numbers, trees, maps, and linked lists.

- In *Visual Studio* you can write a *custom visualizer* to display an object in the format that's appropriate for it.

- In *gdb* the corresponding facility is called a *pretty-printer*.

- In *QtCreator* look for *debug visualizers*.

- When programming in Python, import the pprint module and use its PrettyPrinter method.

- In Perl programs use the Data::Dumper module.

- In JavaScript code display objects with JSON.stringify(obj, null, 4).

- *Python Tutor* allows you to paste Python, Java, JavaScript, or Ruby code into a window, execute it step by step, and see how objects and stack frames point to each other (see Figure 4.1).

- Finally, if you cannot find a suitable option, you can always write a small script to convert your data into input for the *Graphviz dot* program.

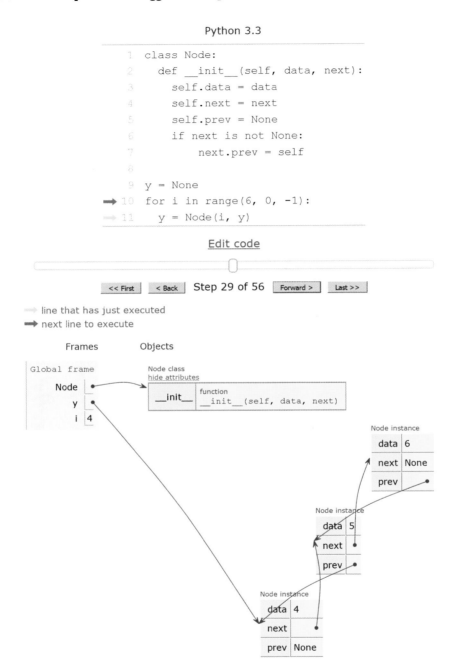

Figure 4.1 Doubly linked list visualization with Python Tutor

Things to Remember

✦ Verify the values of key expressions.

✦ Set up the continuous display of expressions that change during an algorithm's execution.

✦ Follow a routine's logic through its local variables.

✦ Use data visualization facilities to untangle complex data structures.

Item 34: Know How to Attach a Debugger to a Running Process

With a lot of hard work or through serendipity, you manage to reproduce an important but elusive bug. The trouble is that the program where the bug occurred wasn't run from your debugger, and reproducing it again might be difficult. What can you do?

Luckily, debuggers offer you the possibility to attach themselves to a running process. Under *Visual Studio*, use the *Debug – Attach to Process* command. With *gdb*, you first need to find out the numeric process-id of the program you want to debug. Do this by running the *ps* command and looking at the PID column. The *ps* command arguments and output vary between systems. The following invocations query for web server processes given the server's user on a GNU/Linux, an OS X, and a FreeBSD system.

```
$ ps -u apache
  PID TTY       TIME CMD
25582 ?      00:00:00 httpd
25583 ?      00:00:00 httpd
$ ps -u www
  UID  PID TTY       TIME CMD
  70  299 ??      0:00.02 /usr/sbin/httpd -D FOREGROUND
  70 5363 ??      0:00.00 /usr/sbin/httpd -D FOREGROUND
$ ps -U www
 PID TT STAT  TIME COMMAND
1045 -  S   33:39.19 nginx: worker process (nginx)
```

You then run *gdb* with the executable program as its argument, followed by -p and the process-id you want to debug.

```
$ sudo gdb -p 25582
(gdb) where
#0 0x00007f75e115d017 in accept4 () from /lib64/libc.so.6
#1 0x00007f75e18687ba in apr_socket_accept () from /usr/lib64/
   libapr-1.so.0
```

```
#2 0x000055f2aff25513 in ap_unixd_accept ()
#3 0x00007f75d859f717 in ?? () from /etc/httpd/modules/
   mod_mpm_prefork.so
#4 0x00007f75d859f9d5 in ?? () from /etc/httpd/modules/
   mod_mpm_prefork.so
#5 0x00007f75d859fa36 in ?? () from /etc/httpd/modules/
   mod_mpm_prefork.so
#6 0x00007f75d85a0710 in ?? () from /etc/httpd/modules/
   mod_mpm_prefork.so
#7 0x000055f2afef000e in ap_run_mpm ()
#8 0x000055f2afee97b6 in main ()
```

To attach a debugger to Java programs, you must execute the JVM that launches the program with arguments such as the following.

```
-agentlib:jdwp=transport=dt_socket,address=127.0.0.1:8000,\
server=y,suspend=n
```

The preceding incantation has the running program listen to debugger connections from the same host (the IP address 127.0.0.1, also known as localhost) on TCP port 8000. If you're running many Java processes, each one must be listening on a unique port—pick any unused port number in the range 1,024–65,535. You can see used ports by running the command netstat -an and looking for TCP connections in a *listen* state. Then under *Eclipse*, go to *Run – Debug Configurations – New launch configuration*, set the *Host* and *Port* fields to match the arguments you specified in the program's invocation, and click on *Debug* to attach the debugger to the process you specified. Alternately, if you have a misbehaving Java process, you can run the *jstack* command with its process-id as an argument. This will display a stack dump of all executing threads, thereby giving you an idea of what the process is doing.

Once a debugger is attached to a running process, you can stop the process (*Eclipse*: *Run – Suspend*, *Visual Studio*: *Debug – Break All*, *gdb*: break) and examine the context of the executing code by looking at the call stack (see Item 32: "Navigate along the Calls between Routines"). Alternately, you can set breakpoints and wait for the running code to hit them. While the program is running, you can also examine globally accessible variables and objects.

You may also find yourself debugging a process that is executing on another host. This can be useful if you're using a GUI debugger and the program is executing on a computer without a GUI (or a way to access it remotely). This is often the case with embedded software or code running on servers. It's also useful when you're debugging code on devices that lack the resources or the infrastructure to run a full-fledged debugger. In these cases, you run a small debugging monitor on the remote end, and configure your debugger to connect to it. The details vary a lot between debuggers and connection types; consult your setup's documentation for them.

Here is an example of using *gdb* to remotely debug, say, a video recording application running on a TV. On the TV you arrange for the program to be run under the debug server, which will be listening on the (free) TCP port 1234 for the client you will run on your workstation.

```
$ gdbserver your-workstation.example.com:1234 video-recorder
```

Then, on your workstation, you run *gdb* on the same executable file, specifying the remote host and port with the *target* command.

```
$ gdb video-recorder
(gdb) target remote tv-12.example.com:1234
Remote debugging using tv-12.example.com:1234
```

From that point onward, you can control and inspect the process executing on the TV from your workstation with the usual *gdb* commands. If you find the remote debugging methods too complex, consider installing and using the GUI debugger on a remote host by displaying the debugger's window on your desktop or by mirroring the remote host's screen on your screen (see Item 18: "Enable the Debugging of Unwieldy Systems from Your Desk").

Things to Remember

✦ Debug an already running process by attaching your debugger to it.

✦ Debug applications on resource-constrained devices through remote debugging facilities.

Item 35: Know How to Work with Core Dumps

It's often possible to debug an application *after* it has crashed and terminated. On Unix systems native applications that crash can generate a *core dump* file. This is a memory image of the application at the time of crash. (The name comes from the magnetic core memory technology used when the concept got introduced.) There are various requirements and configuration settings for generating the core dump files, ranging from the trivial (the application must be able to create a file name core in its current directory) to the baroque (on Linux you can configure the core dump to be piped into a specified program). The most important is a user limit of the core dump size, which is often configured to be zero. Typically you can see it with the ulimit -c command and change it by appending to it the maximum size of those files in kB. You can make the change permanent by adding the command into a user's or a global shell configuration file, such as .bash_profile or /etc/profile.

To inspect a Unix core dump image with *gdb*, invoke it with the program image and the core dump file as arguments. Then you can issue the where command to see where the program crashed, use the call stack frame navigation commands, and evaluate expressions to determine the program's state. A core dump is so useful that you may wish to generate it from within your program when your program encounters an internal error. You can easily do that by calling the *abort* function.

The process for postmortem debugging of native applications under Windows is different. Windows programs don't generate a dump file by default. Instead, you have to do that from within your application by calling the *MiniDumpWriteDump* function. As with *abort*, you can call it when you encounter an internal error. However, you probably also want to call it when your program encounters an exception, for example, when it tries to access an illegal memory address. For this you need to call the *SetUnhandledExceptionFilter* function, passing to it as an argument your function that calls *MiniDumpWriteDump*. With the dump file at hand, you can open it from *Visual Studio* and examine the application's state at the time of the dump.

If an application hasn't crashed but has stopped responding or has entered another state that you wish to debug, you may want to force the creation of a memory dump file instead of attaching a debugger to it. This can be useful for permanently recording the program's state, sending the file to a colleague, or postponing the debugging for later. You can do this under Unix by sending the program a SIGABRT signal with the command kill -ABRT *process-id*. (You saw how to obtain a program's process-id in Item 34: "Know How to Attach a Debugger to a Running Process.") If the program is running on a terminal window, you can also send it this signal just by pressing Ctrl-\. Under Windows, fire the task manager, right-click on the process that interests you, and select *Create Dump File*. This will generate a dump file in your temporary folder (i.e., in the folder corresponding to the TEMP environment variable). (Run %TEMP% to see it.)

Unfortunately, if you're using language with a managed environment, such as C#, Java, JavaScript, Perl, Python, or Ruby, support for postmortem debugging may be patchy, vendor-specific, or non-existent. This is because the underlying technology is more abstract, sophisticated, and implementation specific (think of just-in-time compilation), the operating system cannot be used directly to create a memory dump, and the requirements from memory dumps are higher (consider thousands of executing threads or JavaScript's pending events). At the time of writing, many of these environments offer no or only rudimentary support for postmortem debugging. If you work in such an environment, armed with the knowledge of what postmortem debugging can do, consult the current documentation to see what's available.

A natural application of postmortem debugging is a system to debug memory dumps obtained from your customers. To do this you need to organize a number of things.

1. You must set up your program to create a memory dump and associated metadata. You already saw how a memory dump can be created. For the metadata, at a minimum, you need the program's version. Other data that might be useful are the environment where the program is executing (e.g., processor, operating system, environment variables, shared library versions), log files, input data (be careful to safeguard the confidentiality of your customers' data), and the history of the program's use (this can be easily stored in a log file).

2. When your program generates a memory dump file, you must arrange to send that your way. Given that your program's state may be corrupt after a crash, it's best to do that through an external program. You can do this by running your program through another one that will check its exit status and send the memory file if it matches a mutually agreed upon value. In such a case, have your program exit with that value in the SIGABRT signal handler (Unix) or the exception filter function (Windows). To send the data, an HTTP POST request is probably the easiest and most reliable method.

3. At your end, you need to write a small server that will receive the HTTP request and store the data for further analysis. It's probably a good idea to store some of the metadata in a database, so that you'll be able to easily analyze it.

4. You also need a way to debug the version that crashed. For the source code, you can simply tag each released source code version in your revision control system (see Item 26: "Hunt the Causes and History of Bugs with the Revision Control System") and include that tag in the sent metadata. Unless you're confident you can recreate bit-identical executables from a tagged source code version (not trivial given embedded timestamps, code randomization, and compiler updates), it's probably easiest to store each version of the shipped executable binary file (and the associated debug—PDB—files in the case of Windows programs).

5. When you want to debug a customer's crash, launch your debugger with the correct source code, the executable, and the corresponding memory dump file.

Given the complexity of this process, you might want to use a framework that performs these tasks, such as *PLCrashReporter* for iOS and OS X and the services built on top of it, or a hosted service, such as those provided by *Crittercism*, *New Relic*, or *Splunk MINT*.

Things to Remember

✦ Debug crashed and hung applications by obtaining and examining their memory dumps.

✦ Debug installed customer applications by setting up a crash report system.

Item 36: Tune Your Debugging Tools

When you are debugging, it pays to invest in your infrastructure (see Item 9: "Set Yourself Up for Debugging Success"). This includes a productive debugger setup. Here are some ideas.

First, use a graphical user interface. Although I love command-line interfaces, and I find myself to be very productive when I use them, debugging is one of the few tasks I believe is almost always better performed through a GUI. The reason for this is that debugging benefits from the simultaneous presentation of diverse data: source code, local variables, call stack, log messages. If you're using *Eclipse* or *Visual Studio*, then you're already set. If you're using *gdb*, then there are several alternatives you can explore. The one with the most features is *DDD* (*DataDisplayDebugger*). This is a Unix-based front end that provides a full-fledged GUI not only to *gdb*, but also to other command-line debuggers, such as those of *Perl*, *Bash* (*bashdb*), *make* (*remake*), and *Python* (*pydb*). In addition to the usual debugger commands, it also provides a powerful way to display a program's data structures. Go ahead and use it if your program runs on a Unix host. (The client can be any computer that supports an X server, which includes Windows and OS X.) Another option is to launch *gdb* with the -tui option or execute the – command to use *gdb*'s text-based user interface. If its *Emacs*-style keyboard bindings aren't your cup of tea, another alternative is *cgdb*, which offers a *vi*-like interface.

Another way to increase the productivity of your debugger sessions is to save commands that are useful for debugging a program into a file and execute it on startup. *Visual Studio* and *Eclipse* automatically save the setup of your debugging session, such as breakpoints and watchpoints, as part of the project you're working on. In *gdb* you have to work a bit harder, but as a compensation you can do more things. You can put *gdb* commands in a file named `.gdbinit` and place that either in your home directory (so that it will be loaded by all *gdb* sessions) or in a project's directory (so that it will be loaded when you run *gdb* in that directory). You can also put *gdb* commands in a file and load it on startup with the `-x` option. You can even combine these three methods:

- Put in `$HOME/.gdbinit` commands you use in all your sessions.

- Put in `myproject/.gdbinit` some definitions useful for the specific project.

- Put in `issue-1234` breakpoints and watchpoints that can help you debug issue 1234.

A particularly useful command to put in your global `.gdbinit` file is `set history save`. This will save the commands you type in each session, allowing you to recall them (with the keyboard's up arrow or by searching) when you run *gdb* again. You can set *gdb*'s input editing interface to match your preferences through commands placed in a file named `.inputrc` in your home directory. For example, a command `set editing-mode vi` or `set editing-mode emacs` will set the keyboard bindings to match those of the *vi* or *Emacs* editors.

Your global `.gdbinit` file is also useful for defining aliases for commonly used commands. For instance, the following script will define a new command, `sf`, that will display the current stack frame.

```
define sf
  where
  info args
  info locals
end
document sf
Display current stack frame
end
```

The *gdbinit* Gist on GitHub offers many more ideas.

You can use more complex scripts to troubleshoot difficult issues, particularly when you can't or don't want to add assertions to a program's source code (see Item 43: "Use Assertions"). As an example, consider the case where a program's resources are protected by enclosing their access in exactly one `lock–unlock` block. You can check for mismatched calls by running the *gdb* script in Listing 4.1 before executing the program.

Listing 4.1 A *gdb* script that verifies lock ordering

```
# Define a counter variable to keep track of locks
set $nlock = 0

# When the lock routine is called, increase the counter
# Define a new breakpoint
break lock
# Commands to execute when the lock routine is called
commands
  silent
  # Increment counter variable
  set $nlock = $nlock + 1
  # Continue the program's execution
  continue
end

# When the unlock routine is called, decrease the counter
break unlock
commands
  silent
  set $nlock = $nlock - 1
  continue
end

# Stop the execution with a backtrace on nested locks
break lock if $nlock > 0
commands
  silent
  echo Nested lock\n
  # Display the stack trace
  backtrace
  # Stop the program's execution
  break
end

# Stop the execution with a backtrace on duplicate unlocks
break unlock if $nlock <= 0
commands
  silent
  echo Duplicate unlock\n
  backtrace
  break
end
```

The preceding script defines a lock counter variable, $nlock. It then sets conditional breakpoints for each of the two functions, which check the $nlock variable and break the execution printing an error message if the function was called in the wrong order. Two additional breakpoints for the same functions are used to maintain the value of the $nlock variable. Note that the conditional breakpoints must be defined before the other two.

If *gdb*'s language isn't powerful enough for your needs, newer versions of *gdb* provide the `compile` command, which allows you to compile and run code in your application's native language. This code can access local and global variables and functions. When you define new commands with compiled elements, the possibilities of what you can achieve are endless. Beware though: sophisticated debugging functionality typically belongs to the program's source code, where it can be properly maintained, shared, and documented (see Item 40: "Add Debugging Functionality"). Unless there are strong reasons that make this impossible, don't get carried away implementing all your debugging infrastructure with *gdb* commands.

Finally, another way to preserve the valuable commands you've entered in a *gdb* session when you modify a program's source code is to run the *make* command within *gdb* (or in another window). When you run the program again, *gdb* will see that its executable image has changed, and will reload it automatically.

Things to Remember

✦ Use a debugger with a graphical interface.

✦ Configure *gdb* to save its history and use your favorite keyboard bindings.

✦ Put commonly used commands inside *gdb* scripts.

✦ Build your program within *gdb* to maintain the commands you entered.

Item 37: Know How to View Assembly Code and Raw Memory

You may occasionally find yourself looking at a single simple line of code, which you know should behave in a particular way, but it doesn't do so. A way to discover the problem's cause is to look at how the code executes at the level of the underlying machine. At that level, what you see is exactly what you get: each machine instruction performs one simple operation, which you can readily observe; there are no hidden abstraction layers harboring treacherous gotchas. By looking at the execution of machine code you may pinpoint unwanted type casts, misunderstood operator precedence rules, unanticipated use of overloaded operators, missing braces, inappropriately typed values (e.g., using an int instead of a long), and unexpected use of polymorphic routines. (You may see some of these problems by stepping into the code, but code inlining may prevent you from doing so.)

Understanding the machine instructions is not as difficult as it sounds. As an example, consider the C program in Listing 4.2 and its (unoptimized) assembly language compilation into two formats: ARM code using the so-called AT&T assembler syntax, which is popular on Unix systems, (Listing 4.3) and Intel x86 code using the Intel assembler syntax, which is popular on Windows systems (Listing 4.4). Most instructions have self-explanatory names, such as add, mov (move), cmp (compare), and call. Instead of the variables you have in high-level languages, you see a fixed small number of registers with names such as eax or edx in Intel processors and r0 to r15 in ARM ones. In most cases, one of the registers (eax or r0) is used to return a function's value. A value in square brackets is used to access the contents of the value's memory location. Local variables and a routine's arguments are accessed on the stack at memory offsets from a register called a *frame pointer* (ebp or fp). The stack is manipulated explicitly using instructions such as push and pop or changes to the frame pointer's value. Loops are implemented by jumping (jmp or b for branch) from the end of the loop to its beginning. Conditionals work by comparing (cmp) two values and then performing a conditional jump based on the comparison's result (e.g., jle or ble for jump or branch if less or equal). A separate set of registers and corresponding instructions is used for performing floating point operations.

Listing 4.2 A simple counting loop in C

```c
#include <stdio.h>
main()
{
        int i;
        for (i = 0; i < 10; i++)
                printf("%d\n", i);
        return 0;
}
```

Listing 4.3 C program compiled into (AT&T syntax) ARM assembly language

```
        .section    .rodata        @ Data area
        .align 2                   @ Align on even memory address
```

```
.LC0:  .ascii "%d\012\000"       @ Printf format string
       .text                     @ Code area
       .global main              @ Export main
main:                            @ Entry point of main
       stmfd sp!, {fp, lr}       @ Function entry boilerplate
       add   fp, sp, #4
       sub   sp, sp, #8
       mov   r3, #0              @ Set register r3 to zero
       str   r3, [fp, #-8]       @ Store register r3 into i
       b     .L2                 @ Branch to loop's end
.L3:                             @ Loop's top label
       ldr   r3, .L4             @ Get printf format address
       mov   r0, r3              @ Set format as first argument
       ldr   r1, [fp, #-8]       @ Set i as second argument
       bl    printf              @ Call printf
       ldr   r3, [fp, #-8]       @ Get i into register r3
       add   r3, r3, #1          @ Increment r3 by one
       str   r3, [fp, #-8]       @ Store register r3 into i
.L2:                             @ Loop's end label
       ldr   r3, [fp, #-8]       @ Get i into register r3
       cmp   r3, #9              @ Compare r3 with 9
       ble   .L3                 @ If less or equal then
                                 @ branch to loops top
       mov   r3, #0              @ Set r3 to zero
       mov   r0, r3              @ Zero r0 as main's return value
       sub   sp, fp, #4          @ Function exit boilerplate
       ldmfd sp!, {fp, pc}
.L4:   .word .LC0                @ Address of printf format arg
```

Listing 4.4 C program compiled into (Intel syntax) x86 assembly language

```
_DATA SEGMENT                    ; Data area
$SG2748 DB  '%d', 0aH, 00H       ; printf format string
_DATA ENDS

PUBLIC _main                     ; Export main
EXTRN _printf:PROC               ; Import printf

_TEXT SEGMENT                    ; Code area
_i$ = -4                         ; Stack offset where i is stored
_main PROC
       push  ebp                 ; Function entry boilerplate
       mov   ebp, esp
```

```
        push   ecx
        mov    DWORD PTR _i$[ebp], 0 ; i = 0
        jmp    SHORT $LN3@main   ; Jump to loop's end
$LN2@main:                       ; Loop's top label
        mov    eax, DWORD PTR _i$[ebp] ; Get i into register eax
        add    eax, 1            ; Increment by one
        mov    DWORD PTR _i$[ebp], eax ; Store eax back to i
$LN3@main:                       ; Loop's end label
        cmp    DWORD PTR _i$[ebp], 10   ; Compare i to 10
        jge    SHORT $LN1@main   ; If greater or equal
                                 ; terminate loop
        mov    ecx, DWORD PTR _i$[ebp] ; Get i into register ecx
        push   ecx               ; Push ecx as argument to printf
        push   OFFSET $SG2748    ; Push printf format string
                                 ; argument
        call   _printf           ; Call printf
        add    esp, 8            ; Free pushed printf arguments
        jmp    SHORT $LN2@main   ; Jump to loop's top
$LN1@main:                       ; Loop's exit label
        xor    eax, eax          ; Zero eax as main's return value
        mov    esp, ebp          ; Function exit boilerplate
        pop    ebp
        ret    0
_main ENDP
_TEXT ENDS
END
```

To view and step through your program's machine code in *Visual Studio*, open a window with the disassembled code (*Debug – Windows – Disassembly* or Alt-8), and then use the step-into and step-over keys. You will also want to see the values of the registers (*Debug – Windows – Registers* or Alt-5). Under *gdb*, run display/i $pc to show each disassembled instruction, and then use the stepi and nexti commands. You can see the register values with info registers or you can issue a command to continuously show a specific register value, for example, display $r0 or display $eax. If you're using Eclipse, consider installing the *bytecode* plugin, which shows you disassembled JVM bytecode.

Looking at register values may also be useful in order to find out the return value of a function that's calculated in the return statement. Simply display the value of the register that's used to return the function's value when the function is about to return to its caller. Note that in cases where a function returns an object larger than the register, the object is typically returned on the stack.

Familiarity with your computer's internal representations is also useful when you're debugging data at a low level. When your program reads binary data from the disk or from other processes, you can easily examine the corresponding memory to see what's there. Under *Visual Studio*, create a memory window (*Debug – Windows – Memory* or Alt–6). At the window's address field, enter the name of the buffer array you want to examine or an expression that yields an address (e.g., &structure_variable). You can also right-click in the memory area to specify the size and type of the units you want to display (e.g., signed 4-byte integers). In *Eclipse*, you can access the corresponding facility (memory monitors) through *Window – Show View – Other – Debug – Memory*, though it does not appear to work for Java programs. The command to use under *gdb* is: x/ followed by the number of elements you want to see, a *print* format character, the size of the elements, and the address of the memory block. For example, x/10xb &a will show the contents of a as 10 byte-size (b) hexadecimal (x) elements.

When examining in-memory representations, keep in mind that there are two ways in which an integer's bytes can be stored in memory. The so-called *little-endian* format has the least significant byte stored first and the most significant stored last. This is the format used by Intel architectures and the one in which most ARM CPUs are configured. Under this format, an integer variable a with the value 0x76543210 would appear as

0x10   0x32   0x54   0x76

The *big-endian* (also known as *network*) format, is adopted by less popular CPU architectures, such as the *SPARC* and *PowerPC*. However, it is the format specified for important Internet protocols (e.g., TCP/IP) and also for reading and writing Java values in binary format. Under this format, the contents of the same variable a would appear as

0x76   0x54   0x32   0x10

Things to Remember

✦ To really understand how your code behaves, work with disassembled machine instructions.

✦ The register eax or r0 can tell you a function's return value.

✦ To really understand how your data is stored, look at its internal representation.

5 Programming Techniques

As a developer, most failures you'll encounter are likely to be associated with the software's code. One method to find the corresponding fault is to stare the code sternly in the eye—with some help.

Item 38: Review and Manually Execute Suspect Code

You can often pinpoint a bug in an algorithm by examining the code or executing the corresponding lines by hand. You want to verify that the code is written correctly and that your understanding of the code is sound. If you find an error while you examine the code, you're done. If not, you can then execute the same code with a debugger (see Item 29: "Step through the Code") and see where you disagree with the computer.

On your first pass through the code, carefully examine each line, and look for common mistakes. Nowadays, you can avoid many such mistakes through appropriate conventions (e.g., by placing additional brackets to avoid operator precedence order mistakes), or a static analysis tool can point them out to you (see Item 51: "Use Static Program Analysis"). Nevertheless, mistakes can slip through, especially in code that does not (ahem) adhere to the necessary coding conventions. Look for errors in operator precedence (the bit operators are particularly risky), missing braces and break statements, extra semicolons (immediately after a control statement), the use of an assignment instead of a comparison, uninitialized or wrongly initialized variables, statements that are missing from a loop, off-by-one errors, erroneous type conversions, missing methods, spelling errors, and language-specific gotchas.

To execute code by hand, have an empty sheet of paper at your side, write down the names of the key variables, and start executing the statements in the order the computer would (Figure 5.1). Every time a variable changes its value, cross out the old value and write the new one. Writing the values with a pencil makes it easier to fix any errors you make.

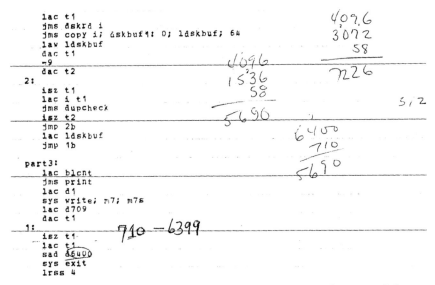

Figure 5.1 Hand-drawn calculations beside a 1970 listing of the PDP-7 Unix file system *check* program, the forerunner of *fsck*

A (real) calculator may help you derive the values of complex expressions more quickly. A programmer's calculator can be helpful if you're dealing with bit operations. Avoid using your computer: manipulating the variable values in a spreadsheet, browsing the code with an editor, or quickly checking whether any new email has arrived will make it difficult to deeply concentrate, which is what this method is all about.

If the code manipulates complex data structures, draw them with lines, boxes, circles, and arrows. Devise a notation to draw the algorithm's most important parts. For example, if you're drawing intervals (it's always difficult to get the corresponding algorithms exactly right), you can draw the closed end (hopefully the interval's start) with a line ending in a square bracket and the open end (the interval's end, if you're following the correct convention) with a round bracket. You may also often find it useful to draw the parts of a program's call graph (how routines call each other) that interest you. If you're fluent in UML, use that for your diagrams, but don't sweat too much about getting the notation right; seek a balance between the ease of drawing and the comprehension of what you've drawn.

A larger paper may help provide you with the space you need for your diagram. A whiteboard provides an even larger surface and also makes it easier to erase parts and collaborate. Add colors to the picture to easily distinguish the elements you draw. If the diagram you've drawn is important, take a picture when you're finished and attach it at the corresponding issue.

One notch fancier is the manipulation of physical objects, such as whiteboard magnets, paper clips, toothpicks, sticky notes, checker pieces, or Lego blocks. This increases the level of your engagement with the problem by bringing into play more senses: 3D vision, touch, and proprioception (the sense of where your body parts are). You can use this method to simulate queues, groupings, protocols, ratings, priorities, and a lot more. Just don't get carried away playing with the objects that are supposed to help you with your work.

Things to Remember

+ Look through the code for common mistakes.

+ Execute the code by hand to verify its correctness.

+ Untangle complex data structures by drawing them.

+ Address complexity with large sheets of paper, a whiteboard, and color.

+ Deepen your engagement with a problem by manipulating physical objects.

Item 39: Go Over Your Code and Reasoning with a Colleague

The *rubber duck technique* is probably the most effective one you'll find in this book, measured by the number of times you can apply it. It involves explaining how your code works to someone else. Typically, half-way through your explanation, you'll exclaim, "Oh wait, how silly of me, that's the problem!" and be done. When this happens, rest assured that this was not a silly mistake that you carelessly overlooked. By explaining the code to your colleague, you engaged different parts of your brain, and these pinpointed the problem. In most cases your colleague plays a minimal role. This is how the technique gets its name: explaining the problem to a rubber duck could have been equally effective. (In the entry on rubber duck debugging, Wikipedia actually has a picture of a rubber duck sitting at a keyboard.)

You can also engage your colleagues in a more meaningful way by asking them to *review* your code. This is a more formal undertaking in which your colleague carefully goes through the code, pinpointing all problems in it: from code style and commenting, to API use, to design and logical errors. So highly regarded is this technique that some organizations have a code review as a prerequisite for integrating code into a production branch. Tools for sharing comments, such as *Gerrit* and GitHub's code commenting functionality can be really helpful because they allow you to respond to comments and leave a record to see how each one is addressed.

Etiquette plays an important role in this activity. Don't take the comments (even the harsh ones) personally, but see them as an opportunity to improve your code. Try to address all review comments; even if a comment is wrong, it is a sign that your code is not clear enough. Also, if you ask others to review your code, you should also offer to review theirs, and do that promptly, professionally, and politely. Code stuck waiting for a code review, trivial comments that overlook bigger problems, and nastiness diminish the benefits gained by the practice of code reviews.

Finally, you can address tough problems in multi-party algorithms through role playing. For example, if you're debugging a communications protocol, you can take the role of one party, a colleague can take the role of the other, and you can then take turns attempting to break the protocol (or trying to make it work). Other areas where this can be effective are security (you get to play Bob and Alice), human-computer interaction, and workflows. Passing around physical objects such as an "edit" token can help you here. Wearing elaborate costumes would be overdoing it though.

Things to Remember

✦ Explain your code to a rubber duck.

✦ Engage in the practice of code reviewing.

✦ Debug multi-party problems through role playing.

Item 40: Add Debugging Functionality

By telling your program that it is being debugged, you can turn the tables and have the program actively help you to debug it. What's needed for this to work is a mechanism to turn on this debugging mode and the code implementing this mode. You can program your software to enter a debugging mode through one of the following:

- A compilation option, such as defining a DEBUG constant in C/C++ code

- A command-line option such as the -d switch used in the Unix *sshd* SSH daemon and many other programs

- A *signal* sent to a process, as was the case in old versions of the *BIND* domain-name server

- A (sometimes undocumented) command, such an unusual key combination (on certain Android versions, you enable the USB debugging mode by tapping seven times on the software's build number)

To avoid accidentally shipping or configuring your software with debugging enabled in a production environment, it's a good practice to include a prominent notice to the effect that the debugging mode is available or enabled. Once you have your program enter a debugging mode there are several things you can program it to do.

First you can make it **log its actions,** so that you can get notified when something happens, and you can later examine the sequence of various events (see Item 56: "Examine Application Log Files" and Item 41: "Add Logging Statements").

For interactive and graphics programs, it may also be helpful to have the debugging mode **display more information on the screen** or enhance the information already there. For example, *Minecraft* has a debug mode (see Figure 5.2) in which it overlays the game screen with performance figures (frames per second, memory used, CPU load), player data (coordinates, direction, light), and operating environment specifications (JVM, display technology, CPU type). It also features a debug mode world, which displays—laid out flat—the thousands of materials in all their conditions that exist in the game. In a rendering application, you could display the edges that make up each object's facets or the points controlling a Bezier curve. In web applications, it can be helpful to have additional data, such as a product's database ID, appear when you hover the mouse over the corresponding screen element.

The debugging mode can also enable **additional commands.** These may be accessible through a command-line interface, an additional menu, or a URL. You can implement commands to display and modify complex data structures (debuggers have difficulty processing these), dump data into a file for further processing, change the state into one that will help your troubleshooting, or perform other tasks described in this item.

A very helpful debugging mode feature is the ability to **enter a specific state.** As an example, consider the task of debugging the seventh step of a wizard-like interface. Your job will be a lot easier if the debugging mode provides you with a shortcut to skip the preceding six steps, perhaps using some sensible default values for them. Similar features are also useful for debugging games, where they can advance you to a high level (depriving you the pleasure and the excuse of playing to get there) or give you hard-to-earn additional powers.

Figure 5.2 Minecraft's debug mode (top) and debug world (bottom)

A debugging mode can also **increase a program's transparency** or **simplify a program's runtime behavior** to make it easier to pin down failures for debugging. For instance, when invoked with debug mode enabled, programs that operate silently in the background (*daemons* in Unix parlance, *services* in the Windows world) may operate in the foreground displaying output on the screen. (The Unix *sshd* daemon is a typical example of such a program.) If a program fires up many threads, you can make it run with just a single thread, simplifying the debugging of problems that are not associated with concurrency. Other changes you can implement can substitute simple or naive algorithms for more sophisticated ones, eliminate peripheral operations to boost performance, use synchronous instead of asynchronous APIs, or use an embedded lightweight application server or database instead of an external one.

For software lacking a user interface, such as that running on some embedded devices or servers, a debugging mode can also **expose additional interfaces.** Adding a command-line interface can allow you to enter debugging commands, and see their results. In embedded devices, you can have that interface run over a serial connection that is set up only in the debug mode. Some digital TVs can use their USB interface in this way. In applications working in a networked environment, you can include a small embedded HTTP server, such as the *libmicrohttpd* one, which can display key details of the application and also can offer the execution of debugging commands.

The debugging mode can also help you **simulate external failures.** These are typically rare events that may require tricky instrumentation to simulate in order to troubleshoot. A debugging mode can offer commands that, by changing the program's state, can simulate its behavior under such conditions. Thus, debugging mode commands can simulate the random dropping of network packets, the failure to write data to disk, radio signal degradation, a malfunctioning real-time clock, a misconfigured smart card reader, and so on.

Finally, the debugging mode provides you with a mechanism to **exercise rare code paths**. This works by changing the program's configuration to favor their execution, instead of a more optimal path. For example, if you have a user input memory buffer that starts with a 1 kB allocation and doubles in size every time it fills, you can have your program's debug mode initialize the buffer with space for a single byte. This guarantees you that the reallocation will be frequently exercised, and that you will be able to observe and fix bugs in its logic. Other cases involve configuring tiny hash table sizes (to stress-test the overflow logic) and very small cache buffers (to stress-test the selection and replacement strategy).

Things to Remember

+ Add to your program an option to enter a debug mode.
+ Add commands to manipulate the program's state, log its operation, reduce its runtime complexity, shortcut through user interface navigation, and display complex data structures.

+ Add command-line, web, and serial interfaces to debug embedded devices and servers.

+ Use debug mode commands to simulate external failures.

Item 41: Add Logging Statements

Logging statements allow you to follow and comprehend the program's execution (see Item 56: "Examine Application Log Files"). They typically send a message to an output device (for example, the program's standard error, a console, or a printer) or store it in a place that you can later browse and analyze (a file or a database). You can then examine the log to find the root cause of the problem you're investigating.

Some believe that logging statements are only employed by those who don't know how to use a debugger. There may be cases where this is true, but it turns out that logging statements offer a number of advantages over a debugger session, and therefore the two approaches are complimentary. First of all, you can easily place a logging statement in a strategic location and tailor it to output exactly the data you require. In contrast, a debugger, as a general-purpose tool, requires you to follow the program's control flow and manually unravel complex data structures.

Furthermore, the work you invest in a debugging session only has ephemeral benefits. Even if you save your setup for printing a complex data structure in a debugger script file, it would still not be visible or easily accessible to other people maintaining the code. I have yet to encounter a project that distributes debugger scripts together with its source code. On the other hand, because logging statements are permanent, you can invest more effort than you could justify in a fleeting debugging session to format their output in a way that will increase your understanding of the program's operation and, therefore, your debugging productivity.

Finally, the output of proper logging statements (those using a logging framework rather than random `println` statements) is inherently filterable and queryable.

There are several logging libraries for most languages and frameworks. Find and use one that matches your requirements, rather than reinventing the wheel. Things you can log include the entry and exit to key routines, contents of key data structures, state changes, and responses to user interactions. To avoid the performance hit of extensive logging, you don't want to have it enabled in a normal production setting. Most of the logging interfaces allow you to tailor the importance of messages recorded either at the source (the program you're debugging) or at the destination (the facility that logs the messages). Obviously, controlling the recorded messages at the source can minimize the performance impact your program will incur; in some cases down to zero. Implementing in your application a *debug mode* allows you to increase the logging verbosity only when needed (see Item 40: "Add Debugging Functionality"). You can also configure several levels or areas of logging to fine-tune what you want to see. Many logging frameworks provide their own configuration facility, freeing you from the effort to create one for your application.

Logging facilities you may want to use include the Unix *syslog* library (Listing 5.1), Apple's more advanced system log facility *ASL* (Listing 5.2), the Windows *ReportEvent* API (Listing 5.3), Java's *java.util.logging* package (Listing 5.4), and Python's *logging* module (Listing 5.5). The interfaces to some of these facilities are not trivial, so refer to the listings as a cheat sheet for using each one in your code. There are also third-party logging facilities that can be useful if you're looking for more features or if you're working on a platform that lacks a standard one. These include Apache's *Log4j* for Java and *Boost.Log v2* for C++.

Listing 5.1 Logging with the Unix *syslog* interface

```
#include <syslog.h>

int
main()
{
    openlog("myapp", 0, LOG_USER);
    syslog(LOG_DEBUG, "Called main() in %s", __FILE__);
    closelog();
}
```

Listing 5.2 Logging with the Apple's system log facility

```
#include <asl.h>

int
main()
{
    asl_object_t client_handle = asl_open("com.example.myapp",
            NULL, ASL_OPT_STDERR);
    asl_log(client_handle, NULL, ASL_LEVEL_DEBUG,
            "Called main() in %s", __FILE__);
    asl_close(client_handle);
}
```

Listing 5.3 Logging with the Windows *ReportEvent* function

```
#include <windows.h>

int
main()
{
   LPTSTR lpszStrings[] = {
      "Called main() in file ",
      __FILE__
   };
   HANDLE hEventSource = RegisterEventSource(NULL, "myservice");

   if (hEventSource == NULL)
      return (1);

   ReportEvent(hEventSource, // handle of event source
      EVENTLOG_INFORMATION_TYPE, // event type
      0,                   // event category
      0,                   // event ID
      NULL,                // current user's SID
      2,                   // strings in lpszStrings
      0,                   // no bytes of raw data
      lpszStrings,         // array of error strings
      NULL);               // no raw data

   DeregisterEventSource(hEventSource);
   return (0);
}
```

Listing 5.4 Logging with the Java's *java.util.logging* package

```
import java.io.IOException;
import java.util.logging.FileHandler;
import java.util.logging.Level;
import java.util.logging.Logger;

public class EventLog {
   public static void main(String[] args) {
      Logger logger = Logger.getGlobal();
      // Include detailed messages
      logger.setLevel(Level.FINEST);
      FileHandler fileHandler = null;
      try {
         fileHandler = new FileHandler("app.log");
```

```
    } catch (IOException e) {
        System.exit(1);
    }
    logger.addHandler(fileHandler); // Send output to file
    logger.fine("Called main");
  }
}
```

Listing 5.5 Logging with the Python's *logging* module

```
import logging;

logger = logging.getLogger('myapp')

# Send log messages to myapp.log
fh = logging.FileHandler('myapp.log')
logger.addHandler(fh)

logger.setLevel(logging.DEBUG)
logger.debug('In main module')
```

In addition, many other programming frameworks offer their own logging mechanisms. For example, if you associate logging with lumberjacks, you'll be happy to know that under *node.js* you can choose between the *Bunyan* and *Winston* packages. If you're using Unix shell commands, then you can log a message by invoking the *logger* command. In Unix kernels (including device drivers), it is customary to log messages with the *printk* function call.

If your code runs on a networked, embedded device lacking a writable file system with sufficient space where you can store the logs (e.g., a high-end TV or a low-end broadband router), consider using *remote logging*. This technology allows you to configure the logging system of the embedded device to send the log entries to a server where these are stored. Thus, the following Unix *syslogd* configuration entry will send all logging associated with local1 to the logmaster host:

```
local1.* @@logmaster.example.com:514
```

Finally, if the environment you're programming in doesn't offer a logging facility, you'll have to roll your own. At its simplest form, this can be a print statement.

```
printf("Entering function foo\n");
```

When you (think) you're done with a print-type logging statement, resist the temptation to delete it or put it in a comment. If you delete it, you lose the work you put to create it. If you comment it out, it will no longer be maintained, and as the code changes it will decay and become useless. Instead, place the print command in a conditional statement.

```
if (loggingEnabled)
   printf("Entering function foo\n");
```

Apart from a print statement, here are some other ways you can have applications log their actions.

- In a GUI application, fire up a popup message.

- In JavaScript code, write to the console and view the results in your browser's console window.

- In a web application, stuff logging output in the resulting page's HTML—as HTML comments or as visible text.

- If you can't modify an application's source code, you can try making it open a file whose name is the message you want to log, and trace the application's system calls with *strace* to see the file's name.

Things to Remember

✦ Add logging statements to set up a permanent, maintained debugging infrastructure.

✦ Use a logging framework instead of reinventing the wheel.

✦ Configure the topic and details of what you log through the logging framework.

Item 42: Use Unit Tests

If a flaw in the software you're debugging doesn't show up in its *unit testing*, then appropriate tests are lacking or completely absent. To isolate or pinpoint such a flaw, consider adding unit tests that can expose it.

Start with the basics. If the software isn't using a unit testing framework or isn't written in a language that directly supports unit testing, download a unit testing package matching your requirements (Wikipedia contains a list of *unit testing frameworks*), and configure your software to use it. With no existing tests in place, this should involve the adjustment of the build configuration to include the testing library and the addition of a few lines in the application's startup code to run any tests. While you're at it, configure your infrastructure to run the tests automatically when code is compiled and committed. This will ensure that your project will benefit from the improved documentation, collective ownership, ease of refactoring, and simplified integration facilitated by the unit testing infrastructure you're adding.

Then, identify the routines that may be related to the failure you're seeing, and write unit tests that will verify their functioning. You can find the routines to test through top-down or bottom-up reasoning (see Item 4: "Drill Up from the Problem to the Bug or Down from the Program's Start to the Bug"). Try writing the tests without looking at the routines' implementation, focusing instead on the documentation of their interface, or, if that's lacking (let's be realistic here) on the code that calls them. This will lessen the probability of you replicating a faulty assumption in the unit test. Ensure that the tests you added become a permanent part of the code by committing them to the software's revision control repository.

As an example, consider the class in Listing 5.6, which tracks the column position of processed text, taking into account the standard behavior of the tab character. This is notoriously difficult to get right: in the 1980s, screen output libraries contained workarounds for display terminals with buggy behavior in this area. The class's functionality can be tested by invoking code such as that in Listing 5.7 to run the *CppUnit* tests in Listing 5.8.

Listing 5.6 A C++ class that tracks the text's column position

```cpp
class ColumnTracker {
private:
    int column;
    static const int tab_length = 8;
public:
    ColumnTracker() : column(0) {}

    int position() const { return column; }

    void process(int c) {
        switch (c) {
        case '\n':
            column = 0;
            break;
        case '\t':
            column = (column / tab_length + 1) * tab_length;
            break;
        default:
            column++;
            break;
        }
    }
};
```

Listing 5.7 Code running the *CppUnit* test suite text interface

```
#include <cppunit/ui/text/TestRunner.h>
#include "ColumnTrackerTest.h"

int
main(int argc, char *argv[])
{
    CppUnit::TextUi::TestRunner runner;

    runner.addTest(ColumnTrackerTest::suite());
    runner.run();
    return 0;
}
```

Listing 5.8 Unit test code

```
#include <cppunit/extensions/HelperMacros.h>
#include "ColumnTracker.h"

class ColumnTrackerTest : public CppUnit::TestFixture {
   CPPUNIT_TEST_SUITE(ColumnTrackerTest);
   CPPUNIT_TEST(testCtor);
   CPPUNIT_TEST(testTab);
   CPPUNIT_TEST(testAfterNewline);
   CPPUNIT_TEST_SUITE_END();
public:
   void testCtor() {
      ColumnTracker ct;
      CPPUNIT_ASSERT(ct.position() == 0);
   }

   void testTab() {
      ColumnTracker ct;
      // Test plain characters
      ct.process('x');
      CPPUNIT_ASSERT(ct.position() == 1);
      ct.process('x');
      CPPUNIT_ASSERT(ct.position() == 2);
      // Test tab
      ct.process('\t');
      CPPUNIT_ASSERT(ct.position() == 8);
      // Test character after tab
      ct.process('x');
      CPPUNIT_ASSERT(ct.position() == 9);
```

```
        // Edge case
        while (ct.position() != 15)
            ct.process('x');
        ct.process('\t');
        CPPUNIT_ASSERT(ct.position() == 16);
        // Edge case
        ct.process('\t');
        CPPUNIT_ASSERT(ct.position() == 24);
    }

    void testAfterNewline() {
        ColumnTracker ct;
        ct.process('x');
        ct.process('\n');
        CPPUNIT_ASSERT(ct.position() == 0);
    }
};
```

Running the unit tests should expose the flawed routine. If the tests succeed, you'll need to expand their coverage or (less frequently) verify their correctness. If more than one test fails, focus on the failing routines that lie at the bottom of the dependency tree—those that call the fewest other routines (clients). Once you've fixed the flawed routine, run the tests again to ensure they all now pass.

Bolting unit tests on existing code isn't trivial because tests and code are typically developed in tandem, so that code can be written in a testable form. Often the tests are even written before the corresponding code. To unit test the suspect routines you may need to refactor the code: splitting large elements into smaller parts and minimizing dependencies between routines to simplify their invocation from the tests (see Item 48: "Improve the Suspect Code's Readability and Structure"). The techniques for doing this are beyond the scope of this book. An excellent treatment of the topic is Michael Feathers' book *Working Effectively with Legacy Code* (Prentice Hall, 2004).

Things to Remember

✦ Pinpoint flaws by probing suspect routines with unit tests.

✦ Increase your effectiveness by adopting a unit testing framework, refactoring the code to accommodate the tests, and automating the tests' execution.

Item 43: Use Assertions

Although unit tests (see Item 42: "Use Unit Tests") are an important tool for locating faulty routines, they can't tell the full story. First, unit tests will point you to the routine that fails a test, but they can't help you find the exact position of the flaw. This is fine when dealing with small routines, but there are complex algorithms that are difficult to break down into small self-contained routines. Second, errors can crop up in the integration of various parts. Higher-level testing should uncover these errors, but again, it rarely pinpoints their cause.

Here's where assertions come in. These are statements containing a Boolean expression that's guaranteed to be true if the code is correct. Should the expression evaluate to `false`, the assertion will *fail*, typically terminating the program with a runtime error displaying data regarding the failure. Debuggers can often direct you to the location of a failed assertion. By placing assertions in key locations of your code, you can narrow down your search for a fault in two ways. Most obviously, you can focus on the location where an assertion failed. In addition, if the assertions you added didn't fail, you may be able to rule out as suspect the code where you placed them.

Most languages support assertions, either through a built-in statement, as is the case for Java and Python, or through a library, as is the case for C. Many programming environments, in order to minimize the possible performance impact of assertion checking, allow you to specify whether this will be performed or not. This can happen at compile time (e.g., in C and C++ by defining the `NDEBUG` macro) or at runtime (e.g., in Java with the `-enableassertions` and `-disableassertions` options). It is common during development to run code with assertion checking enabled. Running production code with assertion checking enabled has both benefits and costs, which you must weigh on a case-by-case basis.

When you're debugging algorithmic code, it's often useful to think in terms of *preconditions* (properties that must hold for the algorithm to function), *invariants* (properties that the algorithm maintains while it's processing data), and *postconditions* (properties that must hold if the algorithm performs according to its specification) (see Item 3: "Confirm That Preconditions and Postconditions Are Satisfied"). Typically, an invariant is true only for the part of the data set that has been processed by the algorithm; at the end of the algorithm's operation, the postcondition will cover the same elements as the invariant.

You can see an example of this style of programming in Listing 5.9, which finds the maximum value in an integer array by assuming the value is the minimum integer and gradually replacing that with higher values it finds in the array. The preconditions tested at the beginning are that the array is non-empty and that the minimum value chosen is indeed less than or equal to all values of the array. This could fail if the input data type was changed without correspondingly adjusting the constant. The loop forming the algorithm's body maintains the invariant that the selected maximum value is greater than or equal to all values traversed. At the end of the loop, after all values have been checked, the same invariant forms the postcondition, which is the algorithm's specification.

Listing 5.9 Using assertions to check preconditions, postconditions, and invariants

```java
class Ranking {
    /** Return the maximum number in non-empty array v */
    public static int findMax(int[] v) {
        int max = Integer.MIN_VALUE;

        // Precondition: v[] is not empty
        assert v.length > 0 : "v[] is empty";

        // Precondition: max <= v[i] for every i
        for (int n : v)
            assert max <= n : "Found value < MIN_VALUE";

        // Obtain the actual maximum value
        for (int i = 0; i < v.length; i++) {
            if (v[i] > max)
                max = v[i];
            // Invariant: max >= v[j] for every j <= i
            for (int j = 0; j <= i; j++)
                assert max >= v[j] : "Found value > max";
        }

        // Postcondition: max >= v[i] for every i
        for (int n : v)
            assert max >= n : "Found value > max";
        return max;
    }
}
```

Apart from this use of assertions to troubleshoot (and document) the operation of algorithms, you can also use assertions in a less formal fashion to pinpoint all sorts of problems. You can thus place assertions

- At the beginning of the program to verify architectural properties of the CPU, such as the sizes of the integer types used

- At the entry point of a routine to verify that the passed parameters are of the expected type (when the language won't check it), and that they hold valid (e.g., non `null`) and reasonable values

- At the exit point of a routine to verify its result

- At the beginning and the end of commonly called or complex methods to verify that the class's state remains consistent

- After calls to API routines that shouldn't fail to verify that this is indeed the case

- After loading resources required by your software to verify that it has been correctly deployed

- After evaluating a complex expression to verify that the result has the expected properties or holds a reasonable value

- In the `default` case of a `switch` statement (with a `false` expression as the assertion's value) to catch unhandled cases

- After initializing a data structure to verify that it holds the expected values

In general, while debugging, add assertions to document your understanding of the code and to test your suspicions.

You can leave in the code most of the assertions you added in order to document its operation and guard against future problems. However, if any of the assertions you added to debug the code has unearthed a problem that can actually crop up in production, then, as part of your debugging work, you must replace it with more robust error handling. Such cases include the verification of input coming from the user or other sources you can't control and the correct execution of APIs that can fail as a matter of course. Also, when a routine can be tested both with an assertion and with unit testing code, the addition of a unit test is preferred because this can be automatically executed and can contribute toward your code's testing code coverage.

Things to Remember

✦ Complement unit testing with assertions to pinpoint more precisely a fault's location.

✦ Debug complex algorithms with assertions that verify their preconditions, invariants, and postconditions.

✦ Add assertions to document your understanding of the code you debug and to test your suspicions.

Item 44: Verify Your Reasoning by Perturbing the Debugged Program

Arbitrarily changing a program to see what will happen is disparagingly described as hacking. However, experimental changes that you make in a thoughtful manner can allow you to test hypotheses and learn more about the system you're trying to debug as well as its underlying platform. The changes are especially valuable if the quality of what you're facing isn't top notch: they may allow you to cover holes in the code's documentation or that of the API.

Here are some examples of questions that might arise when you're debugging a system, which you can easily answer by modifying some code.

- Can I indeed pass null as an argument to this routine?

- Will this code work correctly if the variable contains more than 999 milliseconds?

- Will a warning get logged if a lock is held when entering this routine?

- Is the order of calling these methods related to my problem?

- Could an alternative API work better than the currently used one?

You typically verify the effects of your changes by observing the program's behavior, by logging, or by running the code under a debugger.

One experimental approach involves modifying expressions and values that are embedded in the code, often replacing a runtime expression with a concrete value. For instance, you can pass a correct value constant to a routine (or have a routine return such a value) to verify that the failure you're trying to fix goes away. Or, you can pass or return an incorrect value to see whether a problem you're trying to isolate can be attributed to such a value. Alternately, you can set a parameter to an extreme value in order to make a tiny or rare problem, such as a performance degradation, easier to observe (see Item 17: "Increase the Prominence of a Failure's Effects").

Another experimental avenue involves code changes that allow you to test the correctness of alternative implementations. Here you replace code that might be incorrect with conceivably better code, and see whether this fixes your problem. For example, the Microsoft Windows API provides more than five ways to obtain a string's width on the screen, with little guidance regarding which function is preferable. If your problem is misaligned text, you could exchange one API call (GetTextExtent Point32) with another (GetTextExtentExPoint) and observe the result.

Or, if you have doubts regarding the correct order for calling some routines, you can try an alternative one. In other cases, you can try extreme code simplifications (see Item 46: "Simplify the Suspect Code").

Things to Remember

✦ Set values in the code by hand to identify correct and incorrect ones.

✦ If you can't find guidance to correct the code, experiment by trying alternate implementations.

Item 45: Minimize the Differences between a Working Example and the Failing Code

There are cases where you will have at hand the faulty code you're debugging and an example of related functionality that works just fine. This can often occur when you're debugging a complex API invocation or an algorithm. You may get the working example from the API's documentation, a Q&A site (see Item 2: "Use Focused Queries to Search the Web for Insights into Your Problem"), open-source software, or a textbook. The differences between the working example and your code can guide you to the fault. The approach I describe here is based on manipulating the source code; however, you can also look at differences in the runtime behavior of the two (see Item 5: "Find the Difference between a Known Good System and a Failing One").

Before using the example code to fix the problem you're facing, you first must compile and test it to verify that it actually works. If it doesn't, then probably the problem doesn't lie with your code. It could be that your setup (compiler, runtime environment, operating system) is responsible for the failure, or that your understanding of what the API or algorithm is supposed to be doing is incorrect, or less likely, that you have discovered a bug in third-party code.

With a handy verified working example, there are two approaches for fixing your code. Both involve gradually minimizing the differences between the example and the faulty code. By definition, when there are no differences between the working example and your code, your code will be working.

The first approach involves building on the example to arrive at your code. This works best when your code is simple and self-contained. In small steps, add to the example elements from your code. At each step, verify the example's functioning. The addition that causes the code you're building to stop working is the failure's culprit.

The second approach amounts to trimming your code until it matches the example. This works best when your code has many dependencies that hinder its isolated operation. Here you remove or adjust material in your code to make it match the example. Do this in small steps and, after each change, check that your code keeps failing. The change you perform that makes your code work will point you to the fix you need to make.

Things to Remember

✦ To find the element that causes a failure, gradually trim down your failing code to match a working example or make a working example match your failing code.

Item 46: Simplify the Suspect Code

Complex code is difficult to debug. Many possible execution paths and intricate data flows can confuse your thinking and add to the work you must do to pinpoint the flaw. Therefore, it's often helpful to simplify the failing code. You can do this temporarily, in order to make the flaw stand out (see Item 17: "Increase the Prominence of a Failure's Effects"), or permanently in order to fix it. Before embarking on drastic simplifications, ensure you have a safe way to revert them. All the files you'll modify should be under version control (see Item 26: "Hunt the Causes and History of Bugs with the Revision Control System"), and you should have a way to return the code to its initial state, preferably by working on a private branch version.

Temporary modifications typically entail drastically **pruning the code.** Your goal here is to remove as much code as possible while keeping the failure. This will minimize the amount of suspect code and make it easier to identify the fault. In a typical cycle, you remove a large code block or a call to a complex function, you compile, and then you test the result. If the result still fails, you continue your pruning; if not, you reduce the pruning you performed. Note that if a failure disappears during a pruning step, you have strong reasons to believe that the code you pruned is somehow associated with the failure. This leads to an alternate approach, in which you try to make the failure go away by removing as little code as possible.

Although you can use your version control system to checkpoint the pruning steps, it's often quicker to just use your editor. Keep the code in an open editor window, and save the changes after each modification. If after pruning the failure persists, continue the process. If the failure disappears, undo the previous step, reduce the code you pruned, and repeat. You can systematically perform this task through a binary search process.

Resist the temptation to comment-out code blocks: the nesting of embedded comments in those blocks will be a source of problems. Instead, in languages that support a preprocessor, you can use preprocessor conditionals.

```
#ifdef ndef
  // code you don't want to be executed
#endif
```

In other languages, you can temporarily put the statements you want to disable in the block of an if (false) conditional statement.

Sometimes instead of removing code, it's easier to adjust it to simplify its execution. For example, add a false value at the beginning of an if or loop conditional to ensure that the corresponding code won't get executed. Thus, you will rewrite (in steps) the following code

```
while (a() && b())
  someComplexCode();

if (b() && !c() && d() && !e())
  someOtherComplexCode();
```

in this simplified form.

```
while (false && a() && b())
  someComplexCode();

if (false && !c() && d() && !e())
  someOtherComplexCode();
```

In other cases, you can benefit by **permanently simplifying complex statements** in order to ease their debugging. Consider the following statement.

```
p = s.client(q, r).booking(x).period(y, checkout(z)).duration();
```

Such a statement is justifiably called a *train wreck* because it resembles train carriages after a crash. It is difficult to debug because you cannot easily see the return of each method. You can fix this by adding delegate methods (see Item 48: "Improve the Suspect Code's Readability and Structure") or by breaking the expression into separate parts and assigning each result to a temporary variable.

```
Client c = s.client(q, r);
Booking b = c.booking(x);
```

```
CheckoutTime ct = checkout(z);
Period p = b.period(y, ct)
TimeDuration d = p.duration();
```

This will make it easier for you to observe the result of each call with the debugger or even to add a corresponding logging statement. Given descriptive type or variable names, the rewrite will also make the code more readable. Note that the change is unlikely to affect the performance of the code: modern compilers are very good at eliminating unneeded temporary variables.

Another worthwhile type of simplification involves **breaking one large function into many smaller parts.** Here the benefit for debugging comes mainly from the ability you gain to pinpoint the fault by testing each part individually (see Item 42: "Use Unit Tests"). The process may also improve your understanding of the code and untangle unwanted interactions between the parts. These two positive side effects can also lead to a solution of the problem.

Finally, another more drastic type of permanent simplification involves **ditching complex algorithms, data structures, or program logic.** The rationale for such a move is that the complexity that gives rise to the fault you're trying to locate may, in fact, not be required. Here are some characteristic cases.

- Advances in processing speed may make a particular optimization irrelevant. On a 3MHz VAX computer, a user would sense the difference between an algorithm that responded to a keystroke in 500ms and one that responded in 5ms. On a 3.2GHz Intel Core i5 CPU, the corresponding response times shrink to 500μs and 5μs, which are both imperceptible to the user. In such cases, using a simpler algorithm makes perfect sense when dealing with small fixed-size data sets.

- These days, larger memory and disk capacities as well as network throughput rates rarely justify the complex masking operations required for packing data into bits. You can instead use the language's native types, such as integers and Boolean variables. The same may apply for other complex data compression schemes.

- Changes in hardware technologies may make a particular optimization algorithm irrelevant. For example, operating system kernels used to contain a sophisticated *elevator algorithm* to optimize the movement of disk heads. On modern magnetic disks, it is not possible to know the location of a particular data block on the disk platter, so such an algorithm will not do any useful work. Moreover, solid-state disks have in effect zero seek times, allowing you to scrap any complex algorithm or data structure that aims to minimize them.

- The functionality of the buggy algorithm may be available in the library of the programming framework you're using or it may be a mature third-party component. For example, the code for finding a container's elements' median value in $O(n)$ time can contain many subtle bugs. Replacing the C++ code with a call to `std::nth_element` is an easy way to fix such a flaw. As a larger-scale example, consider replacing a bug-infested proprietary data storage and query engine with a relational database.

- A complex algorithm, implemented to improve performance, may have been overkill from day one. Performance optimizations are only justified when profiling and other measurements have demonstrated that optimization work on a particular code hot spot is actually required. Programmers sometimes ignore this principle, gratuitously creating byzantine, overengineered code. This gives you the opportunity to do away with the code and the bug at the same time.

- Modern user experience design favors much simpler interaction patterns than what was the case in the past. This may allow you to replace the buggy spaghetti code associated with a baroque dialog box full of tunable parameters with simpler code that supports a few carefully chosen options and many sensible defaults.

Things to Remember

✦ Selectively prune large code thickets in order to make the fault stand out.

✦ Break complex statements or functions into smaller parts so that you can monitor or test their function.

✦ Consider replacing a complex buggy algorithm with a simpler one.

Item 47: Consider Rewriting the Suspect Code in Another Language

When the code you're trying to fix refuses to comply, drastic measures may be in order. One such measure is to rewrite the offending code in another language. By choosing a better programming environment, you hope to either side-step the bug completely or find and fix it by using better tools to understand the problem and create a working prototype solution. (For the application of this principle to concurrency problems, see Item 66: "Consider Rewriting the Code Using Higher-Level Abstractions.")

The programming language you'll employ should be more expressive than the one currently used. For example, assessing the performance of sophisticated trading strategies can be more easily expressed in a language with functional programming support, such as *R*, *F#*, *Haskell*, *Scala*, or *ML*. You can also gain more expressiveness through a language's libraries. In some cases, such as in the use of *R* for statistical computing, the gains can be so big so as make it criminal to use a less featureful alternative. As another example, if your code is doing tricky string processing over dynamically allocated collections of elements in C, you may want to try rewriting the code in C++ or Python. Writing the faulty code in a more expressive language will result in a more compact implementation, which offers fewer chances for errors.

Another trait you might find useful is the ability to easily observe the code's behavior, perhaps constructing the code incrementally. Here, scripting languages offer a particular advantage through the read-eval-print loop (REPL) they support. If you implement an algorithm using Unix tool pipelines, then you can build the processing pipeline step by step, verifying the output of each stage before adding a next one. Furthermore, if the development system originally used doesn't offer a decent debugging, logging, or unit testing framework, then adopting an improved implementation environment can provide you with the opportunity to pinpoint the problem by using its shiny support facilities. This can be very useful when you're debugging code in small embedded systems with lackluster development tools.

Once you get the newly written code working, you have two options for fixing the original problem. The first involves adopting the new code and trashing the old one. You can easily do this when there are good bindings between the original language and the new one. For instance, it's typically trivial to call C++ from C with a few plain-data parameters and a simple return value. You can also keep your new implementation by invoking it as a separate process or microservice. However, this makes sense only when you don't particularly care about the invocation's cost.

The other option for fixing your bug involves using the new code as an oracle to correct the old one. You can do this by observing the differences in the behavior between the working code and the failing one (see Item 5: "Find the Difference between a Known Good System and a Failing One") or by gradually converging the two code bases until the bug surfaces (see Item 45: "Minimize the Differences between a Working Example and the Failing Code"). In the first case, you compare the variable and routine return values between the two implementations; in the second one, you proceed by trial and error until you arrive at a correct implementation.

Things to Remember

+ Rewrite code you can't fix in a more expressive language to minimize the number of potentially faulty statements.

+ Port buggy code to a better programming environment to enhance your debugging arsenal.

+ Once you have an alternative working implementation, adopt it, or use it as an oracle to fix the original one.

Item 48: Improve the Suspect Code's Readability and Structure

Disorderly, badly written code can be a fertile breeding ground for bugs. Cleaning up the code can uncover the bugs, allowing you to fix them. However, before embarking on a code-cleaning trip, ensure that you have the time and authority to complete it. Nobody will take kindly to a bug fix that modifies 4,000 lines. At the very least, separate cosmetic changes, from refactorings, from the actual bug fix into distinct commits. In some environments, coordinating with others for the first two changes may be the way to go.

Start with spacing. At the lowest level, ensure that the code follows consistently the language's and local style rules regarding spaces around operators and reserved words. This can help your eye catch subtle errors in statements and expressions. At a slightly higher level, look at the indentation. Again, this should always use the same number of spaces (typically 2, 4, or 8) applied in a consistent way. With orderly indentation, it's easier to follow the code's control flow. Be especially careful with single statements spanning multiple lines: their appropriate indentation will help you verify the correctness of complex expressions and function calls. At the highest level, use your judgment to add spaces where these can aid the user in understanding the code. Aligning similar expressions with some extra spacing can make discrepancies stand out. Separating logic code blocks with an empty line can make it easier for you to understand the code's structure. In general, ensure that the visual appearance of the code mirrors its functionality, so that your eye can catch suspect patterns. If the code's formatting is really beyond manual salvation, consider using your IDE or a tool, such as *clang-format* or *indent*, to fix it automatically.

The code's formatting can improve its visual appearance, but it can only go so far. Therefore, after style fixes, consider whether there's a need to *refactor* the code: maintain its functionality while improving its structure. Your objective here is either to fix the problem through the use of a more orderly structure—akin to rewriting (see Item 47: "Consider Rewriting the Suspect Code in Another Language"), or to make the fault stand out in the more orderly code. Here are some common problems (code smells) that can hide faults and the refactorings you can implement to solve them. Most are derived from Martin Fowler's classic book, *Refactoring: Improving the Design of Existing Code* (Addison-Wesley, 2000), which you can consult for more details.

Duplicated code can introduce bugs when code improvements and fixes fail to update all related instances of the code. By putting the duplicated code into a commonly used routine, class, or template you can ensure that the correct code is used throughout the program. If partial code updates were the source of the failure, then you will discover them as you compare the code instances you remove.

Duplicated code also hides in **switch statements,** which often change the code's flow based on a value representing the data's type. Missing `case` elements in some `switch` statements can easily go unnoticed when new cases are added. As a simple measure, you can add a `default` clause that will log an internal error when it is executed. Even better, restructure the code to eliminate the `switch` statement. This is typically done by moving the behavior associated with each `case` into a method of corresponding subclasses, and replacing the `switch` statement with a polymorphic method call. Alternately, you can express the behavior in subclasses of a *state object*, which is used in the place of the `switch` statement.

A related problem is the **shotgun surgery** code smell, where a single change affects many methods and fields. The bug you're chasing may be a change that someone forgot to implement. By moving all the fields and methods that need change into the same class, you can ensure that these are consistent with each other. The class can be an existing one, a new one, or an internal (nested) one that localizes the required changes.

Also exposed to the risk of inconsistent changes are **data clumps:** data objects that commonly appear together. Group these into a class and use objects of that class both as parameters and as return values. This change will eliminate the multiple data objects and the risk of forgetting one.

When a language's **primitive values,** such as integers or strings, are used to express more sophisticated values, such as currencies, dates, or zip codes, errors in the manipulation of these values can go unnoticed. For example, if currency values are represented as integers, the code can easily add two different currency values. Introduce classes to represent such objects, and replace the primitive values with these objects. Similarly, the use of containers (linked lists or resizable vectors) instead of primitive arrays can help you fix errors associated with array size management. A further step away from primitive types involves the use of bespoke classes, rather than naked floating point types, to represent physical units (time, mass, force, energy, acceleration). With proper methods to combine these (e.g., $F = m \times a$) you can catch errors arising from their improper use—assigning apples to oranges, as it were.

Varying interfaces, such as the set of methods supported by a class, method names, and order and type of their parameters, can cloud the code's structure and thereby hide bugs. Homogenize method names through renaming, and parameters through their reordering. Add, remove, and move methods to homogenize their classes. The classes with their new similar interfaces may reveal more refactoring opportunities, such as the extraction of a superclass.

Long routines can be difficult to follow and debug (see Item 46: "Simplify the Suspect Code"). Break them into smaller pieces, and decompose complex conditionals into routine calls. If a method is difficult to break up due to many temporary variables, consider changing it into a *method object* where these variables become the object's fields.

Code parts that are **inappropriately intimate** with each other can hide incorrect interactions that destroy invariants and disrupt the program's state. Break these by moving methods and fields, and ensure associations between classes are unidirectional rather than bidirectional. Long chains of delegation can provide clients with more access than what is strictly needed, which can in turn be a source of errors. Break these by introducing *delegate methods*. Thus the expression

```
account.getOwner().getName()
```

with the introduction of the `getOwnerName` delegate method becomes

```
account.getOwnerName()
```

Surprisingly, **comments** can also point to trouble spots when they're used to veil incomprehensible or suboptimal code. Often it is enough to replace a commented block of code with a method whose name reflects the original code's comment. The resulting short sequence of method calls will make it easier for you to spot errors in the code's logic. In other cases, an assertion (see Item 43: "Use Assertions") will more effectively express the preconditions written in a comment because the assertion will readily fail when the precondition isn't satisfied.

As a final step, remove **dead code** and **speculative generality.** Remove unused code and parameters, collapse unused class hierarchies, inline classes with a single client, and rename methods with funky abstract names to reflect what they actually do. Your aim here is to eliminate hiding places for bugs.

Things to Remember

✦ Format code in a consistent manner to allow your eye to catch error patterns.

✦ Refactor code to expose bugs hiding in badly written or needlessly complex code structures.

Item 49: Fix the Bug's Cause, Rather Than Its Symptom

A surprisingly tempting way to fix a problem is to hide it under the carpet with a local fix. Here are some examples of a conditional statement "fix" being used:

- To avoid a null pointer dereference

```
if (p != null)
  p.aMethod();
```

- To sidestep the division by zero

```
if (nVehicleWheels == 0)
  return weight;
else
  return weight / nVehicleWheels;
```

- To shoehorn an incorrect number in a logical range

```
a = surfaceArea()
if (a < 0)
  a = 0;
```

- To correct a truncated surname

```
if (surname.equals("Wolfeschlegelsteinha"))
  surname = "Wolfeschlegelsteinhausenbergerdorff";
```

Some of the preceding statements could have a reasonable explanation. If, however, the conditional was put into place merely to patch a crash, an exception, or an incorrect result, without understanding the underlying cause, then the particular fix is inexcusable. (The most egregious example I've seen was C code that cleaned up a string from mysteriously introduced control characters.)

Coding around bugs is bad for many reasons.

- The "fix," by short-circuiting some functionality, may introduce a new more subtle bug.

- By not fixing the underlying cause, other less obvious symptoms of the bug may remain, or the bug may appear again in the future under a different guise.

- The program's code becomes needlessly complex and thus difficult to understand and modify.

- The underlying cause becomes harder to find because the "fix" hides its manifestation—for example, the crash that could direct you to the underlying cause (see Item 55: "Fail Fast").

As you can see, patching a bug's symptom rather than its cause is a false economy, one that saddles your program with *technical debt*.

A related, important, but less serious sin involves trying to debug and fix special cases, when the solution is to generalize their handling in a simpler way (see Item 46: "Simplify the Suspect Code"). For example, the following code, which tries to normalize an angle in the range $0 - 2 \times \pi$, will not handle correctly angles $< 2 \times \pi$ or $> 2 \times \pi$.

```
if (angle < 0)
  angle += Math.PI;
else if (angle > 2 * Math.PI)
  angle -= Math.PI;
```

Instead of fixing code with something like

```
while (angle < 0)
  angle += Math.PI;
while (angle > 2 * Math.PI)
  angle -= Math.PI;
```

which is complex, and can be slow and inaccurate for very large or small values, just use the following expression to calculate the angle's modulus.

```
angle = angle - 2 * Math.PI * Math.floor(angle / (2 * Math.PI)));
```

Things to Remember

✦ Never code around a bug's symptom: find and fix the underlying fault.

✦ When possible, generalize complex cases rather than trying to fix special cases.

Compile-Time Techniques

The transformation of the source code into bytes that will be executed by the CPU or an abstract virtual machine, such as the JVM, offers you ample opportunities to see what's going on and affect the outcome. Both activities can help you zoom in on the fault you're trying to locate.

Item 50: Examine Generated Code

Code often gets compiled through a series of transformations from one form to another until it finally reaches the form of the processor's instructions. For example, a C or C++ file may first get preprocessed, then compiled into assembly language, which is then assembled into an object file; Java programs are compiled into JVM instructions; lexical and parser generation tools, such as *lex*, *flex*, *yacc*, and *bison*, compile their input into C or C++. Various commands and options allow tapping into these transformations to inspect the intermediate code. This can provide you with valuable debugging intelligence.

Consider preprocessed C or C++ source code. You can easily obtain it by running the C/C++ compiler with an option directing it to output that code: -E on Unix systems, /E for Microsoft's compilers. (On Unix systems, you can also invoke the C preprocessor directly as *cpp*.) If the resulting code is anything more than a few lines long, you'll want to redirect the compiler's output into a file, which you can then easily inspect in your editor. Here is a simple example demonstrating how you can pinpoint an error by looking at the preprocessed output. Consider the following C code.

```
#define PI 3.141592653589793238462643383279S;
double toDegrees = 360 / 2 / PI;
double toRadians = 2 * PI / 360;
```

Compiling it with the *Visual Studio* 2015 compiler produces the following (perhaps) cryptic error.

```
t.c(3) : error C2059: syntax error : '/'
```

If you generate and look at the preprocessed code appearing below, you will see the semicolon before the slash, which will hopefully point you to the superfluous semicolon at the end of the macro definition.

```
#line 1 "t.c"

double toDegrees = 360 / 2 / 3.14159265358979323846264433832795;;
double toRadians = 2 * 3.14159265358979323846264433832795; / 360;
```

This technique can be remarkably effective for debugging errors associated with the expansion of complex macros and definitions appearing in third-party header files. When, however, the expanded code is large (and it typically is), locating the line with the culprit code can be difficult. One trick for finding it is to search for a non-macro identifier or a string appearing near the original line that fails to compile (e.g., toRadians in the preceding case). You can even add a dummy declaration as a signpost near the point that interests you.

Another way to locate the error involves compiling the preprocessed or otherwise generated code after removing the #line directives. The #line directives appearing in the preprocessed file allow the main part of the compiler to map the code it is reading to the lines in the original file. The compiler can thus accurately report the line of the original (rather than the preprocessed) file where the error occurred. If, however, you're trying to locate the error's position in the preprocessed file in order to inspect it, having an error message point you to the original file isn't what you want. To avoid this problem, preprocess the code with an option directing the compiler not to output #line directives: -P on Unix systems, /EP for Microsoft's compilers.

In other cases it's useful to look at the generated machine instructions. This can (again) help you get unstuck when you're stumped by a silly mistake: you look at the machine instructions and you realize you've used the wrong operator, or the wrong arithmetic type, or you forgot to add a brace or a break statement. Through the machine code you can also debug low-level performance problems. To list the generated assembly code, invoke Unix compilers with the -S option and Microsoft's compilers with the /Fa option. If you use GCC and prefer to see Intel's assembly syntax rather than the Unix one (see Item 37: "Know How to View Assembly Code and Raw Memory"), you can also specify GCC's -masm=intel option. In languages that compile into JVM bytecode, run the *javap* command on the corresponding class, passing it the -c option. Although assembly code appears cryptic, if you try to map its instructions into the corresponding source code, you can easily guess most of what's going on, and this is often enough.

As an example, consider the following (maybe) innocuous-looking Java code, which builds a long empty string.

```
class LongString {
    public static void main(String[] args) {
        String s = "";
        for (int i = 0; i < 100000; i++)
            s += " ";
    }
}
```

On my computer, the program takes more than nine seconds to execute. Running `javap -c LongString` on the compiled class file to see the JVM instructions it contains will produce the output appearing in Listing 6.1.

Listing 6.1 Disassembled Java Code

```
class LongString {
 public static void main(java.lang.String[]);
  Code:
    0: ldc         #2 // String
    2: astore_1
    3: iconst_0
    4: istore_2
    5: iload_2
    6: ldc         #3 // int 100000
    8: if_icmpge 37
   11: new         #4 // class StringBuilder
   14: dup
   15: invokespecial #5 // Method StringBuilder."<init>":()V
   18: aload_1
   // Method StringBuilder.append:(LString;)LStringBuilder;
   19: invokevirtual #6
   22: ldc         #7 // String
   // Method StringBuilder.append:(LString;)LStringBuilder;
   24: invokevirtual #6
   // Method StringBuilder.toString:()LString;
   27: invokevirtual #8
   30: astore_1
   31: iinc      2, 1
   34: goto  5
   37: return
}
```

As you can see, within the loop in bytes 5–34, the compiler creates a new *StringBuilder* object (bytes 11–15), appends s to it (bytes 18–19), appends " " to it (bytes 22–24), converts it into a String (byte 27), and stores the result back to s (byte 30). You can thus see that the code executed within the loop body is effectively the following expensive Java statement.

```
s = new StringBuilder().append(s).append(" ").toString();
```

Changing the code into a more efficient equivalent, by moving the *StringBuilder* constructor and string conversion out of the loop, results in a program that executes almost instantaneously.

```
StringBuilder sb = new StringBuilder();
for (int i = 0; i < 100000; i++)
    sb.append(" ");
s = sb.toString();
```

Things to Remember

◆ By examining automatically generated code, you can comprehend compilation and runtime problems in the corresponding source code.

◆ Use compiler options or specialized tools to obtain a readable representation of automatically generated code.

Item 51: Use Static Program Analysis

Having tools do the debugging for you sounds too good to be true, but it's actually a realistic possibility. A variety of so-called *static analysis* tools can scan your code without running it (that's where the word "static" comes from) and identify apparent bugs. Some of these tools may already be part of your infrastructure because modern compilers and interpreters often perform basic types of static analysis. Stand-alone tools include *GrammaTech CodeSonar*, *Coverity Code Advisor*, *FindBugs*, *Polyspace Bug Finder*, and various programs whose name ends in "lint." The analysis tools base their operation on formal methods (algorithms based on lots of math) and on heuristics (an important-sounding word for informed guesses). Although, ideally, static analysis tools should be applied continuously during the software's development to ensure the code's hygiene, they can also be useful when debugging to locate easy-to-miss bugs, such as concurrency gotchas (see Item 62: "Uncover Deadlocks and Race Conditions with Specialized Tools") and sources of memory corruption.

Some of the static analysis tools can detect hundreds of different bugs. The following bullets list important bugs that these tools can find and a few toy examples that demonstrate them. In practice, the code associated with an error is typically convoluted through other statements or distributed among many routines.

- Null dereferences

```
Order o = null;
if (x)
  o = new Order();
o.methodCall(); // o might still be null
```

- Concurrency errors and race conditions

```
class SpinWait {
  private boolean ready;
  public void waitForReady() {
    /*
     * The Java compiler is allowed to hoist the field read
     * out of the loop, making this an infinite loop. Calls
     * to wait and notify should be used instead.
     */
    while (!ready)
      ;
  }
}
```

- Spelling errors in languages that don't require variable declarations

```
if (!colour)
  color = getColor(); // Tested colour, but set color
```

- Incorrect array and memory buffer indexing

```
int[] a = new int[10];
for (i = 0; i <= a.length; i++)
      a[i] = 1; // a[a.length] uses an out of bounds index
```

- Incorrect conditionals, loops, case statements, and code that is never executed

```
for (;;)
  n += processRequest();
return n; // This stament will not be executed
```

- Unhandled exceptions

```
public void readData(java.io.InputStream is) {
  try {
    is.read();
```

```
    } catch (java.io.IOException ex) {
      // The exception is ignored
    }
  }
```

- Unused variables and routines

- Math errors

```
int d = 1;
int q = n / --d; // Division by zero
```

- Code duplication

- Missing boilerplate in the implementation of classes, such as the C++ *Rule of three*/*Rule of 0* and `equals`/`hashCode` discrepancies in Java

- Resource leaks

```
void writeDone()
{
    FILE *f = fopen("myfile", "w");
    fprintf(f, "Done\n");
    return;
    // The opened file stream cannot be closed
}
```

- Security vulnerabilities

```
/*
 * Input longer than the buffer size will overflow the
 * buffer allowing a stack smashing attack.
 */
gets(buff);
```

- Language gotchas

```
public static void main(String[] args) {
  // This compares objects rather than strings
  if (args[0] == "--help")
```

Keep in mind that code analysis tools can both miss bugs that a human can catch (these are called *false negatives*) and issue warnings for code that is correct (*false positives*). For example, GCC (4.8.3) fails to warn that r may not become initialized at the end of the following function.

```
int
myFunction(int c)
```

```
{
        int r;

        if (c)
                r = 0;
        return r;
}
```

On the other hand, the *Visual Studio* 2015 C compiler erroneously warns that r may not be initialized at the end of the following function.

```
int
myFunction(int c)
{
        int r, c2 = 0;

        if (c)
                r = 9;
        else
                c2 = 1;
        if (c2)
                r = 0;
        return r;
}
```

No tool will ever be perfect due to both practical limitations (memory required to track the exponentially explosion of the state space) and theoretical constraints (some underlying problems are *undecidable*—there's probably no algorithm that can always solve them correctly). Therefore, although static analysis is useful, you'll sometimes need to use your judgment regarding the correctness of the results it provides you, and be on the lookout for cases it misses.

Your first port of call to obtain the benefits of static analysis should be the compiler or interpreter you're using. Some provide options that will make them check your code more strictly and issue a warning when they encounter questionable code. For example,

- A starting point of options for GCC, *ghc* (the Glasgow Haskell Compiler), and *clang* (the C language family front end of the LLVM compiler) is -Wall, -Wextra, and -Wshadow (many more are available).

- The options for Microsoft's C/C++ compiler are /Wall and /W4.

- In JavaScript code you write "use strict"; (yes, in double quotes).

- In Perl you write use strict; and use warnings;.

(The Perl and JavaScript options enable both static and dynamic checks.) In compilers, also specify a high optimization level: this performs the type of analysis needed for generating some of the warnings. If the level of warnings can be adjusted, choose the highest level that will not drown you in warnings about things you're unlikely to fix. Then methodically remove all other warnings. This may fix the fault you're looking for, and may also make it easier to see other faults in the future.

Having achieved zero number of warnings, take the opportunity to adjust the compilation options so that they will treat warnings as errors (/WX for Microsoft's compilers, -Werror for GCC). This will prevent warnings being missed in a lengthy compilation's output, and will also compel all developers to write warning-free code.

Having securely anchored the benefits of configuring your compiler, it's time to set up additional analysis tools. These can detect more bugs at the expense of longer processing times and, often, more false positives. Wikipedia's *static analysis tools* list contains more than 100 entries. The list includes both popular commercial offerings, such as *Coverity Code Advisor*, and widely used open-source software, such as *FindBugs*. Some focus on particular types of bugs, such as security vulnerabilities or concurrency problems. Choose those that better target your particular needs. Feel free to adopt more than one tool because different tools often complement each other in the bugs they detect. Invest effort to configure each tool in a way that minimizes the spurious warnings it issues by turning off the warnings that don't apply to your coding style.

Finally, make it possible to run the static analysis step as part of the system's build, and make it a part of the continuous integration setup. The build configuration will make it easy for developers to check their code with the static analysis tools in a uniform way. The check during continuous integration will immediately report any problems that slip past developers. This setup will ensure that the code is always clean from errors reported by static analysis tools. All too often, a team will embark on a heroic effort to clean static analysis errors (perhaps while chasing an insidious bug), and then lose interest and let new errors creep in.

Things to Remember

+ Specialized static program analysis tools can identify more potential bugs in code than compiler warnings.

+ Configure your compiler to analyze your program for bugs.

+ Include in your build cycle and continuous integration cycle at least one static program analysis tool.

Item 52: Configure Deterministic Builds and Executions

The following program prints the memory addresses associated with the program's stack, heap, code, and data.

```c
#include <stdio.h>
#include <stdlib.h>

int z;
int i = 1;
const int c = 1;

int
main(int argc, char *arg[])
{
    printf("stack:\t%p\n", (void *)&argc);
    printf("heap:\t%p\n", malloc(1));
    printf("code:\t%p\n", (void *)main);
    printf("data:\t%p (initialized)\n", (void *)&i);
    printf("data:\t%p (constants)\n", (void *)&c);
    printf("data:\t%p (zero)\n", (void *)&z);
    return 0;
}
```

On many environments, each run will produce different results. (I've seen this happening with GCC under GNU/Linux, *clang* under OS X, and Visual C under Windows.)

```
$ dbuild
stack: 003AFDF4
heap: 004C2200
code: 00CB1000
data: 00CBB000 (initialized)
data: 00CB8140 (constants)
data: 00CBCAC0 (zero)
$ dbuild
stack: 0028FC68
heap: 00302200
code: 01331000
data: 0133B000 (initialized)
data: 01338140 (constants)
data: 0133CAC0 (zero)
```

This happens because the operating system kernel randomizes the way the program is loaded into memory in order to hinder malicious attacks against the code. Many so-called code injection attacks work by overflowing a program's buffers with malicious code and then tricking the program being attacked into executing that code. This trick is quite easy to pull off if a vulnerable program's elements are always located at the same memory position. As a countermeasure, some kernels randomize a program's memory layout, thereby foiling malicious code that attempts to use hard-coded memory addresses.

Unfortunately, this *address space layout randomization* (ASLR) can also interfere with your debugging. Failures that happen on one run may not occur in another one; the values of pointers you painstakingly record change when you restart the program; address-based hash tables get filled in a different way; some memory managers may change their behavior from one run to another.

Therefore, ensure that your program stays stable between executions, especially when debugging a memory-related problem. On GNU/Linux, you can disable ASLR by running your program as follows.

```
setarch $(uname -m) -R myprogram
```

On *Visual Studio* you disable ASLR by linking your code with the /DYNAMICBASE:NO option or by setting appropriately the project's *Configuration Properties – Linker – Advanced – Randomized Base Address* option. Some versions of Windows have a registry setting that globally disables ASLR (HKLM/SYSTEM/CurrentControlSet/Control/SessionManager/ MemoryManagement/MoveImages). Finally, on OS X you need to pass the -no_pie option to the linker, through the compiler's -Wl flag. This is the incantation you'll need to use when compiling.

```
-Wl,-no_pie -o myprogram myprogram.c
```

There are other, thankfully less severe, ways through which two builds of the same program may differ. Here are some representative ones.

- Unique randomly chosen symbol names that GCC places into each compiled file. Use the flag -frandom-seed to pin these down.

- Varying order of compiler inputs. If the files to be compiled or linked are derived from a *Makefile* wildcard expansion, their order can differ as directory entries get reshuffled. Specify the inputs explicitly, or sort the wildcard's expansion.

- Timestamps embedded in the code to convey the software's version, through the __DATE__ and __TIME__ macros, for example. Use the revision control system version identifier (e.g., Git's SHA sum) instead. This will allow you to derive the timestamp should you even need it (see Item 26: "Hunt the Causes and History of Bugs with the Revision Control System").

- Lists generated from hashes and maps. Some programming language implementations vary how objects are hashed in order to thwart *algorithmic complexity attacks*. This varies the results of traversing a container. Address this by sorting the listed results. For Perl and Python, you might alternatively set PERL_HASH_SEED or the PYTHONHASHSEED environment variables.

- Encryption salt. Encryption programs typically perturb the provided key through a randomly derived value—the so-called *salt*—in order to thwart pre-built dictionary attacks. Disable the salting when testing and debugging; for example, the *openssl* program offers the -nosalt option. However, do not use this option for production purposes as it will make your system vulnerable to dictionary attacks.

The golden standard for build image consistency is to be able to create bit-identical package distributions by compiling the same source code on different hosts. This requires a lot more work because it also involves sanitizing things such as file paths, locales, archive metadata, environment variables, and time zones. If you need to go that far, consult the *reproducible builds* web site, which offers sound advice on how to tackle these problems.

Things to Remember

✦ Configure your build process and the software's execution to achieve reproducible runs.

Item 53: Configure the Use of Debugging Libraries and Checks

A number of compilation and linking options allow your code and libraries to perform more stringent runtime checks regarding their operation. These options work in parallel with those that configure your own software's debug mode (see Item 40: "Add Debugging Functionality"), which you should also enable at compile time. The options you'll see here mainly apply to C, C++, and Objective-C, which typically avoid the performance penalty of buffer bounds checking. Consequently, when these checks are enabled, programs may run noticeably slower. Therefore, you must apply these methods with care in real-time systems and performance-critical environments. In the following paragraphs, you'll see some common ways in which you can configure the compilation or linking of your code to pinpoint bugs associated with the use of memory.

You can enable a number of checks on software using the C++ standard template library. With the GNU implementation, you need to define the macro _GLIBCXX_DEBUG when compiling your code, whereas under *Visual Studio* the checks are enabled if you build your project under debug mode or if you pass the option /MDd to the compiler. Builds with STL checks enabled will catch things such as incrementing an iterator past the end of a range, dereferencing an iterator of a container that has been destructed, or violating an algorithm's preconditions. As an example, the following code

```
#include <vector>

int
main()
{
      std::vector<int> v;
      v[0] = 3;
}
```

will fail with the error message "attempt to subscript container with out-of-bounds index 0, but container only holds 0 elements" under GCC and with the message "vector subscript out of range" under *Visual Studio*. Moreover, the following set intersection, which requires sorted ranges,

```
#include <vector>
#include <algorithm>
#include <iterator>

int
main()
{
    std::vector<int> s1 = {5, 3, 2};
    std::vector<int> s2 = {1, 3, 2};
    std::vector<int> result;

    std::set_intersection(s1.begin(), s1.end(),
                          s2.begin(), s2.end(),
                          std::back_inserter(result));
}
```

will fail with the error message "elements in iterator range [__first1, __last1) are not sorted" under GCC and with the message "sequence not sorted" under *Visual Studio*. In addition, by defining _GLIBCXX_

DEBUG_PEDANTIC you will also get messages regarding the use of features that are not portable to other STL implementations.

The GNU C library allows you to check for memory leaks—allocated memory that isn't freed over the program's lifetime. To do that, you need to call the mtrace function at the beginning of your program, and then run it with the environment variable MALLOC_TRACE set to the name of the file where the tracing output will go. Consider the following program, which at the time it exits still has an allocated memory block.

```
#include <stdlib.h>
#include <mcheck.h>

int
main()
{
#ifndef NDEBUG
        mtrace();
#endif
        char *c = malloc(42);
        return 0;
}
```

By running the *mtrace* command on the generated trace file, you will get output that precisely identifies where the leaked block was allocated.

```
Memory not freed:
-----------------
   Address   Size   Caller
0x090e5378 0x2a at leak.c:10
```

A more general (and expensive) way to detect all sorts of memory access problems in C and C++ code is *AddressSanitizer* (*ASan*). This system is supported by the GNU compilers and LLVM Clang by specifying the -fsanitize=address option. Adding the -g and -fno-omit-frame-pointer options will get you clearer results. The following program steps out of an array's limits because it mistakenly uses sizeof to obtain the array's size (rather than dividing its result with the elements' size).

```
int
main()
{
        int i, a[5];

        for (i = 0; i < sizeof(a); i++)
                a[i] = i;
}
```

Compiling it with *AddressSanitizer* enabled results in the program failing with the following error message.

```
==59468==ERROR: AddressSanitizer: global-buffer-overflow on
address 0x000100615134 at pc 0x000100614eb0
WRITE of size 4 at 0x000100615134 thread T0
    #0 0x100614eaf in main oob.c:7
    #1 0x7fff926f15ac in start
    #2 0x0 (<unknown module>)

0x000100615134 is located 0 bytes to the right of global
variable 'a' defined in 'oob.c:4:16' (0x100615120) of
size 20
SUMMARY: AddressSanitizer: global-buffer-overflow oob.c:7 main
```

Depending on the compiler you're using, you may need to provide some extra information in order to get an error report in terms of your source code rather than machine code addresses. You can do that by setting the environment variable ASAN_SYMBOLIZER_PATH to point to the program that does this mapping (e.g., /usr/bin/llvm-symbolizer-3.4) and setting the environment variable ASAN_OPTIONS to symbolize=1.

AddressSanitizer is supported on a number of systems, including GNU/Linux, OS X, and FreeBSD running on i386 and x86_64 CPUs, as well as Android on ARM and the iOS Simulator. *AddressSanitizer* imposes a significant overhead on your code: it roughly doubles the amount of memory and processing required to run your program. On the other hand, it is not expected to produce false positives, so using it while testing your software is a trouble-free way to locate and remove many memory-related problems.

The facilities used for detecting memory allocation and access errors in *Visual Studio* are not as advanced as *AddressSanitizer*, but they can work in many situations. You get them to work by linking with the C debug library using the /MDd option, while also defining a macro and calling some functions, as illustrated in the following program.

```
// Define in order to get file and line number information
#define _CRTDBG_MAP_ALLOC

#include <stdlib.h>
#include <crtdbg.h>

int
main()
{
```

```
// Send output to stderr, rather than the VS debug window
_CrtSetReportMode(_CRT_WARN, _CRTDBG_MODE_FILE);
_CrtSetReportFile(_CRT_WARN, _CRTDBG_FILE_STDERR);

// Detect memory leaks on exit
_CrtSetDbgFlag(_CRTDBG_ALLOC_MEM_DF | _CRTDBG_LEAK_CHECK_DF);
{
    char *c = malloc(42);
    c[42] = 'a';
}
// Check all blocks for memory buffer overflows
_CrtCheckMemory( );

    return 0;
}
```

When run, this program will produce the following error report, identifying heap corruption and a memory leak.

```
HEAP CORRUPTION DETECTED: after Normal block (#106) at
0x00688EF0. CRT detected that the application wrote to
memory after end of heap buffer.

Memory allocated at memerror.c(19).
Normal located at 0x00688EF0 is 42 bytes long.

Memory allocated at memerror.c(19).
Detected memory leaks!
Dumping objects ->
memerror.c(19) : {106} normal block at 0x00688EF0,
42 bytes long.
```

Keep in mind that the provided facilities can only identify writes that happen just outside the allocated heap blocks. In contrast to *Address-Sanitizer*, they cannot identify invalid read operations, nor invalid accesses to global and stack memory.

An alternative approach to use under OS X and when developing iOS applications involves linking with the *Guard Malloc* (*libgmalloc*) library. This puts each allocated memory block into a separate (non-consecutive) virtual memory page, allowing the detection of memory accesses outside the allocated pages. The approach places significant stress on the virtual memory system when allocating the memory but requires no additional CPU resources to check the allocated memory accesses. It works with C, C++, and Objective-C. To use the library, set the environment variable

DYLD_INSERT_LIBRARIES to /usr/lib/libgmalloc.dylib. Several additional environment variables can be used to fine-tune its operation; consult the *libgmalloc* manual page for details.

As an example, the following program, which reads outside an allocated memory block, terminates with a segmentation fault when linked with the library.

```
int
main()
{
        int *a = new int [5];
        int t = a[10];
        return 0;
}
```

You can easily catch the fault with a debugger in order to pinpoint the exact location associated with the error.

Finally, if none of these facilities are available in your environment, consider replacing the library your software is using with one that supports debug checks. One notable such library is *dmalloc*, a drop-in replacement for the C memory allocation functions with debug support.

Things to Remember

✦ Identify and enable the runtime debugging support offered by your environment's compiler and libraries.

✦ If no support is available, consider configuring your software to use third-party libraries that offer it.

Runtime Techniques

The ultimate source of truth regarding a program is its execution. While a program is running, everything comes to light: its correctness, its CPU and memory utilization, even its interactions with buggy libraries, operating systems, and hardware. Yet, typically, this source of truth is also fleeting, rushing into oblivion at the tune of billions of instructions per second. Worse, capturing that truth can be a tricky, tortuous, or downright treacherous affair. Tests, application logs, and monitoring tools allow you to peek into the program's runtime behavior to locate the bug that's bothering you.

Item 54: Find the Fault by Constructing a Test Case

You can often pinpoint and even correct a bug simply by working on appropriate tests. Some call this approach DDT for "Defect-Driven Testing"—it is no coincidence that the abbreviation matches that of the well-known insecticide. Here are the three steps you need to follow, together with a running example. The example is based on an actual bug that appeared in *qmcalc*, a program that calculates diverse quality metrics for C files and displays the values corresponding to each file as a tab-separated list. The problem was that, in some rare cases, the program would output fewer than the 110 expected fields.

First, create a test case that **reliably reproduces** the problem you need to solve. This means specifying the *process* to follow and the required *materials* (typically data). For example, a test case can be that loading file foo (material) and then pressing x, y, and z causes the application to crash (process). Another could be that putting Acme's load balancer (material) in front of your application causes the initial user authentication to fail (process).

In the example case, the following commands apply the *qmcalc* program on all Linux C files and generate a summary of the number of fields generated.

```
# Find all C files
find linux-4.4 -name \*.c |
# Apply qmcalc on each file
xargs qmcalc |
# Display the number of fields
awk '{print NF}' |
# Order by number of fields
sort |
# Display number of occurrences
uniq -c
```

The results show that the program fails to generate 110 fields in a small number of cases.

```
    8 100
   19 105
21772 110
   12 80
  472 90
```

The second step is the **simplification** of the test case to the bare minimum (see Item 10: "Enable the Efficient Reproduction of the Problem"). Both methods for doing that, building up the test case from scratch or trimming down the existing large test case, involve an *aha!* moment, where the bug first appears (when building up) or disappears (when trimming down). The test case data will often point you either to the problem, or even to the solution. In many cases you can combine both trimming methods: you first remove as much fat as possible, and, once you think you know what the problem is, you construct a new minimal test case from scratch.

In the same example case, the following shell commands will display the first file that exhibits the problem.

```
# Find C files
find linux-4.4/ -name \*.c |
# For each file
while read f ; do
  # If the number of fields is not 110
  if [ $(qmcalc $f | awk '{print $NF}') != 110 ] ; then
    echo $f  # Output the file name
    break    # Stop processing
  fi
done
```

The result of running the preceding pipeline is the name of a file for which *qmcalc* will output fewer than 110 fields: linux-4.4/drivers/mmc/host/sdhci-pci-o2micro.c.

Can a subset of the file trigger the same problem? Here are the results of counting the number of *qmcalc* output fields for successively fewer lines.

```
$ cp linux-4.4/drivers/mmc/host/sdhci-pci-o2micro.c test.c
$ ./qmcalc test.c | awk '{print NF}'
87
$ head -100 test.c | ./qmcalc | awk '{print NF}'
87
$ head -10 test.c | ./qmcalc | awk '{print NF}'
63
$ head -1 test.c | ./qmcalc | awk '{print NF}'
63
```

Building an artificial test case by applying *qmcalc* to the empty file /dev/null, simplifies the test case even further.

```
$ ./qmcalc /dev/null | awk '{print NF}'
59
```

Looking at the program's output in a form that clearly shows tabs hints at a possible cause of the problem: groups of empty fields.

```
$ ./qmcalc /dev/null | sed -n l
0\t0\t\t\t\t0\t0\t\t\t\t0\t0\t0\t0\t0\t0\t0\t0\t0\t0\t0\t0\t\t\
\t\t0\t0\t\t\t\t0\t\t\t\t0\t\t\t\t0\t0\t0\t0\t0\t0\t0\t0\
\t0\t0\t0\t0\t0\t0\t0\t0\t0\t0\t0\t0\t0\t0\t0\t0\t0\t0\t\
0\t0\t0\t0\t0\t0\t0\t0\t0\t0\t0$
```

A look at the code reveals the problem: a missing field separator (tab) when outputting the descriptive statistics of an empty set.

```
template <typename T>
std::ostream&
operator <<(std::ostream& o, const Descriptive<T> &d) {
    if (d.get_count() != 0)
        o << d.get_count() << '\t' << d.get_min() << '\t' <<
            d.get_mean() << '\t' << d.get_max() << '\t' <<
            d.get_standard_deviation();
    else
        o << "0\t\t\t";
    return o;
}
```

The third step involves consolidating your victory. Having isolated the problem, grab the opportunity to add a corresponding *unit test* or *regression test* in the code (see Item 42: "Use Unit Tests"). If the failure is associated with a fault in isolated code parts, then you should be able to add a corresponding unit test. If the failure occurs through the combination of multiple factors, then a regression test is more appropriate. The regression test should package your test case in a form that can be executed automatically and routinely when the software is tested. While the fault is still in the code, run the software's tests to verify that the test fails, and that it therefore correctly captures the problem. When the test passes, you have a pretty good indication that you've fixed the code. In addition, the test's existence will now ensure that the fault will not resurface again in the future.

This is the *CppUnit* unit test I added in the *qmcalc* example.

```
void testOutputEmpty() {
    std::stringstream str;
    Descriptive<int> a;
    str << a;
    CPPUNIT_ASSERT(str.str() == "0\t\t\t\t");
}
```

As expected, running the program's unit tests before fixing the code results in a failure.

```
$ make test
./UnitTests
...............................................................
..........F.....................................
!!!FAILURES!!!
Test Results:
Run: 110 Failures: 1 Errors: 0

1) test: DescriptiveTest::testOutputEmpty (F) line: 103
DescriptiveTest.h assertion failed
- Expression: str.str() == "0\t\t\t\t"
```

After fixing the code by adding the missing field separator, the test passes.

```
$ make test
................................................................
..................................................
OK (110 tests)
```

To put this in the words of Andrew Hunt and David Thomas: "Coding ain't done 'til all the tests run."

Adding to your code a test for a problem that's already solved is not as pedantic as it sounds. First, you may have missed fixing a particular case; the test will help you catch that problem when that code is exercised. Then, an incorrectly handled revision merge conflict may introduce the same error again. In addition, someone else can commit a similar error in the future. Finally, the test may also catch related errors. There's rarely a good reason to skimp on tests.

When using tests to uncover bugs, it's worthwhile to know which parts of the code are actually tested and which parts are skipped over because bugs may lurk in the less well-tested parts. You can find this through the use of a tool that performs *test coverage analysis*. Examples include *gcov* (C and C++; see Item 57: "Profile the Operation of Systems and Processes"), *JCov*, *JaCoCo*, and *Clover* (Java), *NCover* and *Open-Cover* (.NET), as well as the packages *coverage* (Python) and *blanket.js* (JavaScript).

Things to Remember

+ The process of creating a reliable minimal test case can lead you to the fault and its solution.

+ Embed your test case in the software as a unit or a regression test.

Item 55: Fail Fast

The fast and efficient reproduction of a problem will improve your debugging productivity (see Item 11: "Minimize the Turnaround Time from Your Changes to Their Result" and Item 10: "Enable the Efficient Reproduction of the Problem"). Therefore, configure the software to fail at the first sign of trouble. Such a failure will make it easier for you to pinpoint the corresponding fault because the failing code will be executed relatively soon after the code that caused the failure, and may even be located close to it. In contrast, allowing the software to continue running after a minor failure can lead the code's operation into uncharted territory where a cascade of other problems will make the location of a bug much more difficult.

Failing quickly entails the risk of focusing on the wrong problem. However, if you fix that problem and restart your debugging, you have eliminated forever a source of doubt. Through a process of gradual elimination, you're making progress. Again, allowing minor problems to linger can bring about death from a thousand cuts.

Here are some ways to speed up your program's failures.

- Add and enable assertions to verify the validity of routines' input arguments and the success of API calls (see Item 43: "Use Assertions"). In Java you enable assertions at runtime with the -ea option. In C and C++ you typically enable assertions at compile time by not defining the NDEBUG macro identifier. (This identifier is typically defined in production builds.)

- Configure libraries for strict checking of their use (see Item 53: "Configure the Use of Debugging Libraries and Checks").

- Check the program's operation with dynamic program analysis methods (see Item 59: "Use Dynamic Program Analysis Tools").

- Set the Unix shell's -e option to make shell scripts terminate when a command exits with an error (a non-zero exit status).

Note that while failing fast is an effective way to debug a self-contained program, it may not be a suitable way to run a large production system that has graduated from development to maintenance. There, the priority is likely to be resilience: in many cases, allowing the system to operate after a minor failure (for example, a problem loading an icon image or a crash of one among many server processes) may be preferable to bringing the whole system down. This permissive mode of operation can be counterbalanced by other measures, such as extensive monitoring (see Item 27: "Use Monitoring Tools on Systems Composed of Independent Processes") and logging (see Item 56: "Examine Application Log Files" and Item 41: "Add Logging Statements").

Things to Remember

✦ When debugging, set up trip wires so that your program will fail at the first sign of trouble.

Item 56: Examine Application Log Files

Many programs that perform complex processing, execute in the background, or lack access to a console, log their operations to a file or a specialized log collection facility. A program's log output allows you to follow its execution in real time or analyze a sequence of events at your own convenience. In the case of a failure, you may find in the log either an error or a warning message indicating the reason behind the failure (e.g., "*Unable to connect to example.com: Connection refused*") or data that point to a software error or misconfiguration. Therefore, make it a habit to start the investigation of a failure by examining the software's log files.

The location and storage method of log files differ among operating systems and software platforms. On Unix systems, logs are typically stored in text files located in the /var/log directory. Applications may create in that directory their own log files, or they may use an existing file associated with the class of events they're logging. Some examples include

- Authentication: auth.log

- Background processes: daemon.log

- The kernel: kern.log

- Debug information: debug

- Other messages: messages

On a not-so-busy system, you may be able to find the file corresponding to the application you're debugging by running

```
ls -tl /var/log | head
```

right after the application creates a log entry; the name of the log should appear at the top among the most recently modified files. If the file is located in a subdirectory of /var/log, you may be able to find it as follows:

```
# List all files under /var/log
find /var/log -type f |
# List each file's last modification time and name
xargs stat -c '%y %n' |
# Order by time
sort -r |
# List by the ten most recently modified files
head
```

If these methods do not work, you can look for the log filename in the application's documentation, a trace of its execution (see Item 58: "Trace the Code's Execution"), or its source code.

On Windows systems, the application logs are stored in an opaque format. You can run Eventvwr.msc to launch the *Event Viewer* GUI application, which allows you to browse and filter the logs, use the Windows *PowerShell* GetEventLog command, or use the corresponding .NET API. Again, logs are separated into various categories; you can explore them through the tree appearing on the left of the *Event Viewer*. On OS X, the

GUI log viewer application is named *Console*. Both the Windows and the OS X applications allow you to filter the logs, create custom views, or search for specific entries. You can also use the Unix command-line tools (see Item 22: "Analyze Debug Data with Unix Command-Line Tools") to perform similar processing.

Many applications can adjust the amount of information they log (the so-called log verbosity) through a command-line option, a configuration option, or even at runtime by sending them a suitable signal. Moreover, logging frameworks provide additional mechanisms for expanding or throttling log messages. When you have debugged your problem, don't forget to reset logging to its original level; extensive logging can hamper performance and consume excessive storage space or bandwidth.

On Unix systems, applications tag every log message with the associated facility (e.g., *authorization*, *kernel*, *mail*, *user*) and a level, ranging from *emergency* and *alert* to *informational* and *debug*. You can then configure *syslogd* (or *rsyslogd*), the background program that listens for log messages and logs them into a file, how to handle specific messages. The corresponding file is /etc/syslog.conf (or /etc/rsyslog.conf and the /etc/rsyslog.d directory). There you can specify that log messages up to a maximum level (e.g., all messages up to informational, but not the debug ones) and associated with a given facility will be logged to a file, sent to the console, or ignored. For example, the following specifies the files associated with all messages of the *security* facility, *authorization* up to the *informational* level, and all messages of exactly the *debug* level. It also specifies that messages at the *emergency* level are sent to all logged-in users.

```
security.*    /var/log/security
auth.info     /var/log/auth.log
*.=debug      /var/log/debug.log
*.emerg       *
```

For JVM code, the popular *Apache log4j* logging framework allows the even more detailed specification of what gets logged and where. Its structure is based on *loggers* (output channels), *appenders* (mechanisms that can send log messages to a sink, such as a file or a network socket), and *layouts* (these specify the format of each log message). Log4j is configured through a file, which can be given in XML, JSON, YAML, or Java properties format. Here is a small part of the log4j configuration file used by the *Rundeck* workflow and configuration management system.

```
# This logger covers all of Grails' internals
# Enable to see whats going on underneath.
log4j.logger.org.codehaus.groovy.grails=warn,\
  stdout,server-logger
```

```
log4j.additivity.org.codehaus.groovy.grails=false

# server-logger - DailyRollingFileAppender
# Captures all output from the rundeckd server.
log4j.appender.server-logger=org.apache.log4j.\
  DailyRollingFileAppender
log4j.appender.server-logger.file=/var/log/rundeck/rundeck.log
log4j.appender.server-logger.datePattern='.'yyyy-MM-dd
log4j.appender.server-logger.append=true
log4j.appender.server-logger.layout=org.apache.log4j.\
  PatternLayout
log4j.appender.server-logger.layout.\
  ConversionPattern=%d{ISO8601}[%t] %-5p %c - %m%n
```

By adjusting the level of messages that get logged, you can often get the data needed to debug a problem. Here is an example associated with debugging failing *ssh* connections. The *sshd* configuration file is located in */etc/ssh/sshd_config*. There, a commented-out line specifies the default log level (INFO).

```
#LogLevel INFO
```

Under this log level, when a connection fails, the only thing that gets logged is a message such as the following.

```
Jul 30 12:49:49 prod sshd[5369]: Connection closed by
10.212.204.48 [preauth]
```

Bumping up the log level to DEBUG

LogLevel DEBUG

results in many more informative messages, one of which clearly indicates the problem's cause.

```
Jul 30 12:57:07 prod sshd[5713]: debug1: Could not open
authorized keys '/home/jhd/.ssh/authorized_keys': No such
file or directory
```

There are several ways to analyze a log record in order to locate a failure's cause.

- You can use the system's GUI event viewer and its searching and filtering facilities.

- You can open and process a log file in your editor (see Item 24: "Explore Debug Data with Your Editor").

- You can filter, summarize, and select fields using Unix tools (see Item 22: "Analyze Debug Data with Unix Command-Line Tools").

- You can monitor the log interactively (see Item 23: "Utilize Command-Line Tool Options and Idioms").

- You can use a log management application or service, such as *ELK*, *Logstash*, *loggly*, or *Splunk*.

- Under Windows, you can use the Windows Events Command Line Utility (*wevtutil*) to run queries and export logs.

You typically want to start by examining the entries near the time when the failure occurred. Alternately, you can search the event log for a string associated with the failure, for example, the name of a failed command. In both cases, you then scan the log back in time looking for errors, warnings, and unexpected entries.

For failures lacking a clear manifestation, it's often useful to repeatedly remove from a log file innocuous entries until entries containing important information stand out. You can do this within your editor: under *Emacs* use `delete-matching-lines` *regular-expression*; under *vim* use `:g/`*regular-expression*`/d`; under *Eclipse* and *Visual Studio* find-replace a regular expression that matches the whole line and ends with \n. On the Unix command line, you can pipe the log file through successive `grep -v` commands.

Things to Remember

✦ Begin the investigation of a failing application by examining its log files.

✦ Increase an application's logging verbosity to record the reason of its failure.

✦ Configure and filter log files to narrow down the problem.

Item 57: Profile the Operation of Systems and Processes

When debugging performance problems, your first (and often the only) port of call is a profile of the system's operation. This will analyze the system's **resource utilization** and thereby point to a part that is misbehaving or needs to be optimized. Start by obtaining a high-level overview. Two process viewing tools that will also give you a system's CPU and memory utilization are the *top* command on Unix systems and the *Task Manager* on Windows (see Figure 7.1). On a misbehaving system, a high level of CPU utilization (say, 90% on a single core CPU) tells you that you must concentrate your analysis on processing, whereas a low utilization

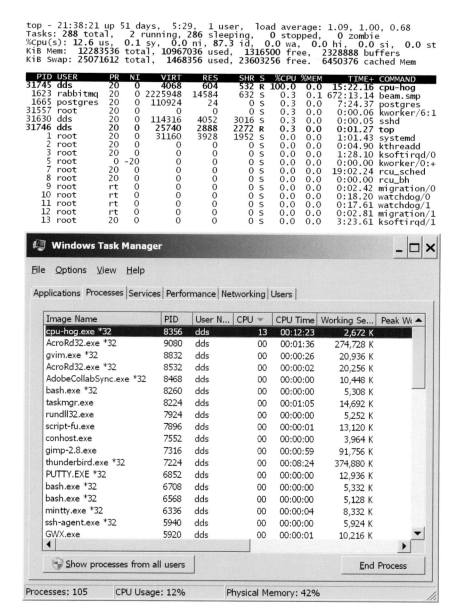

Figure 7.1 A list of running processes obtained with *top* (top) and the Windows *Task Manager* (bottom)

(say, 10%, again on a single core CPU) points to delays that may be occurring due to input/output (I/O) operations. Note that multi-core computers typically report the load over all CPU cores, so if you're dealing with one single-threaded process, divide the thresholds I gave by the total number of available CPU cores. As an example, the two systems appearing in Figure 7.1 have eight cores each, so a single process occupying 100% of a CPU core on an otherwise idle system will make the system load appear as 12% (100%/8).

Also look at the system's physical memory utilization. A high (near 100%) utilization may cause errors due to failed memory allocations or a drop in the system's performance due to virtual memory paging. When looking at the amount of free memory, keep in mind that Linux systems aggressively use almost all available memory as a buffer cache. Therefore, on Linux systems add the memory listed as buffers to the amount of memory you consider to be free.

For systems designed to operate normally near their maximum capacity, you need to look beyond utilization (which will be close to 100%), and examine **saturation.** This is a measure of the demands placed on a resource *above* the level it can service. For this you will use the same tools, but focus on measures indicating saturation of each resource.

- For CPUs, look at a load higher than the number of cores on Unix systems and at the *Performance Monitor System – Processor Queue Length* on Windows systems.

- For memory, look at the rate at which virtual memory pages are written out to disk.

- For network I/O, look for dropped packets and retransmissions.

- For storage I/O, look at the request queue length and operation latency.

For all of the above measures, levels of saturation consistently appearing above 100% (continuously or in bursts) are typically a problem.

Having obtained an overview of what's gumming up your system's performance, drill down toward the process burning many CPU cycles, causing excessive I/O, experiencing high I/O latency, or using a lot of memory.

- If the problem is a high CPU load, look at the running processes. Order the processes by their CPU usage to find the culprit taking up most of the CPU time. In Figure 7.1, this is the process named cpu-hog.

- If the problem is a high memory utilization, look at the running processes ordered by working set (or resident) memory size. This is the amount of physical (rather than virtual) memory used.

- Investigate the possibility of a high I/O load or high I/O latency by using tools such as *iostat, netstat, nfsstat,* or *vmstat* on Unix or the *Performance Monitor* on Windows (run `perfmon`). Look both at the volume of disk and network data and at the corresponding number of I/O operations because either of these can be a bottleneck. Once you've isolated the type of load that's causing you a problem, use *pidstat* on Unix or the Windows *Task Manager* to pinpoint the culprit process. Then trace the individual process's system calls to further understand its behavior (see Item 58: "Trace the Code's Execution").

For cases of high CPU or memory utilization, you should continue by profiling the behavior of the culprit process you've identified. There's no shortage of techniques for monitoring a program's behavior. If you care about CPU utilization, you can run your program under a *statistical profiler* that will interrupt its operation many times every second and note where the program spends most of its time. Alternately, you can arrange for the compiler or runtime system to plant code setting a time counter at the beginning and end of each (non-inlined) function, and thus create a *graph-based profile* of the program's execution. This allows you to attribute the activity of each function to its parents, and thereby untangle performance problems associated with complex call paths. The corresponding GCC option is `-pg`, and the tool you use to view the resulting data is *gprof*. In extreme cases, you can even have the compiler instrument each basic block of your code with a counter, so that you can see how many times each line got executed. The corresponding GCC options are `-fprofile-arcs` and `-ftest-coverage`, and the tool to annotate the code is *gcov*. Other profiling options you can use include the *Eclipse* and *NetBeans* profiler plugins and the stand-alone *VisualVM, JProfiler,* and *Java Mission Control* systems for Java programs (see Figure 7.2), as well as the CLR profiler for .NET code. Memory utilization monitors typically modify the runtime system's memory allocator to keep track of your allocations. *Valgrind* under Unix and, again, *VisualVM* and *Java Mission Control* are useful tools in this category. Aspect Oriented Programming tools and frameworks, such as *AspectJ* and *Spring AOP*, allow you to orchestrate your own custom monitoring. At an even lower level, you can monitor the CPU's performance counters with tools such as *perf, oprofile,* or *perfmon2* to look for cache misses, missed branch predictions, or instruction fetch stalls (for a detailed example see Item 65: "Locate False Sharing by Using Performance Counters").

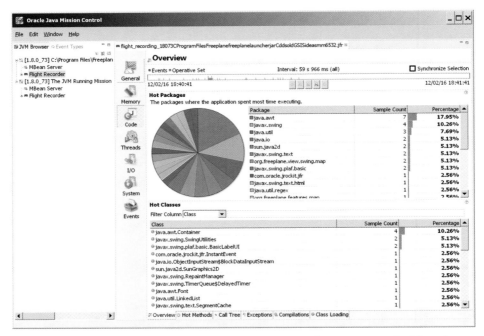

Figure 7.2 An overview of hot packages and classes provided by *Java Mission Control*

Things to Remember

✦ Analyze performance issues by looking at the levels of CPU, I/O, and memory utilization and saturation.

✦ Narrow down on the code associated with a performance problem by profiling a process's CPU and memory use.

Item 58: Trace the Code's Execution

Monitoring and tracing tools and facilities allow you to derive log-like data from the execution of arbitrary programs. This approach offers you a number of advantages over application-level logging.

- You can obtain data even if the application you're debugging lacks logging facilities.

- You don't need to prepare a debug version of the software (see Item 40: "Add Debugging Functionality"), which may obfuscate or hide the original problem.

- Compared to the use of a GUI debugger, it's lightweight, which allows you to use it in a bare-bones production environment.

When you try to locate a bug, an approach you often use involves either inserting logging statements in key locations of your program (see Item 56: "Examine Application Log Files" and Item 41: "Add Logging Statements") or running the code under a debugger, which allows you to dynamically insert breakpoint instructions (see Item 30: "Use Code and Data Breakpoints").

Nowadays, however, performance problems and many bugs involve the use of third-party libraries or interactions with the operating system. One way to resolve these issues is to look at the calls from your code to that other component. By examining the timestamp of each call or looking for an abnormally large number of calls, you can pinpoint performance problems. The arguments to a function can also often reveal a bug. Call tracing tools include *ltrace* (traces library calls), *strace*, *ktrace*, and *truss* (these trace operating system calls) under Unix, *JProfile* for Java programs, and *Process Monitor* under Windows (this traces DLL calls, which involve both operating system and third-party library interfaces). These tools typically work by using special APIs or code-patching techniques to hook themselves between your program and its external interfaces.

As an example, consider a case I was working on where a program processed its input unexpectedly slowly (see Item 10: "Enable the Efficient Reproduction of the Problem"). Running *strace* on the program produced the following output, which indicated that the I/O library's buffer was not used, with the program issuing two system calls for every character used: one to read 8191 bytes and one to move back the file's seek pointer by 8190 bytes.

```
read(6, "ng or publicity pertaining\nto di"..., 8191) = 8191
_llseek(6, -8190, [536], SEEK_CUR) = 0
read(6, "g or publicity pertaining\nto dis"..., 8191) = 8191
_llseek(6, -8190, [537], SEEK_CUR) = 0
read(6, " or publicity pertaining\nto dist"..., 8191) = 8191
_llseek(6, -8190, [538], SEEK_CUR) = 0
read(6, "or publicity pertaining\nto distr"..., 8191) = 8191
_llseek(6, -8190, [539], SEEK_CUR) = 0
read(6, "r publicity pertaining\nto distri"..., 8191) = 8191
_llseek(6, -8190, [540], SEEK_CUR) = 0
```

With this intelligence at hand, it was easy to look at the program's input processing code and hypothesize that the problem was associated with a call to the `tellg` method. The following small test program (see Item 11:

"Minimize the Turnaround Time from Your Changes to Their Result") exhibited the same pathological behavior.

```
ifstream in(fname.c_str(), ios::binary);

do {
  (void)in.tellg();
} while ((val = in.get()) != EOF);
```

With a compact and reliable way to reproduce the problem, it was easy to write a shim class that would independently calculate and cache the file's offset, eliminating the calls to tellg.

Processing the output of *strace* with Unix tools immensely increases your debugging power. Consider the case where a program fails by complaining about an erroneous configuration entry. However, you can't find the offending string in any of its tens of configuration files. The following *Bash* command will show you which of the files opened by the program prog contains the offending string, say, xyzzy.

```
# Send the output of strace to a command
strace -fo >(
  # Isolate and output the path of each opened file
  sed -n 's/.*open("\(\/[^"]*\)".*= [^-].*/\1/p' |
  # Remove special device files
  egrep -v '^/(proc|dev|tmp)/' |
  # Output each file path only once
  sort -u |
  # Search for occurrences of xyzzy within each file
  xargs fgrep xyzzy) prog
```

It works by sending the output of *strace* into a pipeline that isolates the names of files passed to the open system call (sed), removes the filenames associated with devices (egrep -v), keeps a unique copy of each filename (sort -u), and looks for the string xyzzy within those files (fgrep).

Looking at the system calls of Java and X Window System programs can be irritating because these issue a large number of calls associated with the runtime framework. These calls can obscure what the program actually does. Thankfully, you can filter out these system calls with the *strace* -e option. Here are the corresponding incantations.

```
# Trace a Java program
strace -e 'trace=!clock_gettime,gettimeofday,futex,\
timerfd_settime,epoll_wait,epoll_ctl'

# Trace a Unix X Window System program
strace -e 'trace=!poll,recvfrom,writev,read,write'
```

Note that you can also trace an already running program by attaching the tracing tool to it. The command-line tools offer the -p option, whereas the GUI tools allow you to click on the process you want to trace.

System and library call tracing are not the only game in town. Most interpreted languages offer an option to trace a program's execution. Here are the incantations for tracing code written in some popular scripting languages.

- Perl: `perl -d:Trace`

- Python: `python -m trace --trace`

- Ruby: `ruby -r tracer`

- Unix shell: `sh -x`, `bash -x`, `csh -x`, etc.

Other ways to monitor a program's operation include the JavaScript tracing backend *spy-js*, network packet monitoring (see Item 16: "Use Specialized Monitoring and Test Equipment"), and the logging of an application's SQL statements, via the database server. For example, the following SQL statements can turn on this logging for *MySQL*.

```
set global log_output = 'FILE';
set global general_log_file='/tmp/mysql.log';
set global general_log = 1;
```

Most of the tools referred to so far have been around for ages and can be valuable for solving a problem, once you've located its approximate cause. They also have a number of drawbacks: they often require you to take special actions to monitor your code, they can decrease the performance of your system, their interfaces are idiosyncratic and incompatible with each other, each one shows us only a small part of the overall picture, and sometimes important details are simply missing.

A tool that addresses these shortcoming is *DTrace*, a dynamic tracing framework developed originally by Sun that provides uniform mechanisms for monitoring comprehensively and unobtrusively the operating system, application servers, runtime environments, libraries, and application programs. It is currently available on Solaris, OS X, FreeBSD, and NetBSD. On Linux, *SystemTap* and *LTTng* offer similar facilities.

Unsurprisingly, *DTrace*, a gold winner in *The Wall Street Journal*'s Technology Innovation Awards contest, is not a summer holiday hack. The three Sun engineers behind it worked for a number of years to develop mechanisms for safely instrumenting all operating system kernel functions, any dynamically linked library, any application program function or specific CPU instruction, and the Java virtual machine. They also developed a safe interpreted language that you can use to write sophisticated tracing scripts without damaging the operating system's functioning, and aggregating functions that can summarize traced data in a scalable way without excessive memory overhead. *DTrace* integrates technologies and wizardry from most existing tracing tools and some notable interpreted languages to provide an all-encompassing platform for program tracing.

You typically use the *DTrace* framework through the *dtrace* command-line tool. You feed the *dtrace* tool with scripts you write in a domain-specific language named D (not related to the general-purpose language with the same name). When you run *dtrace* with your script, it installs the traces you've specified, executes your program, and prints its results. D programs can be very simple: they consist of pattern/action pairs like those found in the *awk* and *sed* tools and many declarative languages. A pattern (called a predicate in the *DTrace* terminology) specifies a probe—an event you want to monitor. *DTrace* comes with thousands of pre-defined probes (49,979 on an early version of Solaris and 177,398 on OS X *El Capitan* I tried it on). In addition, system programs (such as application servers and runtime environments) can define their own probes, and you can also set a probe anywhere you want in a program or in a dynamically linked library. For example, the command

```
dtrace -n 'syscall:::entry'
```

will install a probe at the entry point of all operating system calls, and the (default) action will be to print the name of each system call executed and the process-id of the calling process. You can combine predicates and other variables together using Boolean operators to specify more complex tracing conditions.

The name `syscall` in the previous invocation specifies a provider—a module providing some probes. Predictably, the `syscall` provider provides probes for tracing operating system calls; 500 system calls on my system. The name `syscall::open:entry` designates one of these probes—the entry point to the open system call. *DTrace* contains tens of providers, giving access to statistical profiling, all kernel functions, locks, system calls, device drivers, input and output events, process creation and termination, the network stack's management information bases (MIBs), the scheduler, virtual memory operations, user program functions and arbitrary code locations, synchronization primitives, kernel statistics, and Java virtual machine operations. Here are the commands you can use to find the available providers and probes.

```
# List all available probes
dtrace -l
# List system call probes
dtrace -l -P syscall
# List the arguments to the read system call probe
dtrace -lv -f syscall::read
```

Together with each predicate, you can define an action. This action specifies what *DTrace* will do when a predicate's condition is satisfied. For example, the following command

```
dtrace -n 'syscall::open:entry {trace(copyinstr(arg0));}'
```

will list the name of each opened file.

Actions can be arbitrarily complex: they can set global or thread-local variables, store data in associative arrays, and aggregate data with functions such as count, min, max, avg, and quantize. For instance, the following program will summarize the number of times each process gets executed over the lifetime of the dtrace invocation.

```
proc:::exec-success { @proc[execname] = count()}
```

By tallying functions that acquire resources and those that release them, you can easily debug leaks of arbitrary resources. In typical use *DTrace* scripts span the space from one-liners, such as the preceding ones, to tens of lines containing multiple predicate action pairs.

If your code runs on a JVM, another tool you might find useful for tracing its behavior is *Byteman*. This can inject Java code into the methods of your application of the runtime system, without requiring you to recompile the code. You specify when and how the original Java code is transformed through a clear and simple scripting language. The advantages of using *Byteman* over adding logging code by hand are threefold. First, you don't need access to the source code, which allows you to trace third-party code as well as yours. Also, you can inject faults and other similar conditions in order to verify how your code responds to them. Finally, you can write *Byteman* scripts that will fail a test case if the application's internal state diverges from the expected norm.

On the Windows ecosystem, similar functionality is provided by the *Windows Performance Toolkit*, which is distributed as part of the *Windows Assessment and Deployment Kit*. The system has a recording component, the *Windows Performance Recorder*, which you run on the system facing performance problems to trace events you consider important, and the *Windows Performance Analyzer*, which, in true Windows fashion, offers you a nifty GUI to graph results and operate on tables.

Things to Remember

✦ System and library call tracing allows you to monitor the behavior of programs without access to their source code.

✦ Learn how to use the *Windows Performance Toolkit* (Windows), *SystemTap* (Linux), or *Dtrace* (OS X, Solaris, FreeBSD).

Item 59: Use Dynamic Program Analysis Tools

A number of specialized tools can instrument your compiled program with check routines, monitor its execution, and report detected cases of probable errors. This type of checking is termed *dynamic analysis* because it is carried out at runtime. The corresponding checks complement the techniques discussed in Item 51: "Use Static Program Analysis," such as writing `"use strict"`; in JavaScript and `use strict; use warnings`; in Perl code, which enable both static and dynamic checks. They also supplement the linking to debug libraries, as described in Item 53: "Configure the Use of Debugging Libraries and Checks," which will also enable some kinds of dynamic checks.

Compared to static analysis tools, dynamic tools have an easier job in detecting errors that actually occur because, rather than having to deduce what code would be executed (as is the case with static analysis tools), they can trace the code as it is being executed. This means that when a dynamic analysis tool indicates an error, it is highly unlikely that this is a false positive. On the other hand, a dynamic analysis tool will only look at code that's actually being executed. Therefore, it can miss faults that are located in code paths that aren't exercised, resulting in a potentially large number of false negatives.

Because dynamic program analysis tools often dramatically slow down a program's execution and can report a slew of low-priority errors, when debugging it's best to employ such a tool with a very specific test script that demonstrates the exact problem you're debugging. Alternately, as a code hygiene maintenance method, you can run the code being analyzed with a realistic and complete test scenario. Through this process you can whitelist all reported errors, so that you can easily catch any new ones that appear when you introduce changes.

Many dynamic analysis tools offer facilities to detect the use of uninitialized values, memory leaks, and accesses beyond the boundaries of available memory space. Other tools can catch security vulnerabilities, suboptimal code, incomplete code coverage (this indicates gaps in your testing), implicit type conversions, dynamic typing inconsistencies, and numeric overflows. You can also read how you can use dynamic analysis tools to catch concurrency errors in Item 62: "Uncover Deadlocks and Race Conditions with Specialized Tools." Wikipedia's page on *dynamic program analysis* lists tens of tools; choose those that match your environment, problem, and budget.

A widely used open-source code dynamic analysis system is the *Valgrind* tool suite, which contains a powerful memory checking component. Consider the following program, which crams into three lines of code a memory leak, an illegal memory access, and the return of an uninitialized value.

```
#include <stdlib.h>

int
main()
{
        char *c = malloc(42);

        c[42] = 1;
        return c[0];
}
```

Running the program with the command

```
valgrind --track-origins=yes --leak-check=yes memory
```

will produce the following output, which identifies all three errors indicating the program location associated with them.

```
Invalid write of size 1
   at 0x400524: main (memory.c:8)
 Address 0x51de06a is 0 bytes after a block of size 42 alloc'd
   at 0x4C28C20: malloc (vg_replace_malloc.c:296)
   by 0x400517: main (memory.c:6)

Syscall param exit_group(status) contains uninitialised byte(s)
   at 0x4EECAB9: _Exit (_exit.c:32)
   by 0x4E6CB8A: __run_exit_handlers (exit.c:97)
   by 0x4E6CC14: exit (exit.c:104)
   by 0x4E56B4B: (below main) (libc-start.c:321)
 Uninitialised value was created by a heap allocation
   at 0x4C28C20: malloc (vg_replace_malloc.c:296)
   by 0x400517: main (memory.c:6)
```

```
HEAP SUMMARY:
    in use at exit: 42 bytes in 1 blocks
  total heap usage: 1 allocs, 0 frees, 42 bytes allocated

42 bytes in 1 blocks are definitely lost in loss record 1 of 1
   at 0x4C28C20: malloc (vg_replace_malloc.c:296)
   by 0x400517: main (memory.c:6)

LEAK SUMMARY:
   definitely lost: 42 bytes in 1 blocks
   indirectly lost: 0 bytes in 0 blocks
     possibly lost: 0 bytes in 0 blocks
   still reachable: 0 bytes in 0 blocks
        suppressed: 0 bytes in 0 blocks

For counts of detected and suppressed errors, rerun with: -v
ERROR SUMMARY: 3 errors from 3 contexts (suppressed: 0 from 0)
```

Another interesting tool is the *Jalangi* dynamic analysis framework for client- and server-side JavaScript. This transforms your JavaScript code into a form that exposes the code's execution through an API. You can then write verification scripts that get triggered when specific things happen, such as the evaluation of a binary arithmetic operation. You can use such scripts to pinpoint various problems in JavaScript code. As an example, consider the following code, which results in the generation of an invalid number (not a number—NaN).

```
var a = "a";
var b = a * 2;
console.log(b);
```

Running the script under *Jalangi* with a checker provided by the tool's authors results in the following errors.

```
[Location: line No.: 2, col: 9]
   binary operation leads to NaN:NaN <- a [string] * 2 [number]
[Location: line No.: 2, col: 9] writing NaN value to
   variable:b: NaN
[Location: line No.: 3, col: 13] read NaN from variable b :NaN
```

Things to Remember

✦ Use dynamic program analysis tools to locate problems that actually occur in your code.

8

Debugging Multi-threaded Code

CPU manufacturers package the constantly increasing number of transistors they can fit onto a chip into multiple cores, and then ask us developers to put the cores to good use. Threads of execution running on the multiple cores avoid coordinating with each other so that each one can run as fast as possible. Consequently, the programs execute in a nondeterministic manner: every time we run them, they may execute in a slightly different order. This throws out the window many of the techniques you saw in other chapters of this book. For example, you can't reliably zoom in to a moving target (see Item 4: "Drill Up from the Problem to the Bug or Down from the Program's Start to the Bug"). Thankfully, there are tools and techniques that specifically address these problems.

Note that many of the techniques described in this chapter are for code that explicitly uses low-level concurrency constructs. These apply to systems code (e.g., an operating system, a database, a game engine, or a library) and to the maintenance of legacy software. Most application-level software developed from scratch should use high-level concurrency abstractions rather than low-level constructs (see Item 66: "Consider Rewriting the Code Using Higher-Level Abstractions"). If you find yourself spending a lot of time debugging new concurrent code, maybe you're doing something wrong.

Item 60: Analyze Deadlocks with Postmortem Debugging

A deadlock is a situation in which threads acquire resources and wait for others in a way that puts them in a deadly embrace: none of the threads can proceed and do any useful work. This can occur when threads need to lock two shared data structures in order to do some work. If one thread has locked one of the two structures and a second one has locked the other structure, both may then block trying to acquire a lock on the data structure they haven't locked. At that point, the two threads are deadlocked. The Kansas legislature has graciously provided us with a charmingly concise example:

"When two trains approach each other at a crossing, both shall come to a full stop and neither shall start up again until the other has gone."

In an excellent *ACM Queue* article titled, "Real-world Concurrency," Bryan Cantrill and Jeff Bonwick write that Cassandras of concurrency are mistaken in portraying deadlocks as a bogeyman because deadlocks are one of the easiest concurrency bugs to analyze. By definition, a deadlocked system is frozen. Saving its state in a *core dump* file (see Item 35: "Know How to Work with Core Dumps") allows you to take the file and analyze it to find the executing threads and the code locations where these are waiting. This will show you the entities participating in the deadlock (for example, two or more locks) and guide you to the corresponding fault, typically a circular wait on a set of resources.

Listing 8.1 A C++ program that deadlocks

```
1   #include <iostream>
2   #include <mutex>
3   #include <thread>
4
5   using namespace std;
6
7   static mutex m1, m2;
8
9   void bob()
10  {
11          lock_guard<mutex> g1(m1);
12          lock_guard<mutex> g2(m2);
13          cout << "Hi, it's Bob" << endl;
14  }
15
16  void alice()
17  {
18          lock_guard<mutex> g1(m2);
19          lock_guard<mutex> g2(m1);
20          cout << "Hi, it's Alice" << endl;
21  }
22
23  int main()
24  {
25          thread t_bob(bob);
26          thread t_alice(alice);
27
```

```
28          t_bob.join();
29          t_alice.join();
30          return 0;
31  }
```

As one example, consider the C++ (11) program in Listing 8.1. The bob and alice functions run in two threads, and each requires two mutual exclusion locks in order to operate: m1 and m2. When run, the program occasionally freezes; if you want to see that happening, you can run it in a shell loop.

```
while true ; do
  deadlock
done &
```

With a frozen program at hand, this is how you would debug it. The following steps use Unix tools and methods, but you can adapt them for any platform.

Assuming that such a program freezes at the customer's premises, the first step is to obtain a *core dump* from the stuck program. You do this by finding its process-id (using the *ps* command), and then using the *kill* command to send it a QUIT signal.

```
$ ps
  PID TTY          TIME CMD
23010 pts/0 00:00:00 bash
23153 pts/0 00:00:00 bash
23175 pts/0 00:00:00 deadlock
23203 pts/0 00:00:00 ps
$ kill -QUIT 23175
-bash: line 15: 23175 Quit (core dumped) deadlock
```

You then obtain a copy of the customer's dump file and run *gdb* on it. The file might be several megabytes in size (here 17 MB on Linux, 9 MB on FreeBSD) because it reflects the process's memory layout. However, most of that space is likely to be empty, and therefore it can be easily compressed to a few kilobytes and sent via email. In the *gdb* invocation, specify both the executable program image and the memory dump file.

gdb deadlock core

Then, list the threads that were executing.

```
(gdb) info threads
  Id    Target Id           Frame
  3     Thread 0x7f6be668c700 (LWP 22096) __lll_lock_wait ()
  2     Thread 0x7f6be6e8d700 (LWP 22095) __lll_lock_wait ()
```

```
*  1     Thread 0x7f6be7e7e740 (LWP 22094) 0x00007f6be72404db
     in pthread_join (threadid=140101412247296, thread_return=0x0)
```

Here exactly two threads appear to be waiting for a lock. On a more complex program you would probably see only some threads waiting for a resource; those would be the threads that you would need to focus on.

Select one of the waiting threads with the thread command by specifying its thread-id, which appears on the left column of the listing.

```
(gdb) thread 2
[Switching to thread 2 (Thread 0x7f6be6e8d700 (LWP 22095))]
#0 __lll_lock_wait ()
     at ../nptl/sysdeps/unix/sysv/linux/x86_64/lowlevellock.S:135
```

Print the thread's stack frame to find the location in your program that tried to obtain the lock.

```
(gdb) backtrace
#0 __lll_lock_wait ()
     at ../nptl/sysdeps/unix/sysv/linux/x86_64/lowlevellock.S:135
#1 0x00007f6be72414b9 in _L_lock_909 ()
   from /lib/x86_64-linux-gnu/libpthread.so.0
#2 0x00007f6be72412e0 in __GI___pthread_mutex_lock (mutex=
   0x6046c0 <m2>) at ../nptl/pthread_mutex_lock.c:79
#3 0x000000000040109e in __gthread_mutex_lock (__mutex=0x6046c0
   <m2>) at /usr/include/x86_64-linux-gnu/c++/4.9/bits/
   gthr-default.h:748
#4 0x000000000040141a in std::mutex::lock (this=0x6046c0 <m2>)
   at /usr/include/c++/4.9/mutex:135
#5 0x00000000004015ce in std::lock_guard<std::mutex>::lock_guard
   (this=0x7f6be6e8ce40, __m=...) at /usr/include/c++/4.9/mutex:
   377
#6 0x0000000000401192 in bob () at deadlock.cpp:12
#7 0x0000000000402785 in std::_Bind_simple<void (*())()>::
   _M_invoke<>(std::_Index_tuple<>) (this=0x2438038) at
   /usr/include/c++/4.9/functional:1700
   [...]
#12 0x00007f6be6f7404d in clone ()
```

As you can see, if you go carefully through the preceding listing, this is line 12 in deadlock.cpp.

Repeat the process for the other stuck threads.

```
(gdb) thread 3
[Switching to thread 3 (Thread 0x7f6be668c700 (LWP 22096))]
```

```
#0  __lll_lock_wait ()
    at ../nptl/sysdeps/unix/sysv/linux/x86_64/lowlevellock.S:135
(gdb) backtrace
#0  __lll_lock_wait ()
    at ../nptl/sysdeps/unix/sysv/linux/x86_64/lowlevellock.S:135
#1  0x00007f6be72414b9 in _L_lock_909 ()
    from /lib/x86_64-linux-gnu/libpthread.so.0
#2  0x00007f6be72412e0 in __GI___pthread_mutex_lock (mutex=
    0x604680<m1>) at ../nptl/pthread_mutex_lock.c:79
#3  0x000000000040109e in __gthread_mutex_lock (__mutex=0x604680
    <m1>) at /usr/include/x86_64-linux-gnu/c++/4.9/bits/
    gthr-default.h:748
#4  0x000000000040141a in std::mutex::lock (this=0x604680 <m1>)
    at /usr/include/c++/4.9/mutex:135
#5  0x00000000004015ce in std::lock_guard<std::mutex>::lock_guard
    (this=0x7f6be668be40, __m=...) at /usr/include/c++/4.9/mutex:
    377
#6  0x000000000040122f in alice () at deadlock.cpp:19
#7  0x0000000000402785 in std::_Bind_simple<void (*())()>::
    _M_invoke<>(std::_Index_tuple<>) (this=0x2438038) at
    /usr/include/c++/4.9/functional:1700
    [...]
#12 0x00007f6be6f7404d in clone ()
```

In the preceding listing, you can see that the other thread is stuck on line 19 in deadlock.cpp. By examining the code around the lines where the two threads got stuck, you can see that the deadlock was caused by bob trying to obtain a lock on m2 (on line 12) while holding a lock on m1, while at the same time alice tried to obtain a lock on m1 (on line 19) while holding a lock on m2.

Systems where a deadlock can occur should include in their design a way to deal with it. Methods for handling the possibility of deadlocks entail ignoring, detecting, preventing, or avoiding them. When debugging a deadlock, check to see which method the system you're debugging employs for handling this possibility. You can do this by consulting the system's documentation, or, more realistically, by examining the code in places where similar conditions can occur. If your luck has it that you are the first person to discover that your system can deadlock, you typically need to go back to the drawing board and come up with a design to handle deadlocks. This could minimize the number of different locks, avoid reentrancy, establish a lock hierarchy, or have the code use primitives where locking can fail rather than block. Otherwise, you must modify the buggy code to follow the system's deadlock handling protocol. One practical prevention approach, which you can readily employ in this case, involves ordering the resources in some way (*partial ordering* is the technical term for complex resource dependencies) and ensuring that resources are always locked in that order. Thus, all you need to do in this case is to swap the order of locks for alice.

```
lock_guard<mutex> g1(m1);
lock_guard<mutex> g2(m2);
cout << "Hi, it's Alice" << endl;
```

Listing 8.2 A Java program that deadlocks

```
 1  public class Deadlock {
 2    public static void main(String[] args) {
 3      Object mutex1 = new Object();
 4      Object mutex2 = new Object();
 5
 6      Runnable bob = () -> {
 7        for (int i = 0; i < 1000; i++)
 8          synchronized(mutex1) {
 9            synchronized(mutex2) {
10              System.out.println("Hi, it's Bob " + i);
11            }
12          }
13      };
14      Runnable alice = () -> {
15        for (int i = 0; i < 1000; i++)
16          synchronized(mutex2) {
17            synchronized(mutex1) {
18              System.out.println("Hi, it's Alice " + i);
19            }
20          }
21      };
22
23      Thread at = new Thread(alice);
24      Thread bt = new Thread(bob);
25
26      bt.start();
27      at.start();
28
29      try {
30        at.join();
31        bt.join();
32      } catch(InterruptedException e) {
```

```
33              System.err.println("Interrupted: " + e);
34          }
35      }
36  }
```

As another example for debugging the same problem in Java code, consider the similar program listed in Listing 8.2. Again, this program typically deadlocks after printing "Hi it's Bob" a few times. Pinpointing the error is easier, thanks to the *jstack* command that comes with Oracle's Java Development Kit. Running the command with the process-id of the deadlocked process as an argument will display information regarding the deadlock and the code involved in it.

```
$ jps
5504 Deadlock
8848 Jps
$ jstack -l 5504
2016-02-15 18:37:53
Full thread dump Java HotSpot(TM) Client VM
Found one Java-level deadlock:
============================
"Thread-0":
  waiting to lock monitor 0x00d66d64 (object 0x0487f930,
  a java.lang.Object), which is held by "Thread-1"
"Thread-1":
  waiting to lock monitor 0x00d66dd4 (object 0x0487f938,
  a java.lang.Object), which is held by "Thread-0"

Java stack information for the threads listed above:
====================================================
"Thread-0":
        at Deadlock.lambda$main$1(Deadlock.java:18)
        - waiting to lock <0x0487f930> (a java.lang.Object)
        - locked <0x0487f938> (a java.lang.Object)
        at Deadlock$$Lambda$2/29293983.run(Unknown Source)
        at java.lang.Thread.run(Thread.java:745)
"Thread-1":
        at Deadlock.lambda$main$0(Deadlock.java:10)
        - waiting to lock <0x0487f938> (a java.lang.Object)
        - locked <0x0487f930> (a java.lang.Object)
        at Deadlock$$Lambda$1/19011157.run(Unknown Source)
        at java.lang.Thread.run(Thread.java:745)

Found 1 deadlock.
```

Things to Remember

✦ Debug deadlocks by obtaining a snapshot of the deadlocked program and pinpointing the threads and the code that are waiting for a set of resources.

Item 61: Capture and Replicate

A powerful way to deal with nondeterministic bugs involves the use of a detailed recording of the program's operations as it runs. Tools that you can use for this purpose include Intel's *PinPlay/DrDebug Program Record/Replay Toolkit*, which you can use with *Eclipse* or *gdb* on Intel architecture binaries, as well as the *Chronon* recorder and debugger, which works with Java applications. These tools record events in a level of detail that allows you to see the actual order of operations that execute truly concurrently (on multiple cores). For example, main memory reads and writes will reflect the order in which these were actually performed.

The way you work with capture and replicate systems involves the following steps.

1. Repeatedly run the application with recording enabled until you manage to replicate the bug. For bugs that seldom occur, it may help to automate this process in a shell script loop (see Item 60: "Analyze Deadlocks with Postmortem Debugging"). When the bug manifests itself, save the recording for further analysis.

2. Analyze the recording to find the point where the bug first occurs. At this step, a technique called *program slice analysis* may help you identify dubious dependencies between threads—check to see whether the tool you're using supports it.

3. Replay the recording running the program under a debugger until you reach the point where the bug occurred.

4. Analyze the program's state at that point to find the underlying fault.

Listing 8.3 A program with a race condition

```
#include <assert.h>
#include <pthread.h>
#include <stdio.h>
#include <stdlib.h>
#include <unistd.h>
```

```
#define C(x) assert((x) == 0)

static int counter;

void *increment(void *threadid)
{
    int i, tmp;

    for (i = 0; i < 100000; i++) {
        tmp = counter;
        tmp++;
        counter = tmp;
    }
    return (NULL);
}

int main()
{
    pthread_t tid[2];
    int i;

    for (i = 0; i < 2; i++)
        C(pthread_create(&tid[i], NULL, increment, NULL));
    for (i = 0; i < 2; i++)
        C(pthread_join(tid[i], NULL));
    printf("counter=%d\n", counter);
    return 0;
}
```

Let's see a concrete example. The program in Listing 8.3 exhibits a race condition because it reads, then increments, and then writes the counter variable in a way that is not atomic. You can see this by running the program a few times.

```
$ ./race
counter=100000
$ ./race
counter=103754
$ ./race
counter=101233
$ ./race
counter=100000
$ ./race
counter=103977
```

The first step involves using *PinPlay* to record a failing run. Alternately, you can perform a similar process by using the corresponding Eclipse plugin. You record by running the *gdb_record* program and specifying the "pin record on" command once the program enters the main function. If a particular run doesn't fail, repeat the recording process until you encounter the failure. Recording slows down your program by at least two orders of magnitude compared to a debug build, so in more complex programs you should start the recording as late as possible.

```
$ gdb_record race
(gdb) break main
Breakpoint 1 at 0x400730: file race.c, line 28.
(gdb) continue
Continuing.
Breakpoint 1, main () at race.c:28
28              for (i = 0; i < 2; i++)
(gdb) pin record on
monitor record on
Started recording region number 0
(gdb) continue
Continuing.
counter=127873
[Inferior 1 (Remote target) exited normally]
(gdb) quit
```

The recording data are stored in a directory named pinball. With the *replay* command, you can run the program with exactly the same sequence of memory operations, which will of course yield the same faulty behavior.

```
$ replay pinball/log_0
counter=127873
$ replay pinball/log_0
counter=127873
$ replay pinball/log_0
counter=127873
```

The next step involves using the *gdb* debugger on the recorded data to monitor the value of the tmp variable on line 16.

```
$ gdb_replay pinball/log_0 ./race
0x0000000000400737 in main () at race.c:28
28              for (i = 0; i < 2; i++)
(gdb) pin trace tmp at 16
monitor trace [ 0x4006ed : %rsp + -12 ] 4 at 0x4006fe #tmp:<16>
Tracepoint #1: trace memory [0x4006ed : %rsp offset -12 ]
```

```
length 4 at 0x4006fe #tmp:<16>
(gdb) break _exit
Breakpoint 1 at 0x7f09dbab22d0: _exit. (2 locations)
(gdb) continue
Continuing.
counter=127873

Breakpoint 1, __GI__exit (status=status@entry=0)
    at ../sysdeps/unix/sysv/linux/_exit.c:28
(gdb) pin trace print to tmp.txt
monitor trace print to tmp.txt
(gdb) quit
```

After the program finishes executing, the generated trace is saved in the file tmp.txt. This has the following contents; as you can imagine, in a correct program the variable's value (appearing on the right of the = sign) should be constantly increasing.

```
0x00000000004006fe: [ 0x0004006ed:rsp + -12] = 0x7f09 #tmp:<16>
0x00000000004006fe: [ 0x0004006ed:rsp + -12] = 0x1 #tmp:<16>
0x00000000004006fe: [ 0x0004006ed:rsp + -12] = 0x2 #tmp:<16>
0x00000000004006fe: [ 0x0004006ed:rsp + -12] = 0x3 #tmp:<16>
0x00000000004006fe: [ 0x0004006ed:rsp + -12] = 0x4 #tmp:<16>
0x00000000004006fe: [ 0x0004006ed:rsp + -12] = 0x5 #tmp:<16>
```

With a trace file at hand, you can then look for duplicate values of tmp; these indicate a problem. You can find such values with the following shell command, which obtains each line's seventh field (the value of tmp), sorts the results, finds duplicate values, and prints the first ones.

```
$ cut -d' ' -f7 tmp.txt | sort | uniq -d | head
0x108e5
0x108e6
0x108e7
```

Now that you know which values of tmp appear multiple times in the execution trace (e.g., 0x108e5), you can issue the command pin break 16 if tmp == 0x108e5 to add a conditional breakpoint. This will stop the execution's replay at the instance where the duplicate tmp value appeared.

```
$ gdb_replay pinball/log_0 ./race
0x0000000000400737 in main () at race.c:28
28              for (i = 0; i < 2; i++)
(gdb) pin break 16 if tmp == 0x108e5
monitor break at 0x4006fe if [ 0x4006ed : %rsp + -12 ]
4 == 0x108e5 #tmp:<16>
```

```
Breakpoint #1: break at 0x4006fe if [0x4006ed :$rsp offset -12]
length 4 == 0x108e5 #tmp:<16>
(gdb) continue
Continuing.
Triggered breakpoint #1: break at 0x4006fe if [0x4006ed :$rsp
offset -12 ] length 4 == 0x108e5 #tmp:<16>[New Thread 13259]

Program received signal SIGTRAP, Trace/breakpoint trap.
[Switching to Thread 13259]
increment (threadid=0x0) at race.c:16
16                     tmp = counter;
```

When the replayed program has stopped its execution with the break-point you specified, you're in a position to examine all threads and variables. This should allow you to see how the problem came about. In the following excerpt, we see that both threads shared the same value for tmp, which indicates that the code that sets tmp and updates counter should be run atomically.

```
(gdb) print tmp
$1 = 67813
(gdb) info threads
[New Thread 13258]
  Id    Target Id          Frame
  3     Thread 13258       0x000000000040070e in increment
    (threadid=0x0) at race.c:18
* 2     Thread 13259       increment (threadid=0x0) at race.c:16
  1     Thread 13248       0x00007f09dbdbf66b in pthread_join (
    threadid=139680249001728, thread_return=0x0)
    at pthread_join.c:92
(gdb) thread 3
[Switching to thread 3 (Thread 13258)]
#0  0x000000000040070e in increment (threadid=0x0) at race.c:18
18                     counter = tmp;
(gdb) print tmp
$2 = 67813
```

Things to Remember

✦ Pinpoint nondeterministic concurrency errors by capturing a failing run, analyzing the recording, and replaying the captured file under a debugger.

Item 62: Uncover Deadlocks and Race Conditions with Specialized Tools

Writing low-level multi-threaded code is only marginally less risky than riding an elephant that is treading on thin ice. There are tens of subtle errors you can make, and each one of them is likely to result in a failure that occurs only on your customer's premises just before an important demo or deadline. Finding concurrency errors with a tool can save you many hours of frustrated head-scratching.

One way involves the *static analysis* of the code to find patterns of likely bugs (see Item 51: "Use Static Program Analysis"). As an example, the *FindBugs* tool can detect 45 errors under the category "Multi-threaded Correctness." These catch faults such as incorrect synchronization elements, mismatched calls to *wait()* and *notify()*, inconsistent synchronization, unguarded fields, and failures to release a lock. You can run *FindBugs* from the command line, a GUI interface, your IDE, or, preferably, as part of your continuous integration process.

Consider the following code

```
 1   class Counter {
 2       private int n = 0;
 3
 4       public synchronized void increment() {
 5           n++;
 6       }
 7
 8       public void decrement() {
 9           n--;
10       }
11
12       public synchronized int value() {
13           return n;
14       }
15   }
```

and a simple program that exercises it (Listing 8.4) by having two threads increment and decrement the counter 100,000 times.

Listing 8.4 Using a counter from multiple threads

```
class ExerciseCounter {
    public static void main(String[] args) {
        final Counter c = new Counter();
        final int ITERATIONS = 100000;
```

```java
    Thread inc = new Thread() {
       public void run() {
          for (int i = 0; i < ITERATIONS; i++)
             c.increment();
     }
    };

    Thread dec = new Thread() {
       public void run() {
          for (int i = 0; i < ITERATIONS; i++)
             c.decrement();
     }
    };

    inc.start();
    dec.start();
    try {
       inc.join();
       dec.join();
    } catch (InterruptedException e) {
       System.err.println(e);
    }
    System.out.println(c.value());
   }
}
```

When the program is run, it typically prints a negative number (e.g., $-6,775$) rather than 0. (I assume you can see the bug. However, can you explain why it always prints a negative rather than a positive number?)

Compiling the Counter class and running *FindBugs* on it reveals that the decrement method is missing the synchronized keyword.

```
$ java -jar findbugs.jar -textui Counter.class

M M IS: Inconsistent synchronization of Counter.n;
locked 60% of time
Unsynchronized access at Counter.java:[line 9]
```

Another category of tools analyzes the *runtime* behavior of your software to locate race conditions, deadlocks, API misuses, and sources of performance degradation. These *dynamic analysis* tools (see Item 59: "Use Dynamic Program Analysis Tools") can locate subtle bugs that occur from interactions of instructions located very far apart—a feat that is beyond the reach of most static analysis tools.

As is common with dynamic analysis tools, executing your software under their control slows it down by multiple orders of magnitude and results in considerably increased memory usage. This is the price you have to pay for having dependencies among multiple threads examined in minute detail. Thankfully, modern powerful 64-bit CPUs addressing tens of gigabytes of RAM allow a task that was completely unrealistic a few years ago to run even on a laptop. Having used dynamic analysis to fix tens of subtle bugs that were introduced when a large legacy code base was parallelized, let me assure you that the slowdown and memory consumption are prices well worth paying.

The following two examples demonstrate how you can use dynamic analysis to locate faults in *OpenMP* and *POSIX Threads* code.

Starting with *OpenMP*, consider the following trivial program, which has multiple threads advancing a counter variable.

```
#include <assert.h>
#include <stdio.h>
#include <stdlib.h>

int main()
{
        int i, counter;
#pragma omp parallel
        for (i = 0; i < 100000; i++)
                counter++;
        printf("counter=%d\n", counter);
        return 0;
}
```

Running it multiple times gives varying results; clearly there are problems in the code.

```
$ ./race
counter=399757
$ ./race
counter=95561
$ ./race
counter=195790
```

Compiling the code with debugging enabled, and running the program with the *Intel Inspector* tool to locate deadlocks and data races, results in a list of two data races listed in Figure 8.1. Apparently, variable i is incorrectly shared between threads, and the variable counter is not atomically incremented.

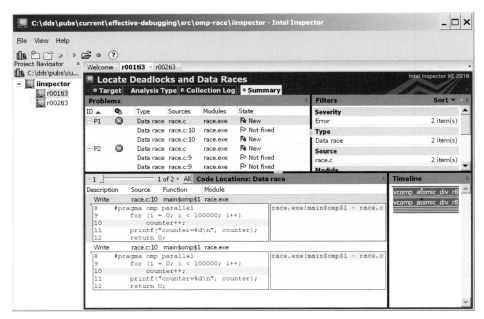

Figure 8.1 *Intel Inspector* identifying race conditions

Fixing the code to have a private version of i in each thread and to increment counter in an atomic fashion fixes the problem.

```c
#include <stdio.h>

static int i, counter;
#pragma omp threadprivate(i)

int main()
{
#pragma omp parallel
    for (i = 0; i < 100000; i++)
#pragma omp atomic
        counter++;
    printf("counter=%d\n", counter);
    return 0;
}
```

The corrected program always outputs the same round number.

```
$ ./fixed
counter=800000
$ ./fixed
counter=800000
```

In addition, running the fixed version under the *Intel Inspector* does not produce any error messages.

In Item 60: "Analyze Deadlocks with Postmortem Debugging," you saw how to debug deadlocks after acquiring a program's memory dump. However, when a failure occurs only very rarely, you may not get a chance to get a dump. Consider again the program in Listing 8.1 with a twist: the call to *sleep* has been removed, making the program's behavior completely nondeterministic. In one computer where I tried it, the program ran 61,266 times before deadlocking.

```
$ while : ; do deadlock ; echo OK ; done >output
^C
$ expr $(wc -l <output) / 3
61266
```

Imagine the difficulty of debugging such a rare failure in a large complex application. Thankfully, dynamic analysis allows the detection of such *potential* problems by establishing a model of the order in which locks get acquired. By distinguishing between a guaranteed order (established, for example, through message passing) and an undeterminable one (the technical term is *partial ordering*), an algorithm can detect a *potential deadlock*, even if an actual deadlock does not occur.

You can find such errors by running the *Helgrind* tool of the *Valgrind* tool suite. This can detect synchronization errors in C, C++, and Fortran programs that use the *POSIX Threads* primitives. You simply invoke the program through the valgrind command, passing it the --tool=helgrind option.

```
valgrind --tool=helgrind deadlock
```

This is (a summary of) the output you get.

```
Helgrind, a thread error detector
Command: deadlock

Thread #3: lock order "0x600F40 before 0x600F80" violated

Observed (incorrect) order is: acquisition of lock at 0x600F80
   at 0x4C30616: pthread_mutex_lock (hg_intercepts.c:593)
   by 0x400834: alice (deadlock.c:24)
 followed by a later acquisition of lock at 0x600F40
   at 0x4C30616: pthread_mutex_lock (hg_intercepts.c:593)
   by 0x40085B: alice (deadlock.c:25)

Required order was established by acquisition of lock
   at 0x600F40
```

```
  at 0x4C30616: pthread_mutex_lock (hg_intercepts.c:593)
  by 0x40077B: bob (deadlock.c:14)
followed by a later acquisition of lock at 0x600F80
  at 0x4C30616: pthread_mutex_lock (hg_intercepts.c:593)
  by 0x4007A2: bob (deadlock.c:15)

Lock at 0x600F40 was first observed
  at 0x4C30616: pthread_mutex_lock (hg_intercepts.c:593)
  by 0x40077B: bob (deadlock.c:14)
Address 0x600f40 is 0 bytes inside data symbol "m1"

Lock at 0x600F80 was first observed
  at 0x4C30616: pthread_mutex_lock (hg_intercepts.c:593)
  by 0x4007A2: bob (deadlock.c:15)
Address 0x600f80 is 0 bytes inside data symbol "m2"
```

ERROR SUMMARY: 1 errors from 1 contexts (suppressed: 18 from 18)

What the preceding report tells you is that the acquisition of locks by bob established a required order for obtaining them: m1 followed by m2. Later on, *Helgrind* observed that this order was violated by alice, which acquired m2 followed by m1. The lack of other locking or synchronization calls that might avoid the intermingling of the two orders allowed *Helgrind* to reason and report that the ordering was incorrect.

Things to Remember

✦ Comb multi-threading source code with static analysis tools to identify possible synchronization and locking errors.

✦ Run multi-threading programs under dynamic analysis tools to find API misuses, potential deadlocks, and data races.

Item 63: Isolate and Remove Nondeterminism

The lack of determinism in the execution of concurrent code can wreak havoc in your attempts to debug it. Unless you resort to extreme measures (see Item 61: "Capture and Replicate"), debugging such code is like trying to build on sand: the code's behavior constantly changes, preventing you from reliably reproducing a bug, zooming in on bugs through repeated trials, or verifying that a bug is indeed fixed. Apart from the various methods and tools described in this chapter, two alternate approaches involve the isolation of nondeterministic code from the rest, and the implementation and configuration of nondeterministic code in a way that makes it deterministic.

The **isolation** approach helps you solve tricky problems in complex concurrent software by splitting the code into two parts. Under this so-called *Humble Object* pattern, you isolate the nondeterministic concurrent code from the rest of the program's logic. The aim of this method is to have on one side just a minimal kernel of all the nondeterministic concurrent code. On the other side, you will have only deterministic code, which you can readily test and debug using traditional, straightforward, tried-and-true tools and techniques. A small nondeterministic kernel is easier to reason about, both formally and semi-formally, individually and collectively, with a walk-through. By keeping the nondeterministic part small, you will hopefully be able to see whether there are any problems in it, or even create an argument regarding their absence (actually *prove* that the code is correct). The small size of the concurrent code may make it easier for you to discern its essence, especially if you transcribe it into pseudocode for the purpose of reasoning. You may also be able to express and rewrite this small kernel in terms of existing reliable ready-made primitives, thus eliminating sources of errors (see Item 66: "Consider Rewriting the Code Using Higher-Level Abstractions"). Finally, the separation of the two parts can be a gateway to further architectural improvements.

Under the **removal** approach, you do away with sources of nondeterminism by replacing them with entities that behave in a predictable way. For instance, you can try configuring a multi-threaded component to run only with a single thread. (This can be easy in a thread pool that you control, but it can be difficult in a third-party component that you use.) Thus, in a Java program you could create a `ForkJoinPool` with `parallelism` set to 1, or in a C/C++ program using *SQLite* you could configure *SQLite* with the `SQLITE_CONFIG_SINGLETHREAD` option. This approach can simplify testing and debugging by allowing your tests to know what to expect and when to expect it, and by giving you repeatable debugging sessions. This can allow you to debug faults in the program's sequential logic with ease, though it doesn't help you deal with concurrency bugs (other than by allowing you to reason that a specific bug stems from a concurrency problem). Obviously the corresponding configuration is built only for debugging and testing and is not included in production.

As another example, if you have an object that responds to requests in an asynchronous manner, you create a *test double* or a *mock object* that internally waits for the response and provides to the test code a way to get the response in a synchronous manner. The following shell function, when run with the `TESTING` variable set, will wait for the specified file download to complete, rather than obtain the file asynchronously.

```
fetch_file()
{
  local url="$1"
  local filename="$2"

  wget -q -O $filename $url &
  if [ "$TESTING" ] ; then
    wait
  fi
}
```

In another case, rather than launching many threads and letting them operate asynchronously, under the test configuration you might launch them one by one and wait for each one to complete. It's best to build this type of behavior into a program during its design. The justification for expending effort on it is that you create software that's easy to test and debug, thus reducing the incidence of future errors and making fixes more traceable.

Things to Remember

✦ Isolate concurrent code from the rest. This allows you to use the most suitable debugging tools and techniques on each part.

✦ Create a testing and debug configuration in which mock objects and other techniques make the code behave in a deterministic manner. This provides you with repeatable code execution.

Item 64: Investigate Scalability Issues by Looking at Contention

When you have a system whose performance (typically latency or throughput) doesn't scale in accordance to the resources it has at its disposal (e.g., CPU cores), start by looking at sources of contention. These include a system's functions that are not parallelized, locks to diverse resources (discussed here), and memory caches (see Item 65: "Locate False Sharing by Using Performance Counters").

Consider the program in Listing 8.5, which creates a map containing a specified number of public-private key pairs by using the specified number of threads.

Listing 8.5 Multi-threaded key pair generation

```
import java.security.*;
import java.util.concurrent.*;
```

```java
import java.util.HashMap;

public class LockContention {
    static public void main(String[] args) {
        int nKeys = Integer.parseInt(args[0]);
        int nThreads = Integer.parseInt(args[1]);
        HashMap<PublicKey, PrivateKey> map =
            new HashMap<PublicKey,
            PrivateKey>();

        Runnable task = () -> {
            try {
                synchronized(map) {
                    KeyPairGenerator keyGen = KeyPairGenerator
                        .getInstance("DSA", "SUN");
                    SecureRandom random = SecureRandom
                        .getInstanceStrong();
                    keyGen.initialize(2048, random);
                    KeyPair pair = keyGen.generateKeyPair();
                    map.put(pair.getPublic(), pair.getPrivate());
                }
            } catch (Exception e) {
              System.out.println("Generation failed: " + e);
            }
        };

        ExecutorService executor = Executors
            .newFixedThreadPool(nThreads);
        for (int i = 0; i < nKeys; i++)
            executor.submit(task);
        try {
            executor.shutdown();
            executor.awaitTermination(5, TimeUnit.SECONDS);
        } catch (InterruptedException e) {
            System.err.println("Interrupted await: " + e);
        }
    }
}
```

Running the program to produce 1,000 key pairs with four threads takes almost as much time as running it with a single thread.

```
$ time java LockContention 1000 4
real  0m11.106s
```

```
$ time java LockContention 1000 1
real   0m11.075s
```

The issue that prevents the performance to scale with more threads is fairly obvious here, but in a larger system it might not be. You can easily debug such problems with a profiling tool that can locate sources of *contention*: cases where threads get blocked while competing to access a shared resource. Two representative tools in this category are Oracle's *Java Flight Recorder* and Intel's *VTune Amplifier*. Here's an example with the former one.

First you run the program under the profiler to collect the required data.

```
$ java -XX:+UnlockCommercialFeatures -XX:+FlightRecorder \
>   -XX:StartFlightRecording=name=test,dumponexit=true,\
>   filename=perf.jfr LockContention 1000 4
Started recording 1. No limit (duration/maxsize/maxage) in use.
```

Alternately, you can attach the profiler to an already running program. In our case, you could do that from the Oracle *Java Mission Control* GUI.

The next step involves exploring and analyzing the collected data—typically using the profiler's GUI. You can see representative images in Figure 8.2. Looking at the time distribution among threads (top left) reveals that something is amiss: time is not equally distributed among them. Examining the top blocked threads (top right), it's clear that threads spend many seconds being blocked. Clicking to see the stack trace of the top blocked thread, you see that there is lock contention on a HashMap object. This is confirmed by looking at sources of latency (bottom left), which show 12.9s of blocked time, and locks (bottom right), which reveals that an equal amount of time was spent on a HashMap lock.

Removing the (excessive) synchronization on map by replacing the Hash Map with a ConcurrentHashMap solves the scalability issue, giving the execution with four threads a decent speedup of 3.2 compared to the single-thread execution.

```
$ time java NoContention 1000 4
real   0m3.503s
```

Things to Remember

+ Solve scalability issues in multi-threaded programs by looking at sources of contention with a profiling tool.

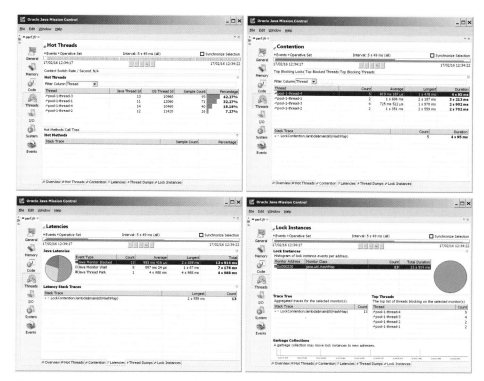

Figure 8.2 Analyzing a contention problem with *Java Flight Recorder*

Item 65: Locate False Sharing by Using Performance Counters

Consider the following example of *OpenMP* C code, which calculates eight sums of the values array scaled down by successive powers of two.

$$\text{sum}_0 = \sum_{i=0}^{N} \left\lfloor \frac{\text{values}_i}{2^0} \right\rfloor, \ldots, \text{sum}_7 = \sum_{i=0}^{N} \left\lfloor \frac{\text{values}_i}{2^7} \right\rfloor$$

```
#include <omp.h>

#define N 100000000
#define NTHREADS 8
int values[N];
```

```
int
main(int argc, char *argv[])
{
    int tid;
    static int sum[NTHREADS];

#ifdef _OPENMP
    omp_set_num_threads(NTHREADS);
#pragma omp parallel private(tid)
    {
        tid = omp_get_thread_num();
#else
    for (tid = 0; tid < NTHREADS; tid++) {
#endif
        for (int i = 0; i < N; i++)
            sum[tid] += values[i] >> tid;
    }
}
```

When compiled with *OpenMP* to run with 8 threads, it takes 2,603ms of wall clock time on an 8-core computer.

```
$ time ./sum-mp
real   0m2.603s
user   0m19.076s
sys    0m0.072s
```

The same code, when compiled without *OpenMP* support, will perform the 8 sums sequentially. In this case it runs faster, taking 2,249ms on the same computer.

```
$ time ./sum-seq
real   0m2.249s
user   0m2.208s
sys    0m0.040s
```

On this embarrassingly parallel task you'd be surprised to see a performance degradation when running multiple threads. Eight workers should finish the work much faster than a single one.

What you're witnessing is the effect of *false sharing*. The code does not contain any synchronization primitives, so the slowdown can't be attributed to them. However, the CPU cores themselves are using a synchronization protocol (a so-called cache coherency protocol) to provide the threads with a consistent view of the memory. The problem solved by the protocol is that all CPU cores share the same main memory, but each CPU core also keeps a private copy of some frequently used memory portions in fast local cache memory attached to it. When one core writes to its local cache in a memory address that is also cached by another core, and the other core attempts to read from that address, some complex magic has to happen for the two caches to present the same picture to their CPU cores. The slowdown you're observing is overhead introduced by the cache synchronization protocol in order to provide all threads with the correct view of the sum array. Normally, independent threads should not tread on each other's feet because they typically operate on distinct memory regions. However, in this case, the sum array is small enough to fit in the same cache area (line) of each core. This in effect makes the sum values shared between the CPU cores, even though each core operates on a separate value—hence the term *false sharing*. Therefore, write operations end up pushing the cached values to the (slow) main memory so that the other cores can see them, and read operations are required to fetch the values from there. (There are actually various ways to implement cache synchronization, but all entail significant overhead.)

A productive way to debug false-sharing problems is to tap into the CPU's performance counters. These track events associated with the CPU's performance, for example, the number of executed instructions and cache misses. Tools such as the *Concurrency Visualizer* extension for *Visual Studio*, Intel's *VTune Performance Analyzer*, and the Linux *perf* command allow you to identify false-sharing (and other) problems when a program is run, and drill down to find the culprit.

Here's an example of using *perf* on the preceding code to measure the number of last-level cache misses (LLC-loads, below). These grow when the cache coherency protocol kicks into action (in our case dramatically due to false sharing).

```
$ perf stat --event=LLC-loads ./sum-seq
 Performance counter stats for './sum-seq':
         17,830   LLC-loads
     2.223350547 seconds time elapsed
$ perf stat -e LLC-loads ./sum-mp
 Performance counter stats for './sum-mp':
     49,264,883  LLC-loads
     2.547188760 seconds time elapsed
```

The next step for locating the place where the false sharing is affecting your code is to run the program under *perf* to record the event that interests you.

```
perf record --event=LLC-loads ./sum-mp
```

You can also attach *perf* to an already running program.

Finally, you can run the command `perf annotate` to go through the obtained results in order to identify the code that's responsible for the many cache misses. The *perf* tool offers a GUI, which is well suited for analyzing large programs. In our case, the textual output plainly illustrates where the problem lies: $25.03 + 14.23 + 14.83 = 54.09\%$ of all last-level cache loads occur in the line that writes to `sum`.

```
Percent |   Source code & Disassembly of sum-mp for LLC-loads
---------------------------------------------------
        :      Disassembly of section .text:
        :        {
        :            tid = omp_get_thread_num();
  0.00 :       4006eb:    callq 400560 <omp_get_thread_num@plt>
  0.00 :       4006f0:    mov   %eax,-0x8(%rbp)
        :      #else
        :          for (tid = 0; tid < NTHREADS; tid++) {
        :      #endif
        :            for (int i = 0; i < N; i++)
  0.00 :       4006f3:    movl  $0x0,-0x4(%rbp)
  0.19 :       4006fa:    cmpl  $0x5f5e0ff,-0x4(%rbp)
  2.42 :       400701:    jg    400738 <main._omp_fn.0+0x59>
        :                sum[tid] += values[i] >> tid;
  0.36 :       400703:    mov   -0x8(%rbp),%eax
  0.79 :       400706:    cltq
  0.22 :       400708:    mov   0x600bc0(,%rax,4),%edx
 25.03 :       40070f:    mov   -0x4(%rbp),%eax
  0.55 :       400712:    cltq
  0.37 :       400714:    mov   0x600c00(,%rax,4),%esi
  2.21 :       40071b:    mov   -0x8(%rbp),%eax
  2.00 :       40071e:    mov   %eax,%ecx
  0.06 :       400720:    sar   %cl,%esi
  2.68 :       400722:    mov   %esi,%eax
  0.06 :       400724:    add   %eax,%edx
  0.83 :       400726:    mov   -0x8(%rbp),%eax
 14.23 :       400729:    cltq
 14.83 :       40072b:    mov   %edx,0x600bc0(,%rax,4)
```

Based on this insight, you can use a stack-based variable to sum up the array's values, and then assign that sum to the `sum` array.

```c
#include <omp.h>

#define N 100000000
#define NTHREADS 8
int values[N];
```

```
int
main(int argc, char *argv[])
{
    int tid;
    static int sum[NTHREADS];

    omp_set_num_threads(NTHREADS);
#pragma omp parallel private(tid)
    {
        int local_sum = 0;
        tid = omp_get_thread_num();
        for (int i = 0; i < N; i++)
            local_sum += values[i] >> tid;
        sum[tid] = local_sum;
    }
}
```

The modified parallel program runs four times faster than the sequential one.

```
$ time sum-mp-noshare
real    0m0.553s
user    0m4.276s
sys     0m0.072s
```

Things to Remember

✦ Use profiling tools that monitor performance counters in order to identify and isolate instances of false sharing.

Item 66: Consider Rewriting the Code Using Higher-Level Abstractions

As you can see in other items of this chapter, controlling low-level multi-threaded code is a fiendishly difficult task. Race conditions, deadlocks, livelocks (a condition where the code runs, but nothing gets done), and suboptimal performance are only some of the bugs that often show up. If the bugs you encounter appear insurmountable, it may be worthwhile to ditch the existing code base (or at least its concurrent component) and adopt a higher-level solution. (See also Item 47: "Consider Rewriting the Suspect Code in Another Language.") There are a number of architectural paths you can follow in order to put multiple processors to work reliably and effectively, such as using a message bus or a job queue. However, these are outside the scope of this book. Instead, this item outlines a few approaches that may help you code around bugs associated with parallelism. The approaches involve faking your application's multicore-handling dexterity by handing over this responsibility to other software. As with all conjuring tricks, it isn't always possible to pull this off, but when you can, the results can be spectacular. With little effort (and maybe some cash), you can achieve remarkable speedups.

At the highest level, it's easy to put multiple cores to work if you can find reliable **ready-made middleware** to take on this task. You can easily do this if your application serves web requests or dishes out SQL statements. Web application servers divide their work into threads or processes and thereby exploit all processing cores at their disposal. The only thing you need to do is to make your application run within the application server's framework, such as Java EE or Node.js. The other easy case involves having a sophisticated relational database management system handle your SQL queries. The query optimization engine of such systems often finds ways to split a query among all available cores—for instance, each WHERE clause filtering a table can be assigned to a separate core. Under this scenario, your main responsibility is to let the database do as much of your work as possible.

Another high-level way to divide the work among multiple cores is to let the operating system do it for you by **splitting your processing among independent processes**. Your application might match the pipes and filters architecture, which has one process generating the output that the next one will consume (see Item 22: "Analyze Debug Data with Unix Command-Line Tools"). The pipeline syntax, popularized by the Unix shell, lets you painlessly join multiple processes together in a series, without having to think about allocating your work among the processor's cores. Any modern operating system worth its salt will do this automatically for you. Let's say your software's threads were tasked to change a data file's compression format from bzip2 into gzip. By running the following pipeline

```
bzip2 -dc data.bz2 | gzip -c >data.gz
```

the decompression program `bzip2` will run concurrently with the compression program `gzip`. As you can see in the following measurements, which run the two commands on a 70 MB compressed file, executing the commands sequentially takes 41 seconds, whereas running them as a pipeline squeezes that number down to 27.

```
$ time { bzip2 -d data.bz2 ; gzip data ; }
real    0m41.367s
user    0m40.325s
sys     0m0.919s
```

```
$ time bzip2 -dc <data.bz2 | gzip -c >data.gz
real    0m27.444s
user    0m40.886s
sys     0m1.278s
```

If the process you're debugging tries to work sequentially through some discrete data chunks (say, files, lines, or other records) then you can easily split the work among multiple cores using *GNU parallel*. All you do is feed your data chunks into it, and it runs as many jobs as needed to keep your CPU cores 100% busy. For instance, if your software was creating thumbnails from camera pictures, you'd invoke the JPEG decompression and compression programs through the parallel command as follows:

```
ls *.jpg | parallel 'djpeg -scale 1/16 {} | cjpeg >thumb/{}'
```

The following measurements show how using this technique will cut the task's running time by half.

```
$ time ls *.jpeg |
> xargs -I '{}' sh -c 'djpeg -scale 1/16 {} | cjpeg >thumb/{}'
real    0m10.493s
user    0m6.428s
sys     0m4.360s
```

```
$ time ls *.[Jj]* |
> parallel 'djpeg -scale 1/16 {} | cjpeg >thumb/{}'
real    0m4.149s
user    0m8.384s
sys     0m6.696s
```

If the code you're debugging is dividing one large task among multiple workers and its input is in one large file, *parallel* can split it among threads as needed. (I know from bitter experience that it can be tricky to get this exactly right when you're implementing it from scratch using low-level thread operations or asynchronous I/O.)

Unfortunately, you can't model all processing tasks as linear processes that can be run as pipelines or as independent processes running under *parallel*. In many cases, the various steps have dependencies. In such cases, you can profit by specifying the dependencies between the various files and the (coarse-grained) actions required to build one from the other as a **Makefile** that the Unix *make* tool can process. Modern versions of *make* accept a -j argument, which instructs the tool to run many jobs in parallel as long as their dependencies allow it. Although this is typically used to speed up a system's compilation, there's nothing preventing you from using the same approach to express the rendering of a movie or the running of a big-data processing job. Here is the speedup occurring when compiling the Linux (4.5) kernel on an 8-core computer. Asking *make* to run 8 jobs in parallel (-j 8) shrinks the time you have to wait for the compilation to finish (wall-clock time) from 14 minutes down to 3.

```
$ time make >/dev/null
real   14m18.053s
user   11m35.152s
sys    1m41.608s

$ time make -j 8 >/dev/null
real   3m12.827s
user   20m32.272s
sys    2m35.600s
```

The *parallel* command works by applying a process on chunks of data. You can do the same trick within your application by employing the **map-reduce** and **filter-reduce** techniques. These allow you to apply a function on the elements of a container (such as a vector) to either change each one of them (map) or select some of them (filter). You can then also use another function to reduce the results into a single element. If the function you're applying is at least moderately expensive, this operation can be profitably split through application-level threads among multiple cores. For example, you can use the Collection.parallelStream method of the java.util.stream package or functions of the *QtConcurrent* C++ library. The only thing you need to do is to use containers and map, filter, or reduce functions compatible with the corresponding API. If the tasks you're parallelizing are relatively big and coarse-grained, you can offload the complete processing to a distributed processing framework, such as *Apache Hadoop*.

Many common, parallelizable, heavy-processing tasks are available in **libraries** hand-tuned to exploit the capabilities of multicore CPUs. Processor vendors, including AMD and Intel, offer libraries with functions covering audio and video encoding and decoding; image, speech, and general signal processing; cryptography; compression; and rendering. More specialized libraries are also available. One example is the ATLAS (Automatically Tuned Linear Algebra Software) implementation of the BLAS (Basic Linear Algebra Subprograms) specification. This dynamically tunes the library's components at build time to match the capabilities of the hardware where the library is built. Another is the NAG Numerical Components Library for SMP and multicore, which provides parallelized implementations of numerical computing and statistical algorithms. If you can express your problem in terms of, say, matrix operations (that's the case for a surprising variety of problems), then you may be able to replace the buggy code with calls to the library.

Here is a demonstration of how the use of an appropriate library utilizes parallelism to improve performance, without the blood, sweat, and tears associated with explicitly concurrent programming. Consider the following *R* program, which calculates the inverse of a 10000 × 10000 matrix.

```
#!/usr/bin/env Rscript

# Matrix size
n <- 10000

# Create a square matrix of random numbers
m <- replicate(n, rnorm(n))

# Calculate the matrix inverse
r <- solve(m)
```

Running the program with a version of the ATLAS library built for a single-core computer takes about three minutes.

```
$ time ./solve.R
real   3m10.285s
user   3m8.476s
sys    0m1.800s
```

Replacing the BLAS library used by *R* with one optimized for a multi-core computer reduces the run time to one minute.

```
$ time ./solve.R
real   1m1.995s
user   3m11.876s
sys    0m3.256s
```

One alternative approach involves using a **programming language** or style that can easily exploit multiple cores. Functional programming has an edge here because the building blocks of the programs you write in this fashion don't step on each other's toes. Thus, if you're working with Java, start by adopting the use of lambda expressions and streams. If your work is tied to existing APIs, try a functional language associated with the corresponding framework, such as *Clojure* (JVM, .NET, and JavaScript), *Scala* (JVM), or *F#* (.NET). Or you might decide to go all the way and use a pure functional language, such as *Haskell*, one tailored to a particular domain, such as *R*, or one explicitly designed to support concurrency, such as *Erlang*. This might make sense if you're starting from scratch and your system performs heavy data processing with little API interaction. Yet another approach for exploiting multiple cores, should you decide to architect the buggy software from scratch, is to adopt a reactive, event-driven framework, such as *Vert.x*.

As an example of the speedup you can obtain by invoking functions in parallel, consider the task of finding those English five-letter words that can be made from a permutation of another word's letters (e.g., "trust" and "strut"). The *R* program in Listing 8.6 generates this set.

Listing 8.6 Parallelizing function application in *R*

```
#!/usr/bin/env Rscript
library(combinat)
library(parallel)

# Read in a file of English words
words <- readLines('/usr/share/dict/words')

# Obtain five letter words
flw <- words[nchar(words) == 5]

# Return words consisting of permutations of the passed word
word.permutations <- function(w) {
  # Obtain all character permutations
  p <- lapply(strsplit(w, NULL), permn)
  # Convert permutations to list of words
  r <- sapply(unlist(p, recursive=FALSE), paste, collapse="")
  # Remove permutations resulting in the original word
  new <- r[r != w]
  # Return the intersection of the two sets
  intersect(flw, new)
}

# Generate list of words that are permutations of others
p <- unlist(lapply(flw, word.permutations))
```

All the work is performed by the word.permutations function; applying it to a single word returns other words that can be generated from its characters.

```
> word.permutations('teams')
[1] "mates" "meats" "steam" "tames"
```

The list of all words is generated by applying the word.permutations to the list of all five-letter words (flw) through *R*'s *lapply* function. Replacing the *lapply* function with its parallelized version cuts down the calculation's time to less than a quarter of the original.

```
> system.time(lapply(flw, word.permutations))
   user  system elapsed
 20.896   0.000  20.896
```

```
> system.time(mclapply(flw, word.permutations, mc.cores=8))
   user  system elapsed
 42.976   0.268   4.623
```

Finally, a number of programming frameworks have tried to address the bugs associated with low-level concurrent code by introducing **higher-level primitives**. Where possible, consider making this switch, instead of battling to fix low-level multi-threaded spaghetti code. Here are some examples from Java's concurrency utilities.

- Use the *Executor* framework's Executor and ExecutorService interfaces (see Item 64: "Investigate Scalability Issues by Looking at Contention") rather than debugging the management of low-level threads.

- Adopt the CountDownLatch, CyclicBarrier, Exchanger, Phaser, and Semaphore classes, rather than trying to correct similar functionality implemented from raw synchronized code blocks.

- Use the concurrent collections available in java.util.concurrent and their weakly consistent iterators, rather than battling with the exceptions, race conditions, and performance problems associated with custom synchronization, the java.util, or the Collections synchronization adapter methods. Classes you might want to use include the following: ArrayBlockingQueue, BlockingDeque, BlockingQueue, ConcurrentHashMap, ConcurrentLinkedDeque, ConcurrentLinkedQueue, ConcurrentMap, ConcurrentNavigableMap, ConcurrentSkipListMap, ConcurrentSkipListSet, CopyOnWriteArrayList, CopyOnWriteArraySet, DelayQueue, LinkedBlockingDeque, LinkedBlockingQueue, LinkedTransferQueue, PriorityBlockingQueue, SynchronousQueue, and TransferQueue.

- Use the CompletableFuture class to organize the parallel execution of tasks with sophisticated dependencies.

- Express filtering and mapping that are to be performed concurrently with parallel streams, future tasks, and lambda expressions.

As an example, consider the program in Listing 8.7, which processes a list of IP addresses contained in a file specified in its first argument and outputs the resolved addresses. For example, if the file contains 8.8.8.8, the program will output google-public-dns-a.google.com.

Listing 8.7 Stream-based IP address resolution

```java
import java.io.IOException;
import java.net.InetAddress;
import java.net.UnknownHostException;
import java.nio.file.Files;
import java.nio.file.Path;
import java.nio.file.Paths;
import java.util.concurrent.ForkJoinPool;
import java.util.concurrent.CompletableFuture;
import java.util.stream.Collectors;
import java.util.List;

/** Resolve IP addressed in file args[0] using 100 threads */
public class Resolve100CF {
    /** Resolve the passed internet address into a name */
    static String addressName(String ipAddress) {
        try {
            return InetAddress.getByName(ipAddress).getHostName();
        } catch (UnknownHostException e) {
            return ipAddress;
        }
    }

    public static void main(String[] args) {
        Path path = Paths.get(args[0]);
        // Create pool of 100 threads to compute results
        ForkJoinPool fjp = new ForkJoinPool(100);

        try {
            // Obtain list of lines
            List<CompletableFuture<String>> list =
                Files.lines(path)
                // Map lines into a future task
                .map(line -> CompletableFuture.supplyAsync(
                        () -> addressName(line), fjp))
                // Collect future tasks into a list
                .collect(Collectors.toList());
            // Wait for tasks to complete, and print the result
            list.stream().map(CompletableFuture::join)
                .forEach(System.out::println);
```

```
        } catch (IOException e) {
            System.err.println("Failed: " + e);
        }
    }
}
```

Through the use of streams and the CompletableFuture class, the program avoids the explicit management of threads and their results. Running the program on a list of 1,000 IP addresses completes the task in 37 seconds—78 times faster than a sequential implementation, which takes 48 minutes.

```
$ time java ResolveFuture 1000.ip >1000p.name
real   0m37.465s
user   0m0.015s
sys    0m0.000s

$ time java ResolveSequential 1000.ip >1000s.name
real   48m40.036s
user   0m0.000s
sys    0m0.015s
```

The remarkable speedup is attributable to the long I/O delays associated with DNS queries. Parallelizing such a task makes perfect sense; avoiding low-level concurrency primitives is even wiser.

Things to Remember

✦ To avoid concurrency pitfalls, consider reimplementing buggy concurrent code at a higher level, using specialized languages, processes, tools, frameworks, or libraries.

Web Resources

Ansible	http://www.ansible.com/
Ant	http://ant.apache.org/
Apache Hadoop	http://hadoop.apache.org/
Apache HTTP Server	http://httpd.apache.org/
Apache JMeter	http://jmeter.apache.org/
Apache log4j	http://logging.apache.org/log4j
"The Art of Command Line"	https://github.com/jlevy/the-art-of-command-line
AutoHotkey	http://www.autohotkey.com/
AutoKey	https://en.wikipedia.org/wiki/AutoKey
Automator	https://en.wikipedia.org/wiki/Automator(software)
Black Duck Open Hub Code Search	https://code.openhub.net/
Boost.Log v2	http://www.boost.org/doc/libs/1_59_0/libs/log/doc/html/index.html
Bugzilla	https://www.bugzilla.org/
Bunyan	https://github.com/trentm/node-bunyan
bytecode	http://andrei.gmxhome.de/bytecode/
Byteman	http://byteman.jboss.org/
CFEngine	http://www.cfengine.com/
cgdb	http://cgdb.github.io
Chef	http://www.chef.io/
Chronon	http://chrononsystems.com/
collectd	https://collectd.org/
CppUnit	http://cppunit.sourceforge.net
Crittercism	http://www.crittercism.com/
ctags	https://en.wikipedia.org/wiki/Ctags
cURL	http://curl.haxx.se/
Cygwin	https://cygwin.com/
DDD	http://www.gnu.org/software/ddd
dmalloc	http://dmalloc.com/
Docker	https://www.docker.com/
Dynamic program analysis	https://en.wikipedia.org/wiki/Dynamic_program_analysis
"Eradicating Non-Determinism"	http://martinfowler.com/articles/nonDeterminism.html

FindBugs	http://findbugs.sourceforge.net/
GCC	https://gcc.gnu.org/
gdbinit	https://gist.github.com/CocoaBeans/1879270
Gerrit	https://www.gerritcodereview.com/
ghi	https://github.com/stephencelis/ghi
Git	https://git-scm.com/
GitHub	https://github.com/
GitLab	https://about.gitlab.com/
GNU Classpath	http://www.classpath.org/
GNU parallel	http://www.gnu.org/software/parallel/
Graphviz	http://graphviz.org/
Homebrew	http://brew.sh/
How To Ask Questions	
The Smart Way	http://www.catb.org/~esr/faqs/smart-questions.html
Humble Object	http://xunitpatterns.com/Humble%20Object.html
Intel Inspector	https://software.intel.com/en-us/intel-inspector-xe
Jalangi	https://www.eecs.berkeley.edu/~gongliang13/jalangi_ff/index.html
JProfile	http://www.ej-technologies.com/products/jprofiler/overview.html
jq	http://stedolan.github.io/jq/
JRuby	http://jruby.org/
JSFiddle	https://jsfiddle.net/
Launchpad	https://launchpad.net/
libmicrohttpd	http://www.gnu.org/software/libmicrohttpd/
LLVM	http://llvm.org/
Log4j	http://logging.apache.org/
LTTng	http://lttng.org/
Lua	http://www.lua.org/
Magic Number	https://en.wikipedia.org/wiki/Magic_number_%28programming%29
make	https://en.wikipedia.org/wiki/Make(software)
Maven	https://maven.apache.org/
Mono	http://www.mono-project.com/
mruby	http://www.mruby.org/
Nagios	https://www.nagios.org/
New Relic	http://newrelic.com/
OpenJDK	http://openjdk.java.net/
OTRS	http://www.otrs.org/
Outwit	http://www.spinellis.gr/sw/outwit/
PLCrashReporter	https://www.plcrashreporter.org/
Process Monitor	https://technet.microsoft.com/en-us/sysinternals/processmonitor
Program Record/	
Replay Toolkit	http://www.pintool.org/
Pull request	https://help.github.com/articles/using-pull-requests/
Puppet	http://www.puppetlabs.com/
Python Tutor	http://www.pythontutor.com/
qmcalc	https://github.com/dspinellis/cqmetrics

Raspberry Pi	http://raspberrypi.org/
Redmine	http://www.redmine.org/
Reproducible builds	https://reproducible-builds.org/
RRDtool	http://oss.oetiker.ch/rrdtool/
Rubinius	http://rubinius.com/
Rule of three	https://en.wikipedia.org/wiki/Rule_of_three_%28C%2B%2B_programming%29
saleae	https://www.saleae.com
Salt	http://saltstack.com/
Selenium	http://www.seleniumhq.org/
SourceLair	https://www.sourcelair.com/
Splunk MINT	http://www.splunk.com
spy-js	http://spy-js.com/
sscce.org	http://sscce.org/
Stack Overflow	http://www.stackoverflow.com
StackExchange	http://www.stackexchange.com
Static analysis tools	https://en.wikipedia.org/wiki/List_of_tools_for_static_code_analysis
tcpdump	http://www.tcpdump.org/
TeamViewer	https://www.teamviewer.com/
"TestDouble"	http://martinfowler.com/bliki/TestDouble.html
Trac	http://trac.edgewall.org/
Unit testing frameworks	https://en.wikipedia.org/wiki/List_of_unit_testing_frameworks
Valgrind	http://valgrind.org/
Vert.x	http://vertx.io/
vim	http://www.vim.org/
VisualVM	https://visualvm.java.net/
VLC	http://www.videolan.org/index.html
Wat	https://www.destroyallsoftware.com/talks/wat
Winston	https://github.com/flatiron/winston
Wireshark	https://www.wireshark.org/
zzuf	http://caca.zoy.org/wiki/zzuf

Look at the book's web site www.spinellis.gr/debugging for updates to this list.

Index

REGISTER YOUR PRODUCT at informit.com/register
Access Additional Benefits and SAVE 35% on Your Next Purchase

- Download available product updates.

- Access bonus material when applicable.

- Receive exclusive offers on new editions and related products.
  (Just check the box to hear from us when setting up your account.)

- Get a coupon for 35% for your next purchase, valid for 30 days. Your code will
  be available in your InformIT cart. (You will also find it in the Manage Codes
  section of your account page.)

Registration benefits vary by product. Benefits will be listed on your account page
under Registered Products.

InformIT.com—The Trusted Technology Learning Source
InformIT is the online home of information technology brands at Pearson, the world's foremost
education company. At InformIT.com you can

- Shop our books, eBooks, software, and video training.
- Take advantage of our special offers and promotions (informit.com/promotions).
- Sign up for special offers and content newsletters (informit.com/newsletters).
- Read free articles and blogs by information technology experts.
- Access thousands of free chapters and video lessons.

Connect with InformIT—Visit informit.com/community
Learn about InformIT community events and programs.

informIT.com
the trusted technology learning source

Addison-Wesley · Cisco Press · IBM Press · Microsoft Press · Pearson IT Certification · Prentice Hall · Que · Sams · VMware Press

ALWAYS LEARNING   PEARSON